ABRAHAM, ISAAC, AND JACOB
Servants and Prophets of God

ABRAHAM, ISAAC, AND JACOB
Servants and Prophets of God

by

Dr. Norman L. Heap

VANTAGE PRESS
New York / Atlanta
Los Angeles / Chicago

FIRST EDITION

Copyright © 1986 by Dr. Norman L. Heap

Published by Vantage Press, Inc.
516 West 34th Street, New York, New York 10001

Manufactured in the United States of America
ISBN: 0-533-07272-7

Library of Congress Catalog Card No.: 86-91700

Dedication

This book is dedicated to the descendants of Abraham, Isaac, and Jacob through Levi, Judah, and Joseph. They faithfully kept the records from which the Holy Scriptures are derived. Through them the rights of priesthood, kings and birth, were continued or restored.

Through Levi and his posterity were to come other priests and prophets including Aaron and Moses with power to act for God, that whatsoever is bound on earth might be bound in heaven.

Through Judah and his posterity were to come kings of nations, and more importantly, the King of Kings, and Lord of Lords, even Messiah, the Son of Man and the Son of God who would save the world from the sins of its people.

Through Joseph the birthright blessings would be continued. Through his posterity salvation would be made possible to the house of Israel and to all the world in the latter days.

Indeed, through Abraham, Isaac, Jacob, Levi, Judah, and Joseph and their posterity all of the families of the earth have been, and will continue to be blessed.

Acknowledgements

Translations of the Holy Scriptures are generally in the public domain. Nonetheless, the compiler gratefully acknowledges The Jewish Publication Society of America, The Church of Jesus Christ of Latter Day Saints, and The Reorganized Church of Jesus Christ of Latter Day Saints for quotations he used from their respective copyrighted scriptures.

Grateful acknowledgement is given to The J.H. Parry Company for extensive use of the Book of Jasher which was translated from the original Hebrew into English, published in 1887 and reprinted in 1973. Other copyrighted material is used by permission and courtesy of several publishers. Their works are listed in a bibliography. Special thanks to The Jewish Publication Society, Farrar, Straus and Giroux, Doubleday and Company, Deseret Book Company, and Kregel Publications for the use of selected quotations from the works listed. The compiler is most grateful for an understanding companion and wife, Virginia Thayer, without her this book would not be possible.

Prologue

Amos declared,

"For surely the Lord God will do nothing, but he revealeth His counsel (secret) unto His servants the prophets."[1]

The record in Genesis was revealed to Moses, a servant and indeed a prophet of God. Genesis is sometimes referred to as the First Book of Moses. It contains some, but not all, of God's counsel or secrets revealed to the world through Abraham, Isaac and Jacob (Israel), each of whom preceded Moses as prophets/servants of God. Acting as His messenger, Moses made known God's role in the creation or organization of the earth in which we live.

The Lord God counseled Abraham, Isaac and Jacob (Israel) to "walk (uprightly) before me and be perfect."[2] To Abraham, the Lord God revealed His decision to work through a covenant people not yet born, a people through whom "all of the families of the earth shall be blessed."[3] The covenant people were to be born through Abraham and Sarah. They were to become as numerous as the sands of the sea, and as the stars of the sky. They were to be given a land of promise. Kings and nations were to come from them. Abraham and Sarah were to keep their covenants with Him, ie to walk uprightly before Him and be perfect, as a condition of these promises or blessings.

Any attempt to reconstruct the life histories of people who lived 3600 to 4000 years ago is open to challenge. There are few, if any, original source documents extant, and few people capable of reading and translating them if the documents do exist.

Other writings with roots in the ancient past, however, shed light on the lives of these three great men and their wives, and their relationship to the Mighty God Jehovah. The writings include the Masoretic Text of the Holy Scriptures and the Legends of the Jews, published by

---

1. Amos 3:7, MT, KJV, JST
2. Genesis 17:1 KJV, JST, "Be thou whole hearted;" MT
3. Genesis 12:3, KJV, MT, (12:2) JST

the Jewish Publication Society of America, the King James version of the Bible and the Book of Abraham as translated by Joseph Smith, the writings of Josephus an historian of Antiquity, the Book of Jasher, Jubilees, Rivers in the Desert by Nelson Glueck and others.

The limitations inherent in reconstructing the lives of Abraham, Isaac and Jacob are duly noted. The need to pursue such a study is great enough, however, to assume the risks related thereto.

The central themes underlying this work are:

1) That all the families of the earth have been blessed in the past, are currently being blessed, and will continue to be blessed in the future by the Mighty God, Jehovah, through His covenant people, as they strive to walk uprightly before Him and become perfect.

2) That the Mighty God's counsel "to walk uprightly before me and be perfect" is of great significance to all of the families of the earth today.

The life spans of the prophets as reported in Genesis have been taken at face value. No attempt has been made to critique them. Some may claim it is physically impossible for human beings to live 950, 600, 205, or even 175 years, as Genesis reports the respective ages of Noah, Shem, Terah and Abraham to have been at their deaths.

One might as well claim the great flood of Noah's day didn't actually happen, or that Sarah didn't actually have a baby at ninety years of age, that angels didn't actually destroy the first born of Israel's captures, and at the same time, pass over the first born of Israel's obedient; or that Moses, using power from the Lord, didn't actually part the waters of the Red Sea to allow safe passage of the children of Israel, with corresponding destruction of their pursuers by those same waters.

This volume assumes that a God, who organizes or creates a heaven and earth and sets in motion millions of plant and animal organisms with delicately interrelated life cycles ranging from single cell organisms to the complexity of human beings, is quite capable of modifying the length of life each of His creatures is to live. If He could program some trees, such as the giant sequoia redwoods of California, to live more than 2,000 years and others to live less than 100 years, why couldn't He do the same with man?

Further, that such a God could bring about a flood of waters to cover the earth, or reverse life's aging processes so that a woman well beyond child bearing age (by today's standards) could indeed bear a child, or send His angels to destroy some of His disobedient creatures as in the cities of Sodom and Gomorrah, and to spare others who were obedient. He could vest in Moses the power to countermand the law of gravity and part waters for the safe passage of His covenant people, the House of Israel. He could do likewise as His people crossed the Jordan River led by twelve representatives of Israel and the Ark of the Covenant, as the waters were stayed and Israel crossed over and entered the promised land.

In this context the life spans of the antedeluvian prophets Adam, Seth, Enoch, Methuselah and Lamech are credible. Noah's life spanned the flood and covered a period of 600 years before and 350 years after, for 950 years total. His life span is also credible.

The life span's of those after the flood decreased sharply from 600 years, the life of Shem, to 110 years in Joseph's day. Shem, who also spanned the flood, lived 600 years, Eber 464 years, Abraham 175 years, Isaac 180 years, Jacob (Israel) 147 years, and Levi 137 years.

The shortening of the life of man was reportedly prophesied by Eber and took place soon after the earth was divided. The Legends of the Jews contains a report that the earth was divided by lot by Noah with Shem getting the Temporate Zones, Japheth the cold or Frigid Zones, and Ham the Hot Zones. Further that the division of the earth took place toward the end of the life of Peleg, the name given to him by his father Eber, who being a prophet, knew that the division of the earth would take place in the time of his son (Peleg). The brother of Peleg was called Joktan, because the duration of the life of man was shortened in his time.[4]

The query of an angel is echoed. "Is anything too hard for the Lord"?[5]

This volume covers events in the lives of Abraham, Isaac and Jacob and their contemporaries, from the birth of Abram in Ur to the death of Jacob (Israel) in Egypt and his subsequent burial in Canaan alongside his father Isaac and his grandfather Abraham in the cave of Mach-pelah some 307 years later.

It is intended to sensitize readers to knowledge Abraham, Isaac, and Jacob had of the living God, and His plans and purposes for the world and all who live in it. Knowledge of God's plans and purposes for the human family is of great significance for people today.

---

4. The Legends of the Jews vol 1 page 172.
5. Genesis 18:14, KJV, MT, (18:13) JST

The compiler relies heavily on those records accepted as scripture by most Judeo-Christian peoples, supplemented by other records accepted as scripture by some Judeo-Christian people. Other records, which might be classified as aprocryphas, are also used.

He accepts full responsibility for what is written attributing any truth this book contains to the living God, Jehovah. To himself he consigns any error which might have been inadvertantly reported. Hopefully and prayerfully such errors are few and far between.

Concord, CA
Norman L. Heap

ABRAHAM, ISAAC AND JACOB
SERVANTS AND PROPHETS OF GOD

TABLE OF CONTENTS

ABRAHAM, ISAAC, AND JACOB
Servants and Prophets of God

CHAPTER I

ABRAHAM, ABRAHAM, BEHOLD MY NAME IS JEHOVAH, AND I HAVE HEARD THEE

From Genesis we may infer that Abram was born about 292 years after the flood or about 1948 years after the fall of Adam and Eve, in the 892nd year in the life of Noah, the 400th year in the life of Shem and the 225th year in the life of Eber. That Noah, Shem and Eber were still living at Abram's birth is supported by the Antiquities and the Legends of the Jews, the Book of Jasher and by extrapolation of dates contained in Genesis Chapter 11.[6]

The earth having been cleansed of all human inhabitants except for the eight souls saved from the flood[7] was repeopled through Noah, his wife and Shem, Ham and Japheth and their wives...."of them was the whole earth overspread,"[8] especially the area surrounding the resting place of the Ark.[9]

Genesis briefly mentions the development of a secular form of government by Nimrod, son of Cush, son of Ham, who

> ..."began to be a mighty one in the earth. He was a mighty hunter before the Lord...And the beginning of his kingdom was Babel, and Erech, and Accad and Calneh in the land of Shinar."[10]

Noah, however, had proclaimed "blessed be the Lord God of Shem" and added "God shall enlarge Japheth and he shall dwell in the tents of Shem."[11]

---

6. Antiquities VI:5; Legends I:201, 205; Jasher IX, Genesis II; KJV, MT, JST
7. Genesis 7:23, 8:1-22, KJV, MT, (8, 9) JST
8. Ibid 9:19, KJV, MT, (9:26) JST
9. Ibid 8:4, KJV, MT, (8:49) JST
10. Ibid 10:6-10, KJV, MT, (10:5-9) JST
11. Ibid 9:26-27, KJV, MT, (9:30-31) JST

While the covenants of the Lord God with mankind continued through Shem, whose descendants provided spiritual leadership, secular leadership or control of the area was assumed or seized by the descendants of Ham.

Nimrod, born of Cush in his old age, was king of Shinar in whose land the City and Tower of Babel were built. Nimrod presumably presided over its construction.[12] Sustained by the children of Phut, Mitzraim, Cush and Canaan[13] King Nimrod attempted to..."build us a city and a tower, whose top may reach unto heaven."[14]

No explanation is given in Genesis as to why the Lord was displeased with their works or why He scattered them abroad and they ceased to build the city.[15] Other writings attribute the Lords displeasure to the motives for building the tower. i.e. they were planning to war against God by ascending into heaven to fight against Him.[16]

The City of Babel and its tower were probably built near the time of Abram's birth. The descendants of Ham through his sons Cush, Mitzraim, Phut and Canaan including Nimrod, son of Cush controlled a wide area from Egypt through the middle east to Ur. Wherever Abraham lived throughout his life, in Ur, in Haran, in Canaan or in Egypt, secular control was in the hands of Ham's descendants headed by kings and pharaohs. Tighter control over the peoples of these areas was maintained by some kings and pharaohs than others, the least control seemed to be in Canaan.

"The borders of the Canaanites were from Sidon, as thou comest into Gerar unto Gaza;" and included the cities of Sodom, Gomorrah, Admah and Zeboim which were settled by the Canaanites.[17] Abraham was able to move about within the land of Canaan, build altars, acquire cattle and sheep, worship God, and become wealthy with the blessing of the Lord without incurring the wrath of the Canaanite people.

The land of Abram's birth however, was different. Things were happening which made it necessary for Abram to leave Ur and move into Canaan. Before discussing them, a little more background material is needed.

---

12. Jasher IX:21-39
13. Ibid IX:21
14. Genesis 11:4, KJV, MT, (11:3) JST
15. Ibid 11:8, KJV, MT, (11:5-6) JST
16. Jasher IX:25-26; Antiquities IV 2-3
17. Genesis 10:19, KJV, MT, (10:10) JST

Immediately following a description of the confusion of tongues and the scattering of peoples the Genesis account gives Abraham's lineage beginning with Shem, son of Noah (from whom Semites get their name), Arphaxad (whose land was Chaldea), Salah, Eber (from whom the Hebrews derived), Peleg (in whose days the earth was divided, and in whose days the life of man was shortened), Reu (who prophesied Abram's birth), Serug, Nahor, and Terah, Abraham's father.

That Abram was a special soul to be born yet in the future is supported by the prophecy of Reu at the birth of his son Serug, preserved in the Legends of the Jews.

"From this child (Serug) he shall be born in the fourth generation that shall set his dwelling over the highest, and he shall be called perfect and spotless and shall be the father of nations, and his covenant shall not be dissolved, and his seed shall be multiplied for ever."[18]

All ten of his direct ancestors were still living at Abram's birth. Three of them died before Abram's 60th birthday. Peleg died first, when Abram was forty eight, followed by his grandfather Nahor when Abram was forty nine, and Noah, the patriarch of the earth, died in Abram's fifty eighth year.

With the death of Noah, Abram's seven direct ancestors still alive were Shem in his 458th year, Arphaxad in his 348th year, Salah in his 313th year, Eber in his 283rd year, Reu in his 219th year and Serug in his 187th year, and Terah in his 128th year, (See paragraph 1 page 1).

Shem, apparently became the Lord's prophet and patriarch of the earth and its spiritual leader at Noah's death. There is little reference to Shem in Genesis. Such an important person would not likely have faded from existence. He may well have been given another name; Melchizedek for example, king of Salem, by whom Abraham was blessed and to whom he paid tithes.[19]

The Legends of the Jews reports that Melchizedek was Shem and that his wife's name was Zedeketelbab: Jasher declares Shem's name to be Adonizedek. Melchizedek means King of Righteousness, Adonizedek means Lord of Righteousness.[20]

---

18. Legends I:185
19. Genesis 14:18-20, KJV, MT, (14:17-20) JST
20. Legends I:171; Jasher XVI:11-12

Abraham's story in Genesis begins with a reference to his (Abram's) birth along with his two brothers Nahor and Haran, born in the seventieth year of the life of their father Terah.[21]

It is unlikely however, that all three were born in the same year. Haran was probably the oldest followed by Nahor and Abram. One account puts Haran thirty two years older than Abram. Abram likely married Sarah at about fifty years of age when she was forty.

The Genesis account says nothing more about Abram's early life, moving directly to the departure of the family from Ur of Chaldees:

"And Terah took Abram his son, and Lot the son of Haran his son's son, and Sarai his daughter in law, his son Abram's wife; and they went forth with them from Ur of the Chaldees, to go into the land of Canaan; and they came unto Haran, and dwelt there. And the days of Terah were two hundred and five years: And Terah died in Haran"[22]

"Now the Lord had said unto Abram, Get thee out of thy country, and from thy kindred, and from thy father's house, unto a land that I will shew thee: And I will make of thee a great nation, and I will bless thee, and make thy name great; and thou shalt be a blessing: And I will bless them that bless thee, and curse them that curseth thee: and in thee shall all (the) families of the earth be blessed. So Abram departed, as the Lord had spoken unto him; and Lot went with him: And Abram was seventy and five years old when he departed out of Haran"[23]

Thus in a few sentences Genesis covers the first seventy five years of Abram's life. The brief account leaves the reader with many questions: Was something occuring in Ur which made it difficult for Abram to stay there? Why did the Lord want Abram to move into Canaan? Was the Lord's command to get out of Ur away from his kindred and father's house issued to Abram in Ur or in Haran? Was His command to leave his father's house Abram's first encounter with the Lord, or had he had prior experiences with Him? Why was Terah left behind in Haran where he lived his final sixty years? What was Abram's first seventy five years like? Who were his friends and associates?

---

21. Genesis 11:26-30, KJV, MT, (11:15-18) JST
22. Genesis 11:31-32, KJV, MT, (11:19-20) JST
23. Ibid 12:1-4, KJV, MT, (12:1-2) JST

None of these questions is answered by Genesis. Fortunately there are other writings which shed some light on them.

Ancient records written by the hand of Abraham on papyrus and translated by Joseph Smith Jr. in the year 1835 AD illuminate Abram's motivations for leaving the residence of his father, Terah, in the Ur of Chaldeas. These records sharpen our understanding of his relationship with God and Abraham's place in the history of this earth.

The Book of Abraham,[24] as this record is called, is written in the first person. It briefly parallels the Genesis account of Abram's departure from the Ur of Chaldees, his stay in Haran, Canaan and in Egypt. It also contains information important to our understanding of what was going on in Ur and why the Lord wanted Abram to leave. We learn that this was not Abram's first encounter with the Lord God Jehovah. We also learn that Abram had been given a special instrument by the Lord, the Urim and Thummim through which he, Abram, discerned the heavens and something about life as it existed before this earth was formed.

Abram encountered...the Lord face to face as one man talketh with another, and he told me of the works which his hands had made.[25] Abram learned that he (Abram) was chosen in advance to perform the work he was to do on this earth.

Abram, preceded Moses by at least 400 years, and had revealed to him the creation of the earth (through the Urim and Thummim). This revelation to Abram parallels the story of the creation revealed to Moses recorded in Genesis, and known to the world as the First Book of Moses.

"And I, Abraham, had the Urim and Thummim, which the Lord my God had given unto me, in the Ur of Chaldees; And I saw the stars, that they were very great, and that one of them was nearest unto the throne of God,"

"and there were many great ones which were near unto it; And the Lord said unto me; These are the governing ones; and the name of the great one is Kolob, because it is near unto me, for I am the Lord thy God: I have set this one to govern all those which belong to the same order as that upon which thou standest."[26]

24. The Book of Abraham, Pearl of Great Price
25. Ibid 3:11
26. Ibid 3:1-3

Abraham also affirms that he had in his possession ancient records previously kept by "the fathers, even the patriarchs, concerning the right of Priesthood," before his departure from the Ur of Chaldees and had

..."therefore a knowledge of the beginning of the creation, and also of the planets, and of the stars, as they were made known unto the fathers, have I kept even unto this day, and I shall endeavor to write some of these things upon this record for the benefit of my posterity that shall come after me."[27]

We learn from this passage that not only did Abraham have a knowledge of the beginning of the creation and also of the planets and the stars, but so did his fathers, meaning no doubt, Eber, Shem, Noah, Enoch and Adam. Abraham wrote it down for the benefit of his posterity, none of whom had yet been born. That Abraham had a great understanding of celestial bodies is supported by the writings in Antiquities and in the Legends of the Jews.[28]

In the record written by his own hand, Abraham declares:

..."I sought for the blessings of the fathers and the right whereunto I should be ordained to administer the same; having been myself a follower of righteousness, desiring also to be one who possessed great knowledge, and to be a greater follower of righteousness, and to possess a greater knowledge, and to be a father of many nations, a prince of peace, and desiring to receive instructions, and to keep the commandments of God, I became a rightful heir, a High Priest, holding the right belonging to the fathers."[29]

Continuing, Abraham declared:

"It (the right of Priesthood) was conferred upon me from the fathers; it came down from the fathers from the beginning of time, yea, even from the beginning, or before the foundations of the earth to the present time, even the right of the firstborn, on the first man, who is Adam, our first father, through the fathers unto me. I sought for mine appointment unto the Priesthood accord-

27. Ibid 1:31; see also Legends V:118; Abraham had Book of Adam
28. Antiquities VII:2; see also Legends I:225
29. Book of Abraham 1:2

6

ing to the appointment of God unto the fathers concerning the seed."[30]

Apparently in referring to the fathers, Abraham meant Eber, Shem and Noah and others further back in his ancestry, for Abraham continues:

"My fathers (probably meaning Terah, Nahor, Serug and Reu) having turned from their righteousness, and from the holy commandments which the Lord their God had given unto them, unto the worshiping of the gods of the heathen, utterly refused to hearken to my voice; For their hearts were set to do evil, and were wholly turned to the God of Elkenah, and the God of Libnah, and the God of Mahmackrah, and the God of Korash, and the god of Pharaoh, king of Egypt. Therefore they (including Terah) turned their hearts to the sacrifice of the heathen in offering up their children unto their dumb idols, and hearkened not unto my voice, but endeavored to take away my life by the hand of the priest of Elkenah. The priest of Elkenah was also the priest of Pharaoh"[31]

While Genesis is silent on the subject of Terah's idolatry Joshua is not;

"And Joshua said unto all the people, Thus saith the Lord God of Israel: your fathers dwelt of old time beyond the (river) flood even Terah, the father of Abraham, and the father of Nahor, and they served other gods....Now therefore fear the Lord, and serve Him in sincerity and in truth: and put away the gods which your fathers served on the other side of the flood (river) and in Egypt; and serve ye the Lord."[32]

The Antiquities and Legends of the Jews, the Book of Jasher, and the Apocalypse of Abraham also record Terah's idolatry. They report that idol worship was introduced by Nimrod who spred it through his political power since secular control of the whole region was in his

---

30. Ibid 1:3&4
31. Book of Abraham 1:5-7
32. Joshua 24:2-14 KJV, MT, JST

7

hands. Idol worship by the people including Terah was pervasive, as this passage indicates:

...."And all the sons of the earth in those days greatly transgressed against the Lord, and they rebelled against him and they served other gods, and they forgot the Lord who had created them in the earth; and the inhabitants of the earth made unto themselves, at that time, every man his god; gods of wood and stone which could neither speak, hear, nor deliver, and the sons of men served them and they became their gods. And the king (Nimrod) and his servants and Terah with all his household were then the first of those that served gods of wood and stone."[33]

Abraham continues his account:

"Now at this time it was the custom of the priest of Pharaoh, the king of Egypt, to offer up upon the altar which was built in the land of Chaldea, for the offering unto these strange gods, men, women, and children....Now this priest had offered upon this altar three virgins at one time, who were the daughters of Onitah, one of the royal descent directly from the loins of Ham. These virgins were offered up because of their virtue; they would not bow down to worship gods of wood or stone, therefore they were killed on this altar, and it was done after the manner of the Egyptians."[34]

The practice of human sacrifice including child sacrifice as reported in the Book of Abraham is supported by archeological evidence found by Glueck:

"When Abraham and his people traveled through the Negev, they probably did not recognize the sorry remains of the Chalcolithic villages that had been destroyed many centuries earlier. But the fashion of child sacrifice, which was in vogue in the Chalcolithic period, prevailed also in his time and for long thereafter. The pottery and sculptures and copper mace heads and loom

33. Jasher IX:6-7; Legends I:195,197; see also Antiquities IV:2-3, 209, 210, 211, 237, & VI:185-186, and Apocalpse of Abraham, pseudepigrapha I:681-704
34. Book of Abraham 1:8-11

weights of such Chalcolithic sites as Tell Abu Matar, Khirbet Samra and Teleilat Ghassul revealed only part of the story of their culture and period. Even more revealing is the skeleton of a new born babe found under a fireplace at Tell Abu Matar and of a child buried as a foundation offering under a stone wall there, and of an infant stuffed into a jar that had been placed under a threshold at Teleilat Ghassul."

"The firstborn of man and woman were offered to the gods so that the hearth might be full, the women conceive easily and bear many sons, the tilled acres yield their crops in unfailing abundance, the herds and flocks increase with numberless calves, and lambs and kids, the newly built house be full of blessing. Such gifts were intended to placate their wrath and elicit their favor."[35]

Even Abraham was not exempt as an intended sacrifice.

"And it came to pass that the priests laid violence upon me, that they might slay me also, as they did those virgins upon this altar....And as they lifted up their hands upon me, that they might offer me up and take away my life, behold I lifted up my voice unto the Lord my God, and the Lord hearkened and heard, and he filled me with the vision of the Almighty, and the angel of his presence stood by me, and immediately unloosed my bands; And his voice was unto me: Abraham, Abraham, behold my name is Jehovah, and I have heard thee, and have come down to deliver thee, and to take thee away from thy father's house, and from all thy kinfolk into a strange land which thou knowest not of; And this because they have turned their hearts away from me, to worship the god of Elkenah, and the god of Libnah and the god of Mahmackrah, and the god of Korash, and the god of Pharaoh, king of Egypt; therefore I have come down to visit them, and to destroy him who hath lifted up his hand against thee, Abraham, my son, to take away thy life. Behold, I will lead thee by my hand, and I will take thee, to put upon thee my name, even the Priesthood of thy father, and my power shall be over thee. As it was with Noah, so shall it be with thee, but through thy ministry my name shall be known in the earth forever, for I am thy God."[36]

35. Rivers in the Desert Chapter III p. 61
36. Book of Abraham 1:12-19

The Lord then followed through with His promise to destroy the priest who sought to take Abraham's life...."And the Lord broke down the altar of Elkenah, and of the gods of the land, and utterly destroyed them, and smote the priest that he died; and there was great mourning in Chaldea and also in the court of Pharaoh...."[37]

Jehovah, thus foreshadowed the first of His commandments later given to Abraham's posterity through Moses when He declared "Thou shalt have no other gods before me."

We see that Abraham's move into Canaan was at the command of the Lord, precipitated by state mandated worship of idols of wood and stone, instituted by Pharaoh, king of Egypt and of Chaldees. Further, Abraham's father Terah had worshipped dumb idols and had acceded to the practice of human sacrifice to appease those idols, even to the sacrifice of his own son, Abraham. Jehovah intervened, saved Abraham's life and commanded him to leave Ur of Chaldees and his kindred there.

Explaining his father's behavior, Abraham said that Terah was deceived by the Pharoah's claim to the priesthood, and that he was led away by their idolatry even to participation in their effort to take away his (Abraham's) life.

Genesis moves directly from a declaration of Abram's lineage and a listing of his family to his removal from Ur of Chaldees to Haran in six verses.[38]

From these verses we learn of Abram's brothers Nahor and Haran, his nephew Lot, his wife Sarai, who was barren at the time, Nahor's wife Milcah, daughter of Haran.

Back to Abraham's account:

"Now after the priest of Elkenah was smitten that he died, there came a fulfillment of those things which were said unto me concerning the land of Chaldea, that there should be a famine in the land.

Accordingly, a famine prevailed throughout all the land of Chaldea, and my father was sorely tormented because of the famine, and he repented of the evil which he had determined against me, to take away my life....

---

37. Ibid 1:20
38. Genesis 11:27-32, KJV, MT, (11:16-20) JST

10

Now the Lord God caused the famine to wax sore in the land of Ur, insomuch that Haran my brother died; but Terah my father yet lived in the land of Ur of the Chaldees. And it came to pass that I, Abraham took Sarai to wife, and Nehor took Milcah to wife, who were the daughters of Haran. Now the Lord had said unto me: Abraham get thee out of thy country, and from thy kindred, and from thy fathers house, unto a land I will show thee. Therefore, I left the land of Ur, of the Chaldees, to go into the land of Canaan; and I took Lot, my brother's son, and his wife, and Sarai my wife; and also my father followed after me, unto the land we denominated Haran. And the famine abated; and my father tarried in Haran and dwelt there, as there were many flocks in Haran; and my father turned again unto his idolatry therefore he continued in Haran."[39]

Remembering that the Lord God had spared his life by delivering him from the priest of Elkenah and had commanded him to leave his kindred and country Abraham and Lot his brother's son, prayed for guidance and received a blessing and a promise:

"But I, Abraham, and Lot my brother's son, prayed unto the Lord, and the Lord appeared unto me, and said unto me: Arise, and take Lot with thee; for I have purposed to take thee away out of Haran, and to make of thee a minister to bear my name in a strange land which I will give unto thy seed after thee for an everlasting possession, when they hearken to my voice. For I am the Lord thy God; I dwell in heaven; the earth is my footstool; I stretch my hand over the sea, and it obeys my voice; I cause the wind and the fire to be my chariot; I say to the mountains - Depart hence - and behold, they are taken away by a whirlwind, in an instant, suddenly. My name is Jehovah, and I know the end from the beginning; therefore my hand shall be over thee. And I will make of thee a great nation, and I will bless thee above measure, and make thy name great among all nations, and thou shalt be a blessing unto thy seed after thee, that in their hands they shall bear this ministry and Priesthood unto all nations;"

---

39. Book of Abraham 1:29-30, 2:1-5

"And I will bless them through thy name; for as many as receive this Gospel shall be called after thy name, and shall be accounted thy seed, and shall rise up and bless thee as their father; And I will bless them that bless thee and curse them that curse thee; and in thee (that is, thy priesthood) and in thy seed (that is thy Priesthood), for I give unto thee a promise that this right shall continue in thee, and in thy seed after thee (that is to say, the literal seed or the seed of the body) shall all the families of the earth be blessed, even with the blessings of the Gospel, which are the blessings of salvation, even of life eternal."[40]

This blessing and promise was most remarkable in that it was given to Abraham when he, as yet, had no children. Indeed, this was a prophecy concerning the future of Abraham and his yet unborn posterity, through whom the right of Priesthood was to continue, through whose ministry the Gospel, which are the blessings of salvation and life eternal, was/is to be spread, and through whom all the families of the earth were to be blessed.

The Legends indicate that the significance of Abram's being a blessing would "be fulfilled only in the future world, when the seed of Abraham shall be known among all nations and his offspring among the peoples as the seed which the Lord hath blessed".[41]

The right of priesthood, kings and birth were sometimes referred to as three crowns of (1) priesthood, (2) kingdom, & (3) gospel (Torah).[42]

More than four hundred years later during a similar encounter with Moses, the Lord God Jehovah declared

"For behold, this is my work and my glory to bring to pass the immortality and eternal life of man".[43]

The significance of this declaration of God's purpose will be discussed more fully in a subsequent volume.

---

40. Book of Abraham 2:6-11
41. Legends I:218
42. Ibid V:219
43. Book of Moses 1:39 Pearl of Great Price

Overwhelmed by these great blessings and promises Abraham's heart was filled with gratitude and he said:

"Now, after the Lord had withdrawn from speaking to me, and withdrawn his face from me, I said in my heart: Thy servant has sought thee earnestly; now I have found thee; Thou didst send thine angel to deliver me from the gods of Elkenah, and I will do well to hearken unto thy voice, therefore let thy servant rise up and depart in peace."[44]

Abraham and his family then left from Haran enroute to Canaan, in his seventy fifth year according to Genesis, in his sixty second year according to the Book of Abraham and in his fifty fifth year according to the Book of Jasher.

Before discussing Abrahams journey into Canaan let us return to his first fifty years.

---

44. Book of Abraham 2:12-13

CHAPTER II

ABRAHAM'S EARLY LIFE

But what of Abraham's early life and upbringing. If his immediate fathers, including Terah had turned to the worhip of dumb idols and to the practice of human sacrifice, how and when did Abraham become a follower of righteousness and how did he learn to call upon the living God for deliverance? How did he become so favored as to receive the Urim and Thummim and to be able to talk with the Lord face to face?

Where was the abode of his older fathers or ancestors who were still living during Abraham's first fifty eight years? Did Abraham have any contact with Noah, Shem and Eber? Was he influenced by them?

Explanations are not available in Genesis. The Antiquities and Legends of the Jews, the Book of Jasher and other writings each contain accounts of Abraham's birth and early life. While these accounts are apocryphal and may be questioned, they offer plausible answers to the above questions.

These writings place Terah as prince of Nimrod's hosts, an important and powerful position at the time of Abram's birth. Special heavenly manifestations surrounded Abram's birth, so much so that the life of the newly born son of Terah was threatened. To preserve Abram's life Terah tricked Nimrod into believing he had killed Abram. He then took Abram his son, secretly together with Abram's mother, Emetelo and nurse, and concealed them in a cave where they were brought provisions on a regular basis.

(From Jasher) "And the Lord was with Abram in the cave and he grew up, and Abram was in the cave ten years, and the king and his princes, sooth sayers and sages thought that the king had killed Abram...."[45]

"And when Abram came out from the cave, he went to Noah

45. Jasher VII:49-51, VIII:36

14

and his son Shem, and he remained with them to learn the instruction of the Lord and his ways, and no man knew where Abram was, and Abram served Noah and Shem his son for a long time."

"And Abram was in Noah's house thirty-nine years, and Abram knew the Lord from three years old, and he went in the ways of the Lord until the day of his death, as Noah and his son Shem had taught him; and all the sons of the earth in those days greatly transgressed against the Lord, and they rebelled against him and they served other gods, and they forgot the Lord who had created them in the earth; and the inhabitants of the earth made unto themselves, at that time, every man his god; gods of wood and stone which could neither speak, hear, nor deliver, and the sons of men served them and they became their gods."[46]

We see from these accounts that Abram learned the ways of the Lord from Noah and Shem in whose presence he dwelt for thirty-nine years from age ten to about age forty nine.

While Abram was gaining spiritual strength through righteous living and by learning to call upon the living God in the household of Noah and Shem, his father Terah was under the influence of Nimrod,

(From Jasher) "the king and all his servants and Terah with all his household were then the first of those that served gods of wood and stone....And all that generation were wicked in the sight of the Lord, and thus made every man his god, but they forsook the Lord who created them."

"And there was not a man found in those days in the whole earth, who knew the Lord (for they served each man his own god) except Noah and his household, and all those who were under his counsel knew the Lord in those days. And Abram the son of Terah was waxing great in those days in the house of Noah, and no man knew it, and the Lord was with him. And the Lord gave Abram an understanding heart, and he knew all the works of that generation were vain, and that all their gods were vain and were of no avail."[47]

---

46. Ibid IX:5-6
47. Book of Jasher IX:7-12

15

What better place for Abram to learn the ways of Lord God, then, than in the house of Noah and Shem, the only place where the living God was still being worshipped.

Jasher indicates that during his growth to manhood and maturity Abram first worshipped the sun, then concluded the sun could not be God, and next he worshipped the stars and the moon, again concluding they could not be the God that made the earth and all mankind, but rather, the sun, the moon and the stars are the servants of a living God:

(From Jasher) "And Abram said unto himself, Surely these are not gods that made the earth and all mankind, but these are the servants of God, and Abram remained in the house of Noah and there knew the Lord and his ways, and he served the Lord all the days of his life."[48]

Antiquities adds that Abram was the first to publish the notion "that there was but one God, the creator of the universe; and that as to other (gods), if they contributed anything to the happiness of men, that each of them afforded it only according to his appointment and not by their own power".

Further Abram had concluded from his observations of heavenly bodies that planets, stars, suns and moons were subservient to Him who commands them, and it is to Him we ought justly to offer our honour and thanksgiving.[49]

By contrast the rest of the world was under the influence of Nimrod "And king Nimrod reigned securely and all the earth was under his control, and all the earth was of one tongue and words of union."[50]

Jasher goes on to imply that the tower of Babel was built during Abram's stay with Noah and Shem and that the confusion of tongues, the scattering of people, and the shortening of the life of man were near simultaneous events, also which took place during Abram's first fifty years.

The Jasher and Antiquities accounts indicate the tower of Babel was of gigantic proportions which took many years and thousands on

---

48. Ibid IX:19
49. Antiquities Book I Ch VII:1
50. Jasher IX:20

thousands of laborers to build, that burnt brick and bitumen mortar were used in its construction.[51]

Further that "the building of the tower was unto them a transgression and a sin", which in the end resulted in the judgement of God upon them which included changing some of the builders of the towers into apes and elephants,* through killing one man through the hand of his neighbor, as a second means of judgement, and thirdly, through the scattering of those others who remained alive as humans.

The punishment or judgement of each of the three groups pertained to the motives each had for building the tower. The first group wanted to ascend to heaven and place their own gods of wood and stone there and worship them: they became like apes and elephants. The second group shot arrows from the top of the tower towards heaven attempting to slay those in the heavens; they turned on one another and slayed each other. And those who sought to actually ascend into heaven and fight against Him, the Lord, were scattered throughout the earth.

The scattering of the third and remaining group was largely self imposed, for they had seen the punishment of the first two groups and knew the wrath of God would shortly come upon them. They vacated the tower and took off in many directions and in many sub groups.

The Lord God destroyed the tower by opening up the earth which swallowed a third (and probably the largest) circumference of it. Another third was burnt by fire from heaven and the final third was left standing aloft. The part remaining aloft was three days walk in circumference.

It was during this period, according to Jasher, that Peleg died in the forty-eighth year of the life of Abram. Abram was still in the house of Noah and Shem at this time.[52]

The tower of Babel was destroyed, the language of the remaining people in the land of Shinar was confounded, and they broke into many divisions and scattered throughout the earth where they built many cities. Sodom, Gomorrah, Admah and Zeboyim were built by descendants of Ham, as was the city of Seir. Seir was the son of Hur,

---

51. Ibid IX:4-39; Antiquities Book I Ch IV:2-3
52. Ibid IX:21-39, X:1

*Is anything too hard for the Lord, if He wanted to judge people this way?

17

son of Hivi, son of Canaan, son of Ham. Shem's sons built the cities of Elam, Ashur, Arpachshad, Lud and Elam and named them after their own names. Shem's descendants also built Ninevah, Resen, Calach, Rehobother as well as Uz and Bela. According to Antiquities, Shem's five sons, inhabited the land that began at Euphrates and reached the Indian Ocean; Elam, left behind the Elamites, the ancestors of the Persians; Ashur lived at the City of Nineve and named his descendants Assyrians; Arphaxad named the Arphaxadites later called Chaldeans; Aram the Aramites which the Greeks called Syrians, and Laud (Lud) founded the Laudites later called Lydians. Japheth's descendants apparently left the entire area and built their cities there.

Nimrod stayed in the vicinity of Shinar, however, and built Erech, Eched, and Calneh, in addition to Babel. The names of his cities were descriptive of the events in the land of Shinar; Babel, because the Lord confounded the language of the whole earth, Erech because God dispersed them (the people), Eched, because of the great battle where members of the group killed each other off, and Calneh because his princes and men were consumed there.[54]

Nimrod placed the remainder of his people (subjects) within these cities. He dwelt in Babel and again consolidated his power, calling himself Amraphel saying that at the tower his princes and men fell through his means.[55]

Even so, Nimrod still would not return to the Lord, for he continued in wickedness and in teaching wickedness to the sons of men; and Marden, his son, was worse than his father, and continued to add to the abominations of his father.

"And he caused the sons of men to sin, therefore it is said, from the wicked goeth forth wickedness."[56]

As Abram's thirty-nine year stay with Noah and Shem came to a close, that is in his forty eighth year, Peleg died, and Nahor his grandfather died in his forty ninth year. In Abram's fiftieth year he returned to his father Terah's house.

(From Jasher) "And in the fiftieth year of the life of Abram son of Terah, Abram came forth from the house of Noah, and went to his

53. Ibid X:2-39
54. Ibid XI:1-4 Antiquities Book I Ch VI:4-5
55. Ibid XI:5-6
56. Ibid XI:7-8

fathers house. And Abram knew the Lord, and he went in his ways and instructions, and the Lord his God was with him. And Terah his father was in those days, still captain of the host of king Nimrod, and he still followed strange gods."[57]

Returning home after a thirty nine year absence, full of knowledge of the living God, full of instruction in His ways, and full of righteousness, Abram was appalled at the conditions in his father Terah's house. For he saw in his father's house twelve gods of wood and stone standing in their temples, with scores of other little gods and images. Abram appealed to his father Terah. He tried to win him over to the living God of Noah and Shem, without success. Abram devised a scheme to show him the folly of worshipping false gods. Ultimately Abram destroyed his father's idols (false gods) and was called before Nimrod at Terah's request to account for his deeds - Abram tried to convince Nimrod of his folly in worshipping false gods, again without success.

Abram was put in prison for ten days while the king was trying to decide what to do with him.

The king consulted his advisers asking what should be done with this destroyer of Terah's gods. They asked for Abram to be burned. They thought Terah should be burned too, since it was through Terah Abram was preserved rather than killed at birth.

The king was angry with Terah for having disobeyed him fifty years previously and sought now to kill him along with Abram through burning. Seeking an explanation the king asked Terah who advised him to disobey his command to kill Abram fifty years ago. Terah falsely blamed it on his son Haran. Haran was sentenced to die with Abram. The two were cast into the fire. Haran was consumed in the fire, but Abram was saved.

Haran's death by fire is at variance with Abraham's own story in the Book of Abraham where Haran's death was reportedly caused by famine. Of significance, in these stories, however, is Abraham's effort to persuade his father Terah and king Nimrod to worship the living God. For example:

(From Jasher) "And Abram asked his father saying, Father tell me where is God who created heaven and earth, and all the sons of

---

57. Ibid XI:13-15

19

men upon earth, and who created thee and me. And Terah answered his son Abram and said, Behold those who created us are all with us in the house."

"And Abram said to his father, My lord, shew them to me, I pray thee; and Terah brought Abram into the chamber of the inner court, and Abram saw, and behold the whole room was full of gods of wood and stone, twelve great images and others less than they without number."

"And Terah said to his son, Behold these are they which made all thou seest upon earth, and which created me and thee and all mankind. And Terah bowed down to his gods, and he then went away from them, and Abram his son went away with him."[58]

After having his mother fix a fine meal for Terah's gods which was placed before them, (to make a point with his father) and which the gods did not eat, Abram clothed with the spirit of the living God broke down Terah's images or false gods.

(From Jasher) "And in the evening of that day in that house Abram was clothed with the spirit of God. And he called out and said, Wo unto my father and this wicked generation, whose hearts are all inclined to vanity, who serve these idols of wood and stone which can neither eat, smell, hear nor speak, who have mouths without speech, eyes without sight, ears without hearing, hands without feeling, and legs which cannot move; like them are those who made them and that trust in them."[59]

Abram filled with righteous indignation took a hatchet and broke down all the gods except the greatest (largest) in whose hand he placed the hatchet. Terah heard the noise of Abram's activity and came into the room of his gods. Terah confronted Abram "What is this work thou hast done to my gods?" Abram replied that the destruction was the work of the large god in whose hands the hatchet was seen.

---

58. Ibid XI:19-22
59. Ibid XI:31-32

Terah replied:

(From Jasher) "What is this tale that thou hast told? Thou speakest lies to me. Is there in these gods spirit, soul or power to do all thou hast told me? Are they not wood and stone, and have I not myself made them, and canst thou speak such lies, saying that the large god that was with them smote them? It is thou that didst place the hatchet in his hands, and then sayest he smote them all."[60]

And Abram answered his father and said to him:

(From Jasher) "And how canst thou then serve these idols in whom there is no power to do anything? Can those idols in which thou trustest deliver thee? can they hear thy prayers when thou callest upon them? can they deliver thee from the hands of thy enemies, or will they fight thy battles for thee against thy enemies, that thou shouldst serve wood and stone which can neither speak nor hear?"

"And now surely it is not good for thee nor for the sons of men that are connected with thee to do these things; are you so silly, so foolish or so short of understanding that you will serve wood and stone, and do after this manner? And forget the Lord God who made heaven and earth, and who created you in the earth, and thereby bring a great evil upon your souls in this matter by serving stone and wood?"

"Did not our fathers in days of old sin in this manner, and the Lord God of the universe brought the waters of the flood upon them and destroyed the whole earth? And how can you continue to do this and serve gods of wood and stone, who cannot hear, or speak, or deliver you from oppression, therby bringing down the anger of the God of the universe upon you? Now therefore my father refrain from this, and bring not evil upon thy soul and the souls of thy household."[61]

---

60. Ibid XI:41-42
61. Ibid XI:43-48

21

After completing this appeal to his father Terah, Abram took the hatchet and broke down the largest and remaining idol and departed. Terah, seeing what Abram had done appealed to the king, rehearsed what happened fifty years before, and asked the king to call Abram to account for breaking down his (Terah's) gods. Abram was apprehended and brought before the King. Abram again blamed the destruction on the large god. The king asked, "Had they power to speak and eat and do as thou has said?" The king's question gave Abram the opening he wanted.

For Abram replied:

(From Jasher) "And if there be no power in them why dost thou serve them and cause the sons of men to err through thy follies? Dost thou imagine that they can deliver thee or do anything small or great, that thou shouldst serve them? And why wilt thou not serve the God of the whole universe, who created thee and in whose power it is to kill and keep alive? O foolish, simple, and ignorant king, woe unto thee forever."

"I thought thou wouldst teach thy servants the upright way, but thou has not done this, but hast filled the whole earth with thy sins and the sins of thy people who have followed thy ways. Dost thou not know, or hast thou not heard, that this evil which thou dost, our ancestors sinned therein in days of old, and the eternal God wrought the waters of the flood upon them and destroyed them all, and also destroyed the whole earth on their account? And wilt thou and thy people rise up now and do like unto this work, in order to bring down the anger of the Lord God of the universe, and to bring evil upon thee and the whole earth?"

"Now therefore put away this evil deed which thou doest, and serve the God of the universe, as thy soul is in his hands, and then it will be well with thee. And if thy wicked heart will not hearken to my words to cause thee to forsake thy evil ways, and to serve the eternal God, then wilt thou die in shame in the latter days, thou, thy people and all who are connected with thee, hearing thy words or walking in thy evil ways."

"And when Abram had ceased speaking before the king and princes, Abram lifted up his eyes to heaven, and he said, The Lord seeth all the wicked, and he will judge them."[62]

We note that Abraham had testified to his father and again to Nimrod that idol worhip, and all that goes with it, was one of the principal reasons for the destruction of the peoples of the earth by flood. Noah, his three sons and their wives were the only survivors.

Nimrod was not convinced. Abram was cast into prison for calling Nimrod to repentance, spent ten days there, and was sentenced to death by burning. He was cast into the fire but was not burned. The king was astounded. He asked Abram why he was not burned. Abram replied:

(From Jasher) "The God of heaven and earth in whom I trust and who has all in his power, he delivered me from the fire into which thou didst cast me."[63]

The king thought Abram was a god and bowed down to him.

(From Jasher) "And Abram said to them, Do not bow down to me, but bow down to the God of the world who made you, and serve him, and go in his ways for it is he who delivered me from out of this fire, and it is he who created the souls and spirits of all men, and formed man in his mother's womb, and brought him forth unto the world, and it is he who will deliver those who trust in him from all pain."[64]

The king still marvelled how Abram was saved from the fire. He gave Abram many gifts including two servants, one named Oni and the other named Eleaser. Abram went forth from the king in peace, but many of the servants of the king had heard Abram and followed him,

---

62. Ibid XI:54-61
63. Ibid XII:35
64. Ibid XII:38

even about three hundred. Taking these followers with him Abram returned to Terah's house:

> (From Jasher) "he and the men that followed him, and Abram served the Lord his God all the days of his life, and he walked in his ways and followed his law. And from that day forward Abram inclined the hearts of the sons of men to serve the Lord."[65]

Abram married Sarai and Nahor married Milca, at this time, the two women being the daughters of their brother Haran, according to Jasher, Antiquities, and the Legends of the Jews.

Abram had had at least two brushes with death as he persisted in serving the living God. Divine intervention saved him each time, from the furnace, and again from the being offered as a sacrifice: During Abram's trials his message was not lost, for he had won souls to God, and they adhered to him.

Failing to destroy Abram by fire, Nimrod and the Pharaoh tried another means, sacrifice to their gods. They laid violence upon Abram that they might slay him. But Abram prayed mightily for deliverance. The Lord God of this earth intervened, introduced himself as Jehovah and informed Abram that he should leave his father's house and his kinfolk and go into a strange land. Abram was promised he would be led by the Lord's hand, and that the Lord's name and His priesthood (i.e. the power to act for God) would be put upon him. The Lord's power would also be over Abram. See Chapter I.

Thus the stage was set for Abram to leave Ur of Chaldees, and go into a land where his family and followers could worhip the living God, Jehovah, and walk uprightly before Him, without secular interference.

In conversations with his father, Abram invited Terah to come with them, and counseled him to leave his high station with Nimrod, his idols and riches, and serve the Lord who created him in the earth. Terah repented of his attempts to take Abram's life, left King Nimrod, his idols and riches and came as requested.

> (From Jasher) "And Abram said to his father. . .Arise, let us go together to the land of Canaan, that we may be delivered from his (King Nimrod's) hand, lest thou perish also through him in the latter days. Dost thou not know or has thou not heard, that it is

---

65. Ibid XX:42-43

24

not through love that Nimrod giveth thee all his honor, but it is only for his benefit that he bestoweth all this good upon thee? And if he do unto thee greater good than this, surely these are only vanities of the world, for wealth and riches cannot avail in the day of wrath and anger. Now therefore hearken to my voice, and let us arise and go to the land of Canaan, out of the reach of injury from Nimrod; and serve thou the Lord who created thee in the earth and it will be well with thee, and cast away all the vain things which thou pursuest ....And Terah hearkened to the voice of his son Abram, and Terah did all that Abram said, for this was from the Lord, that the king should not cause Abram's death."[66]

As Genesis, the Book of Abraham, the Legends of the Jews and the Book of Jasher recorded, Abram and Sarai and their party stopped in a land denominated as Haran and stayed there for a time before moving on to Canaan.

While in Haran, where there was good pasture, and many flocks, the famine, which the Lord had imposed and which had caused Terah to repent of his intent to take his sons Abram's life, abated. Terah returned again to his idolatry after the famine abated and lived out the remaining years of his life, more than sixty years, in Haran.

Abram was successful in winning over many souls to the living God Jehovah, and away from idol worship while in Haran. Genesis records only that the souls Abram "had gotten in Haran" followed him into Canaan. Jasher describes Abram's behavior and the conversions more fully.

(From Jasher) "And the people of the land of Haran saw that Abram was good and upright with God and men, and that the Lord his God was with him, and some of the people of the land of Haran came and joined Abram, and he taught them the instruction of the Lord and his ways; and these men remained with Abram in his house and they adhered to him."[67]

Jasher goes on to report that Abram remained in the land of Haran for three years, and moved on to Canaan at the request of the Lord who appeared to him and rehearsed again the promises and

---

66. Jasher XII:65-70
67. Jasher XIII:2

blessings in store if Abram would obey. Jasher gives Abram's age when he departed Ur of Chaldees at fiftytwo and fiftyfive when the Lord appeared and urged him to move on to Canaan. Abram obeyed, however, Nahor his brother, Terah his father and Lot his nephew and all their families remain in Haran. Abram and all belonging to him arrived in Canaan, and built an altar. The Lord God appeared again and reiterated His future promises and blessings.

Noah died while Abram (age 58) was in Canaan. In his seventieth year the Lord God appeared to Abram again, identified Himself as that God who brought Abram out of Ur and challenged him "to walk before me and be perfect and keep my commands", and again reiterated His promises and future blessings.

After this wonderful experience, desiring to ascertain the welfare of his father, mother, brother, and nephew and their families, Abram returned to Haran where he remained five years.

(From Jasher) "And many of the people of Haran, about seventy two men followed Abram and Abram taught them in the instruction of the Lord and his ways, and he taught them to know the Lord."[68]

Once again the Lord appeared to Abram, this time while he visited his family in Haran. He rehearsed His promises and future blessings and commanded Abram to:

"go forth from this place, thou, thy wife, and all belonging to thee, also every one born in thy house and all the souls thou hast made in Haran, and bring them out with thee from here and rise to return to the land of Canaan".[69]

Abram left his father Terah and mother Emtelai in Haran where Emtelai is believed to have died as well as Terah. The Legends claim Abram forsook his father because Terah wanted to "ruin Abram".[70]

This time Lot and his family went with Abram. Apparently his

---

68. Jasher XIII:1-22
69. Ibid XIII:24
70. Legends I:218

26

brother Nahor stayed behind with Terah and was likely idolatrous again, as was Terah.

(From Jasher) "And Abram arose and took his wife Sarai and all belonging to him and all that were born to him in his house and the souls which they had made in Haran, and they came out to go to the land of Canaan. And Abram went and returned to the land of Canaan, according to the word of the Lord. And Lot the son of his brother Haran went with him, and Abram was seventy five years old when he went forth from Haran to return to the land of Canaan."[71]

We return now to the description of Abram and his entourage as they depart from Haran and move into Canaan given by his own hand in the Book of Abraham, by Genesis, by the Antiquities, the Legends of the Jews and by Jasher.

---

71. Jasher XXIII:25-26

CHAPTER III

SO I ABRAHAM DEPARTED AS THE LORD HAD SAID UNTO ME

(From the Book of Abraham) "So I, Abraham, departed as the Lord had said unto me, and Lot with me; and I, Abraham, was sixty and two years old when I departed out of Haran. And I took Sarai, whom I took to wife when I was in Ur, in Chaldea, and Lot, my brother's son, and all our substance that we had gathered, and the souls that we had won in Haran, and came forth in the way to the land of Canaan, and dwelt in tents as we came on our way. Therefore, eternity was our covering and our rock and our salvation, as we journeyed from Haran by the way of Jershon, to come to the land of Canaan."

"Now I, Abraham, built an altar in the land of Jershon, and made an offering unto the Lord, and prayed that the famine might be turned away from my father's house, that they might not perish. And then we passed from Jershon through the land unto the place of Sechem; it was situated in the plains of Moreh, and we had already come into the borders of the Canaanites, and I offered sacrifice there in the plains of Moreh, and called on the Lord devoutly, because we had already come into the land of this idolatrous nation."

"And the Lord appeared unto me in answer to my prayers, and said unto me: Unto thy seed shall I give this land. And I, Abraham, arose from the place of the altar which I had built unto the Lord, and removed from thence unto a mountain on the east of Bethel, and pitched my tent there, Bethel on the west, Hai on the east; and there I built an altar unto the Lord and called again upon the name of the Lord."

"And I, Abraham, journeyed, going on still towards the south; and there was a continuation of a famine in the land; and I Abraham, concluded to go down into Egypt, to sojourn there, for the famine became very grievous."[71]

The Legends note that each altar raised was a center of missionary activity for Abram. He would pitch a tent for Sarai and one for himself, then he would proceed at once to make proselytes, thus he accomplished his purpose to proclaim the Name of God.[72]

Abram was a stranger in the land of Canaan, a land the Lord has promised would belong to him and his (Abram's) posterity. Why would the Lord want to evict the Canaanites? Because, say the Legends, the Canaanites occupied a land not given to them by the Lord. The Legends report that Canaan settled in land the Lord had given to Shem. When the lots were drawn by Noah's sons, Shem was to receive the temperate zones, Japheth the frigid or cold zones and Ham the hot zones. Canaan ignored his father's (Ham) plea and that of his brother's Cush and Mizraim to vacate the land belonging to Shem and his children. Abram, a descendant of Shem, was a rightful heir of the land in which he was a stranger.

"Though the Canaanites had taken unlawful possession of the land, yet Abraham respected their rights; he provided his camels with muzzles to prevent them from pasturing on the properties of others."[74]

The famine was too severe, however, and he went on to Egypt to escape it.

Thus the account of Abraham's departure from Haran with Sarah, Lot, and with all their substance, and the souls they had won in Haran, is consonant with this segment of Abraham's life as reported in KJV Genesis, JST Genesis, MT Genesis, Jasher, and the Antiquities

71. Book of Abraham 2:14-21
72. Legends I:219
73. Ibid I:172
74. Ibid I:220

29

and Legends of the Jews.[75] Two differences in the accounts are noted, the Book of Abraham records Abraham's age at departure at 62, all others record his age as 75 at this departure. Another difference is that the Book of Jasher reports this as a second departure for Abraham, having been in Canaan for fifteen years previously. See Chapter XIII for details.

As previously mentioned Abraham had already learned much about the planets and the stars and their relationship to one another, one being greater than another. He learned also that it was likewise with the spirits of men and women, or intelligences, one may be greater than another. He learned that he, Abraham, was one of the great ones who would be made rulers, and that he was chosen to be so before he was born. For the complete text see Book of Abraham Chapters 3-5. These things were learned from records he had received from the fathers. They were revealed to Abraham with the assistance of the Urim and Thummim given to him by the Lord before he left Ur of the Chaldees.

In Hebrew, Urim and Thummim meant Lights and Perfection. An Urim and Thummim is an instrument prepared of God to assist man in obtaining revelation from Him and in translating languages. See Exodus 28:30 etc. The Egyptians were astrologers. It was important, therefore, that Abraham could discern the heavens, with the Lord's help, before encountering them. Other information important for Abraham to know before entering Egypt dealt with the Pharaoh, his power and origins. Abraham already knew a lot about the Pharaoh as his own record indicates.

(From Abraham) "Now this king (Pharaoh) of Egypt was a descendant from the loins of Ham, and was a partaker of the blood of the Canaanites by birth. From this descent sprang all the Egyptians, and thus the blood of the Canaanites was preserved in the land. The land of Egypt being first discovered by a woman, who was the daughter of Ham, and the daughter of Egyptus, which in Chaldean signifies Egypt, which signifies that which is forbidden."

"When this woman discovered the land it was under water,

---

75. Book of Abraham 2:14-21, Genesis 12:4-10, KJV, MT, JST 12:3-8, Jasher XIII:25-28, 15:1

who afterward settled her sons in it, and thus from Ham, sprang that race which preserved the curse in the land. Now the first government of Egypt was established by Pharaoh, the eldest son of Egyptus, the daughter of Ham, and it was after the manner of the government of Ham, which was patriarchal. Pharaoh, being a righteous man, established his kingdom and judged his people wisely and justly all his days, seeking earnestly to imitate that order established by the fathers in the first generations, in the days of the first patriarchal reign, even in the reign of Adam, and also of Noah, his father, who blessed him with the blessings of the earth, and with blessings of wisdom, but cursed him as pertaining to the Priesthood. Now, Pharaoh, being of that lineage by which he could not have the right of Priesthood, notwithstanding the Pharaohs would fain claim it from Noah through Ham, therefore my father was led away by their idolatry."[76]

Earlier in the Genesis record we read of Canaan and his posterity being cursed by Noah, the Patriarch.[77] The curse apparently included a denial of the Priesthood and its blessings. On the other hand, Pharaoh received the blessings of the earth, and of wisdom. Though Pharaoh could not have the right of Priesthood, he fain claimed that right anyway from Noah through Ham.

Abraham's father Terah and grandfather Nahor were therefore influenced by the false claims of the Pharaoh's and Nimrod. Nimrod, son of Cush, son of Ham; and the Pharaoh, eldest son of Egyptus, daughter of Ham both claimed the right of Priesthood through Ham and through Noah. Through Nimrod and the Pharaohs, the worship of gods of wood and stone, that neither speak, hear nor deliver, was introduced and maintained through their political powers. Thus Terah and his fathers were led away by Nimrod and the Pharaoh's idolatry.

Nibley adds, "In the Abraham traditions the great perverter Nimrod marries his mother Sachlas and claims to possess the priesthood through his inheritance of the garment of Noah that was stolen by Ham and passed down as an illegal inheritance to his descendants."[78]

Ham had seen the nakedness of his father Noah, "And Noah awoke from his wine, and knew what his younger son had done to him,

---

76. Book of Abraham 1:21-27
77. Genesis 9:25, 27 KJV, MT, JST
78. Nibley, Abraham in Egypt Page 212, Legends I:177, Antiquities I:8:1

and he said Cursed be Canaan;"[79]....one wonders why Noah would curse Canaan, because Ham had seen Noah's nakedness? One explanation is that Ham had stolen the garment of the priesthood from Noah. When Noah cursed Ham's son Canaan, Ham gave the garment to his son Cush, instead.

(From Jasher) "And the garments of skin which God made for Adam and his wife, when they went out of the garden, were given to Cush. For after the death of Adam and his wife, the garments were given to Enoch, the son of Jared, and when Enoch was taken up to God, he gave them to Methuselah, his son. And at the death of Methuselah, Noah took them and brought them to the ark, and they were with him until he went out of the ark."

"And in their going out, Ham stole those garments from Noah, his father, and he took them and he hid them from his brothers (Shem and Jepheth). And when Ham begat his first born Cush, he gave him the garments in secret, and they were with Cush many days. And Cush also concealed them from his sons and brothers and when Cush had begotten Nimrod, he gave him those garments through his love for him, and Nimrod grew up and when he was twenty years old he put on those garments."[80]

Abraham, with the help of the Urim and Thummim, his many personal encounters with, and direct interventions by the Lord, was now prepared to meet the astrologers and idolatrous Pharaohs of Egypt.

The very grievous famine encountered in Canaan motivated Abraham and those with him to go down to Egypt where food was more plentiful.

Genesis, the Book of Abraham, Jasher, the Antiquities and the Legends of the Jews all report this event in Abraham's life.

"And it came to pass when I was come near to enter into Egypt, the Lord said unto me: Behold, Sarai, thy wife, is a very fair woman to look upon; Therefore it shall come to pass, when the Egyptians shall see her, they will say - She is his wife; and they

79. Genesis 9:21-25 KJV
80. Jasher VII:24-29, Abraham in Egypt 212, Legends I:178

will kill you, but they will save her alive; therefore see that ye do on this wise: Let her say unto the Egyptians, she is thy sister, and thy soul shall live. And it came to pass that I, Abraham, told Sarai, my wife, all that the Lord had said unto me - Therefore say unto them, I pray thee, thou art my sister, that it may be well with me for thy sake, and my soul shall live because of thee."[81]

Note that in this account, Abraham was acting under instructions from the Lord, while in the other three accounts it is reported as Abraham's own idea. Confusion over the ancestrial relationship between Abraham and Sarah stems in part from the report of the second difficulty with Sarah's beauty, this time with Abimelech when Abraham said, "And yet indeed she is my sister, she is the daughter of my father, but not the daughter of my mother; and she became my wife."[82]

Was Sarah Abraham's full sister, half-sister, or was she his niece? If Sarah were Abraham's niece she would have been "the (grand) daughter of my father."

It is clear from Genesis and other accounts that Abraham was ten years older than Sarah. It is also clear from that account that Nahor, Abraham's brother, married Milcah the daughter of Haran, Abraham's other brother, and that Lot was also Haran's son. Mentioned in the same sentence is Sarah as follows:

"And Abram and Nahor took them wives: the name of Abram's-wife was Sarai; and the name of Nahor's wife, Milcah, the daughter of Haran, the father of Milcah and the father of Iscah."[83]

Sarai is referred to in the Legends of the Jews as "Iscah, the Seer".[84] She was so called because of her prophetic gift. If Sarai and Iscah are one and the same, it is clear, from Genesis quoted in the above verse, that Sarai is the daughter of Haran and granddaughter of Terah.

Jasher reports that Haran was thirty two years older than Abraham, that Haran took a wife when Abraham was seven years old, and that Lot was their firstborn when Abraham was about eight years old. Further, that Milca was the first daughter of Haran and Sarah the

81. Book of Abraham 2;22-25 see also Genesis 12:12-13, KJV, MT (12:9) JST
82. Genesis 20:12 KJV, MT, (20:13) JST
83. Ibid 11:29 KJV, MT, (11:18) JST
84. Legends I:203, 276, V:214, 215, 231, 272

second born daughter, when Haran was forty two years of age and Abraham was ten.[85]

Jasher and the Legends of the Jews also report that Terah had taken a second wife.

(From Jasher) "And Terah took a wife and her name was Amthelo, the daughter of Cornebo; and the wife of Terah conceived and bare him a son in those days. Terah was seventy years old when he begat him, and Terah called his name Abram, because the king raised him in those days, and dignified him above all the princes that were with him."[86]

One may conclude that Sarah is Abraham's niece; Terah being Abraham's father and Sarah's grandfather. Sarah is Terah's granddaughter by his first wife, and Abraham is his son by his second wife, giving credence to the "She is the daughter of my father, but not the daughter of my mother" report. One may also conclude Sarah is Abraham's step-sister. As Nelson Glueck puts it "Abraham deceived the Egyptian Pharaoh with the truth".[87]

The Book of Abraham's report ends with his appeal to Sarah to say she is his sister. Genesis, Jasher, Antiquities and the Legends continue the story.

Having been forewarned by the Lord as to what might happen concerning Sarai, and having received counsel from Him in handling the problem, Abram and his entourage went into Egypt to escape the famine in Canaan.

(From Genesis) "And it came to pass that, when Abram was come into Egypt, the Egyptians beheld the woman that she was very fair. The princes also of Pharaoh saw her and commended her before Pharaoh; and the woman was taken into Pharaoh's house. And he entreated Abram well for her sake; and he had sheep, and oxen and he asses, and menservants and maidservants, and she asses, and camels."

"And the Lord plagued Pharaoh and his house with great

---

85. Jasher VII 7:22, 9:1-4
86. Jasher VII 7:50-51 see also Legends I:186, 191, 213, V:208, 209, VI:463
87. Rivers in the Desert Page 66-67; see also Antiquities VI:5

plagues because of Sarai, Abram's wife. And Pharaoh called Abram and said, What is this that thou hast done unto me? why didst thou not tell me that she was thy wife? Why saids't thou, She is my sister? so I might have taken her to me to wife: now therefore, behold thy wife, take her, and go thy way."

"And Pharaoh commanded his men concerning him: and they sent him away, and his wife and all that he had. And Abram went up out of Egypt, he and his wife, and all that he had, and Lot with him, into the south. And Abram was very rich in cattle, in silver and in gold."[88]

Jasher, the Antiquities and Legends of the Jews embellish the story. When the Pharaoh took Sarai into his house, Abram and Sarai both prayed for her deliverance. In Sarai's prayer she rehearsed the Lord's command for them to leave Ur, how they had been obedient in coming into the land of Canaan and how they went on into Egypt to escape the famine in Canaan. In closing her prayer she asked for mercy and deliverance from the Pharaoh.[89]

The Lord heard their prayers, and sent an angel to deliver her from the power of the Pharaoh.

(From Jasher) "And the king (Pharaoh) came and sat before Sarai and behold an angel of the Lord was standing over them, and he appeared to Sarai, and said to her, Do not fear, for the Lord has heard thy prayer."[90]

The king (Pharaoh) having been told Sarai was Abram's sister, then gave Abram silver and gold and precious stones in abundance together with cattle, menservants and maidservants.[91]

Genesis gives no other reason why the Lord plagued the Pharaoh and his house with great plagues than to say it was because of Sarai, Abram's wife.[92]

Jasher, the Antiquities and Legends of the Jews report that after giving Abram many riches, the King (Pharaoh) approached Sarai, and

88. Genesis 12:14-20, 13:1-2 KJV, MT, (12:10-15, 13:1-2) JST
89. Jasher XV:1-19 also Legends I:223
90. Ibid XV:19-20, Legends I:223
91. Ibid XV:21-22, Legends I:223
92. KJV Genesis 12:17 KJV, MT (12:13) JST

reached out to touch her that night. The angel, standing over her, smote the Pharaoh heavily. As the Pharaoh approached Sarai a second time, the angel smote him to the ground, "and acted thus the whole night and the king (Pharaoh) was terrified."[93]

The king (Pharaoh) stayed away from Sarai the rest of the night. The next day the Pharaoh, having been told by Sarai that she was Abram's wife, called Abram and queried him about her.

> (From Jasher) "Why didst thou say, She is my sister, owing to which I took her unto me for a wife, and this heavy plague has therefore come upon me and my household. Now, therefore, here is thy wife, take her and go from our land, lest we all die on her account."

> "And Pharaoh took more cattle, men servants, and maid servants, and silver and gold, to give to Abram, and he returned unto him Sarai his wife. And the king took a maiden whom he begat by his concubines, and he gave her to Sarai for a handmaid. And the king said to his daughter, It is better for thee my daughter to be a handmaid in this man's house than to be a mistress in my house, after we have beheld the evil that befell us on account of this woman."[94]

The plaque of affliction upon the Pharaoh and his people was leprosy, according to the Legends of the Jews.[95] No wonder the Pharaoh wanted to get rid of Abram, Sarai and their party. Jasher and the Legends of the Jews identifies the handmaid given to Sarai by the Pharaoh as Hagar.[96] In other words, Abram later married Hagar, the daughter of the Pharaoh. Ishmael born of this union, would then be a descendant of Shem through Abraham and of Ham through the Pharaoh.

In Antiquities of the Jews we see that this experience gave Abram leave "to enter into conversation with the most learned among the Egyptians, from which conversation, his virtue and his reputation became more conspicuous than they had been before....Whereupon he

---

93. Jasher XV:23-25
94. Ibid XV:26-34 see also Legends I:224
95. Legends I:224
96. Jasher XV:26-34, XVI:24-26; Legends I:224

(Abram) was admired by them in those conferences as a very wise man; and one of great sagacity, when he discoursed on any subject....He communicated to them arithmetic and delivered to them the science of astronomy, for before Abram came into Egypt, they were unacquainted with those parts of learning; for that science came from the Chaldeans into Egypt, and from thence to the Greeks also."[97]

(From Jasher) "And Abram arose and he and all belonging to him went away from Egypt, and Pharaoh ordered some of his men to accompany him and all that went with him. And Abram returned to the land of Canaan, to the place where he had made the altar, where he at first had pitched his tent."[98]

97. Antiquities Book I Ch VIII:1-2 see also Legends I:225
98. Jasher XV:33-34

CHAPTER IV

AND MELCHIZEDEK KING OF SALEM BROUGHT FORTH BREAD AND WINE

The Genesis account of Abram and Sarai's return to Canaan from Egypt continues;

"And he went on his journeys from the south even to Bethel unto the place where his tent had been at the beginning, between Bethel and Hai; Unto the place of the altar, which he had made there at the first: and there Abram called on the name of the Lord. And Lot also, which went with Abram, had flocks and herds and tents. And the land was not able to bear them, that they might dwell together: for their substance was great, so that they could not dwell together."[99]

Acquiring much of their wealth in flocks and herds and servants from Egypt, Abraham's and Lot's movement of their animals precipitated a pasture crisis, because the land of Canaan was less able to sustain them.

(From Genesis) "And there was a strife between the herdman of Abram's cattle and the herdman of Lot's cattle: and the Canaanite and Perizite dwelled then in the land. And Abram said unto Lot, Let there be no strife, I pray thee, between me and thee, and between my herdman and thy herdman; for we are brethren."

"Is not the whole land before thee? separate thyself, I pray thee, from me: if thou will take the left hand, then I will go to the

---

99. Genesis 13:3-6 KJV, MT, (13:2-4) JST

right;or if thou depart to the right hand, then I will go to the left. And Lot lifted up his eyes, and beheld all the plain of Jordan, that it was well watered everywhere, before the Lord destroyed Sodom and Gomorrah, even as the garden of the Lord, like the land of Egypt, as thou comest unto Zoar."

"Then Lot chose him all the plain of Jordan; and Lot journeyed east: and they separated themselves the one from the other. Abram dwelled in the land of Canaan, and Lot dwelled in the cities of the plain, and pitched his tent toward Sodom."[100]

Thus Abram and Lot, his nephew, part company after many years of daily contact. Jasher and the Legends of the Jews puts most of the blame for the separation on Lot, who, they say, fed his cattle in the fields of the Canaanites, who, in turn, complained to Abram of Lot's behavior. Abram bade them to separate and assured Lot that if he needed help and protection in the future he, Abram, would come to his aid.[101] Abram chose to live in or near Hebron in Canaan a city more ancient than Tanis of Egypt.[102] In separating himself from Abram, Lot also separated himself from the God of Abraham as well, and he fell into trouble.

Lot's need for Abram's assistance soon came to be, for Lot had located himself among wicked people. "But the men of Sodom were wicked and sinners before the Lord exceedingly," declared Genesis.[103]

"And the Lord was angry with them."[104]

The Lord spoke again to Abram and bade him to remember their covenants.

(From Genesis) "And the Lord said unto Abram, after Lot that was separated from him, Lift up now thine eyes, and look from

---

100. Ibid 13:7-12 KJV, MT, (13:4-10) JST
101. Jasher XV:35-47
102. Antiquities Book I Ch VIII:3
103. Genesis 13:13 KJV, MT, (13:11) JST
104. Genesis 13:11 JST

the place where thou art northward, and southward and eastward and westward;"[105]

"And remember the covenant which I make with thee; for it shall be an everlasting covenant; and thou shalt remember the days of Enoch thy father;"[106]

"For all the land which thou seest, to thee will I give it, and to thy seed forever. And I will make thy seed as the dust of the earth: so that if a man can number the dust of the earth, then shall thy seed also be numbered. Arise, walk through the land in the length of it and in the breadth of it; for I will give it unto thee. Then Abram removed his tent, and came and dwelt in the plain (by the terebinth) of Mamre, which is in Hebron, and built there an altar unto the Lord."[107]

Lot chose to dwell in the plain of Jordan where five cities had been built: Sodom, Gomorrah, Admah, Zeboiim and Bela. The first four were believed to have been founded by men of the same name from the family of Ham.[108] The fifth city, Bela, was apparently founded by a man of the same name, Bela, of the house of Ashur, son of Shem.[109] Bela also was called Zoar and was adjacent to Sodom.[110]

Nimrod, son of Cush (descendant also of Ham) also called Amraphel, and Abram's old enemy, had built four cities Babel, Erech, Eched and Calneh.[112] The descendants of Shem's sons Elam, Ashur, Arphaxad, Lud and Aram also built cities and called the names of their cities after their names.[113]

Such a city was Elam, over which Chedorlaomer reigned as king. Chedorlaomer fought with the families of Ham and subdued them, and he also fought against the five cities of the plain and brought them under his control and made them subject to his tax.[114]

---

105. Genesis 13:14 KJV, MT (13:12) JST
106. Genesis 13:13 JST
107. Genesis 13:15-18 KJV, MT (13:14-15) JST
108. Jasher X:24-28
109. Ibid 10:31-36
110. Genesis 14:2 KJV, MT, JST
111. Legends I:229, V:85 Yashar Noah 29a
112. Jasher XI:1-6
113. Ibid X:31
114. Ibid XI:9-11

For twelve years the five cities of the plain, Sodom, Gomorrah, Admah, Zebouin and Bela or Zoar were under Chedorlaomer's control and taxation. In the thirteenth year they rebelled against him and in the fourteenth year Chedorlaomer launched a counter attack, defeated them and spoiled their cities.[115]

Chedorlaomer did not do it alone, however. He engaged the assistance of Amraphel (Nimrod) king of Shinar, Arioch, king of Ellasar, and Tidal, king of Nations.[116]

These four kings made war with five kings of the plain, Bera, king of Sodom, Birsha, king of Gomorrah, Shinab king of Admah, and Shemeber King of Zeboiim, and the king of Bela, which is Zoar.[117] Before reaching these five cities however, they destroyed and plundered other cities.[118]

By the time the five cities of the plain joined the battle, the fighting was taking place in the vale or valley of Siddim which was filled with s/lime pits, where the kings of Sodom and Gomorrah fell.[119]

The four kings of Elam et al pursued the remainder of the other five kings armies who had fled to the mountain Hanabel. In pursuit, the armies of the five kings of Elam et al, stopped at Sodom, taking all that was there, plundering it and Gomorrah,"And they took Lot, Abram's brother's son, who dwelt in Sodom, and his goods and departed."[120]

Word was brought to Abram, his friends and confederates Amorite brothers Anar, Aschol and Mamre, that Lot had been taken captive by Elam's armies. The messenger is identified by Genesis as one that had escaped the battles. Jasher identified him as Unic, Abram's servant who was in the battle and saw what happened.[121]

Abram assembled 318 of his trained men and pursued the army of Elam unto Dan where he smote them, recaptured all the goods, and more importantly, recovered Lot and his family.[122]

The remnants of Sodom's defeated army including Bera the King emerged from the s/lime pits, where they had fallen, to meet Abram

---

115. Genesis 14:1-12 KJV, MT, (14:1-11) JST
116. Ibid 14:1 KJV, MT, JST
117. Ibid 14:1-12 KJV, MT, (14:1-11) JST
118. Ibid 14:5-7 KJV, MT, (14:5-6) JST
119. Ibid 14:10 KJV, MT (14:9) JST
120. Ibid 14:12 KJV, MT (14:11) JST
121. Jasher XVI:6
122. Genesis 14:13-16; KJV, MT, (14:12-15) JST, Jasher XVI:6-8

and his men.[123] Abram's impressive victory also brought out Melchizedek, King of Salem or Jerusalem, who came with bread and wine. Being the priest of the Most High God, Melchizedek received from Abram tithes of all he had taken, and then blessed him.[124]

There is no indication Melchizedek or his city participated in these battles. However, the Antiquities account records that Melchizedek had supplied Abram's army in a hospitable manner.[125]

JST Genesis provides additional information about Melchizedek:

"And Melchizedek, king of Salem, brought forth bread and wine; and he break bread and blest it; and he blest the wine, he being the priest of the most high God. And he gave to Abram, and he blessed him, and said, Blessed Abram, thou art a man of the most high God, possessor of heaven and earth; And blessed is the name of the most high God, which hath delivered thine enemies into thine hand. And Abram gave him tithes of all he had taken."[126]

The King of Sodom, a wicked man, wanted to strike a deal with him, offering to give Abram all the goods recovered from Elam in the battle, in exchange for the persons recovered.[127]

The righteous Abram was incensed by this proposal for he replied:

(From Genesis)..."I have lift up mine hand unto the Lord, the most high God, the possessor of heaven and earth, That I will not take from a thread even to a shoe latchet, and that I will not take any thing that is thine, lest thou shouldst say, I have made Abram rich; Save only that which the young men have eaten, and the portion of the men which went with me, Aner, Eshcol, and Mamre; let them take their portion."[128]

---

123. Ibid 14:17 KJV, MT, (14:16) JST
124. Ibid 14:18-20 KJV, MT, (14:17-40) JST
125. Antiquities Book I,X:2
126. Genesis 14:17-20 JST
127. Genesis 14:21 KJV, MT, JST
128. Ibid 14:22-24 KJV, MT, JST

Apparently pleased with Abram's stance, "Melchizedek lifted up his voice and blessed Abram."[129] A more complete description of Melchizedek to whom Abram paid tithes and by whom he was blessed is presented in JST Genesis as follows:

"Now Melchizedek was a man of faith, who wrought righteousness; and when a child he feared God, and stopped the mouths of lions, and quenched the violence of fire. And thus having been approved of God, he was ordained an high priest after the order of the covenant which God made with Enoch. It being after the order of the Son of God; which order came, not by man, nor the will of man, neither by father nor mother; neither by beginnings of days nor ends of years; but of God; And it was delivered unto men by the calling of his own voice, according to his own will, unto as many as believed on his name."

"For God having sworn unto Enoch and unto his seed with an oath by himself; that every one being ordained after this order and calling should have power by faith to break mountains, to divide the seas, to dry up waters, to turn them out of their course; To put at defiance the armies of nations, to divide the earth, to break every band, to stand in the presence of God; to do all things according to his will, according to his command, subdue principalities and powers, and this by the will of the Son of God which was before the foundation of the world. And men having this faith, coming up unto this order of God were translated and taken up unto heaven."

"And now, Melchizedek was a priest of this order; therefore, he obtained peace in Salem, and was called the Prince of peace. And his people wrought righteousness, and obtained heaven, and sought for the city of Enoch which God had before taken, separating it from the earth, having reserved it unto the latter days, or the end of the world;"

"And hath said, and sworn with an oath, that the heavens and the earth should come together; and the sons of God should be tried so as by fire. And this Melchizedek, having thus estab-

---

129. Genesis 14:25 JST

43

lished righteousness, was called the king of heaven by his people, or in other words, the King of peace. And he lifted up his voice, and he blessed Abram being the high priest, and the keeper of the storehouse of God; Him whom God had appointed to receive tithes for the poor. Wherefore, Abram paid unto him tithes of all that he had, of all the riches which he possessed, which God had given him more than that which he had need."[130]

Jasher's account of this meeting is thus:

..."Adonizedek, King of Jerusalem, the same was Shem, went out with his men to meet Abram and his people, with bread and wine, and they remained together in the valley of Melech. And Adonizedek blessed Abram, and Abram gave him a tenth from all he had brought from the spoil of his enemies, for Adonizedek was a priest before God."[131]

Adonizedek means Lord of Righteousness, Melchizedek means King of Right eousness. The JST Genesis translation and the Legends of the Jews each report Melchizedek as being an high priest who blessed Abram. The Legends also note that God Himself changed Shem's name to Melchizedek.[132] The account of this same meeting between Abram and Melchizedek as contained in the Legends of the Jews reads as follows:

"When Abraham returned from the war Shem, or as he is sometimes called Melchizedek, the king of righteouness, priest of God, Most High, and king of Jerusalem, came forth to meet him with bread and wine. And this high priest instructed Abraham in the laws of the priesthood and in the Torah (gospel) and to prove his friendship for him. He blessed him, and called him the partner of God in the possession of the world seeing that through him the name of God (Jehovah) had first been made known among men."[133]

---

130. Genesis 14:26-40 JST
131. Jasher XVI:11-12, Legends I:233
132. Legends V:225, I:233
133. Legends I:233

Returning to JST Genesis:

"And it came to pass, that God blessed Abram, and gave unto him riches, and honor, and lands for an everlasting possession, according to the covenant which he had made and according to the blessing wherewith Melchizedek had blessed him"[134]

The Lord revealed to Joseph Smith, the prophet, that Melchizedek was a great high priest, and that His priesthood or power was called the Melchizedek Priesthood out of respect or reverence to the name of the Supreme Being. Before Melchizedek's day it was known as the Holy Priesthood after the order of the Son of God.[135] By calling it the Melchizedek Priesthood the Lord's name would not be mentioned too frequently.

Abram's contact with the Lord and his messengers had been frequent. The Lord had intervened and saved Abram's life in Ur, and had saved Sarai's life before the Pharaoh. Abram also had help from above when he rescued Lot. He had learned of the Lord's ways through Noah and Shem/Melchizedek. Melchizedek had blessed Abram and had conferred the priesthood upon him. Abram was promised repeatedly that his descendants would be as numerous as the sands of the sea, and as numerous as the dust of the earth or stars in the sky, and that through them (his descendants) all the families of the earth would be blessed.

Not surprising, then, as Abram reached eighty years of age, and still childless, he wondered why the Lord had given him no seed. No doubt reflecting on the great blessing Melchizedek had given him, Abram pondered his childlessness. Appearing again in another vision in Hebron the Lord reassured Abram once more.

"After these things the word of the Lord came unto Abram in a vision saying, Fear not Abram; I am thy shield, and thy exceeding great reward. And Abram said, Lord God, what wilt thou give me, seeing I go childless, and the steward of my house is this Eliezer of Damascus? And Abram said, Behold, to me thou hast given no seed: and lo, one born in my house is mine heir."

"And behold, the word of the Lord came unto him saying:

---

134. Genesis 14:40 JST
135. D&C 107:1-8

45

This shall not be thine heir; but he that shall come forth out of thine own bowels shall be thine heir. And he brought him (Abram) forth abroad and said, Look now, toward heaven, and tell the stars, if thou be able to number them: and he said unto him (Abram), so shall thy seed be."[136]

In other words Abram was to be the natural father of an heir, even at his age. The heir was not to be one of his servants but of Abram's own flesh.

The JST Genesis adds,

"And Abram said, Lord God, how wilt thou give me this land for an everlasting inheritance? And the Lord said Though thou wast dead, yet am I not able to give it to thee? And if thou shalt die, yet thou shalt possess it, for the day cometh, that the Son of Man shall live; but how can he live, if he be not dead? he must first be quickened. And it came to pass that Abram looked forth and he saw the days of the Son of Man, and he was glad, and his soul found rest, and he believed in the Lord: and the Lord counted it unto him for righteousness."[137]

The Lord then reemphasized that it was He who brought Abram out of the Ur of Chaldees to "give thee this land to inherit it," and forecast the experiences Abram's descendants would have in Egypt, the next 400 years reckoned from the birth of Isaac. The Lord assured Abram he had much more time to live and have children, assured him his descendants would break free of their captures in Egypt and come back to inherit their land of promise, which the Lord said, could not be given to them yet, because the land of inheritance was currently occupied by people whose iniquity was not yet full.[138]

(From Legends) "It is worth noting here that God required no other sacrifices under the law of Moses, than what were taken from these five kinds of animals where He here required of Abram, (sometimes referred to as the Covenant of the pieces).

---

136. Genesis 15:1-5 KJV, MT, (15:1-8) JST
137. Genesis 15:9-12 JST, also 15:6 KJV, MT
138. Genesis 15:7-21 KJV, MT, (15:13-22) JST

Nor did the Jews feed upon any other domestic animals than the three here named."[139]

(From Genesis) "And he said unto him, I am the Lord that brought thee out of the Ur of Chaldees, to give thee this land to inherit it. And he said, Lord God whereby shall I know that I shall inherit it? And he said unto him, Take me an heifer of three years old, and a she goat of three years old, and a ram of three years old, and a turtle dove, and a young pigeon. And he took out him all these, and divided them in the midst, and laid each piece one against another: but the birds divided he not. And when the fowls came down upon the carcasses, Abram drove them away. And when the sun was going down, a deep sleep fell upon Abram; and lo an horror of great darkness fell upon him."

"And he said unto Abram, Know of a surety that thy seed shall be a stranger in a land that is not theirs, and shall serve them; and they shall afflict them four hundred years; And also that nation, whom they shall serve, will I judge: and afterward shall they come out with great substance."

"And thou shalt go to thy fathers in peace, thou shalt be buried in a good old age. But in the fourth generation they shall come hither again; for the iniquity of the Amorites is not yet full."

"And it came to pass, that, when the sun went down, and it was dark, behold a smoking furnace, and a burning lamp that passed between those pieces."

"In the same day the Lord made a covenant with Abram saying, Unto thy seed have I given this land, from the river of Egypt unto the great river Euphrates: The Kenites, and the Kenzzites and the Kadmonites. and the Hittites, and the Perizzites and the Rephaims, and the Amorites, and the Canaanites and the Girgashites and the Jebusites."[140]

Approaching their eighty-fifth and seventh-fifth birthdays respec-

---

139. Legends I:237
140. Genesis 15:7-21 KJV, MT (15:13-22) JST

tively, Abram and Sarai still had no children. Abram entreated God to grant that he might have male issue. Sarai felt it was her fault. At God's command she did something about it. Sarai gave Abram her handmaid Hagar whereby Abram could have children. Hagar was an Egyptian and the probable daughter of the Pharaoh of Egypt. Sarai had been a good example for Hagar and Hagar had "learned all the ways of Sarai, as Sarai taught her, she was not in any way deficient in following her good ways."[141] "Taught and bred by Sarah she walked in the same paths of righteousness as her mistress, and thus was a suitable companion for Abraham, Abram, instructed by the holy spirit, acceded to Sarah's proposal."[142]

"Now, Sarai, Abram's wife bare him no children: and she had a handmaid, an Egyptian, whose name was Hagar. And Sarai said unto Abram, Behold now, the Lord hath restrained me from bearing: I pray thee, go in unto my maid, it may be that I may obtain children by her. And Abram hearkened to the voice of Sarai. And Sarai, Abram's wife took Hagar her maid the Egyptian, after Abram had dwelt ten years in the land of Canaan, and gave her to her husband Abram to be his wife."

"And he went in unto Hagar, and she conceived: and when she saw that she had conceived, her mistress was despised in her eyes. And Sarai said unto Abram, My wrong be upon thee: I have given my maid into thy bosom; and when she saw that she had conceived, I was despised in her eyes: the Lord judge between me and thee."[143]

Sarai had waited years for children without success. Hagar conceived almost immediately. Sarai was despondent and jealous, Hagar was proud, and despised Sarai. Friction developed in the family. Abram reminded Sarai that Hagar was her maid. "But Abram said unto Sarai Behold, thy maid is in thy hand; do to her as it pleaseth thee. And when Sarai dealt hardly with her, she fled from her face."[144]

---

141. Jasher XVI:24-25; Antiquities Book I Ch X:4
142. Legends I:237
143. Genesis 16:1-5 KJV, MT, JST
144. Genesis 16:6; KJV, MT, (16:6-7) JST Legends I:238, V:20 Yasher Lek 34a

48

Jasher embellishes the event:

"And Abram hearkened to the voice of his wife Sarai, and he took her handmaid Hagar, and Abram came to her and she conceived. And when Hagar saw that she had conceived she rejoiced greatly, and her mistress was despised in her eyes, and she said within herself, This can only be that I am better before God than Sarai my mistress, for all the days that my mistress had been with my lord, she did not conceive, but me the Lord has caused in so short a time to conceive by him."

"And when Sarai saw that Hagar had conceived by Abram, Sarai was jealous of her handmaid, and Sarai said within herself, This is surely nothing else but that she is better than I am. And Sarai said unto Abram, My wrong be upon me, for at the time when thou didst pray before the Lord for children why didst thou not pray on my account that the Lord should give me seed from thee?"

"And when I speak to Hagar in thy presence, she despiseth my words, because she has conceived, and thou wilt say nothing to her; may the Lord judge between me and thee for what thou has done to me. And Abram said to Sarai, Behold thy handmaid is in thy hand, do unto her as it may seem good in thy eyes, and Sarai afflicted her, and Hagar fled from her to the wilderness."[145]

The Genesis account continues,

"And the angel of the Lord found her by a fountain of water in the wilderness, by the fountain in the way to Shur. And he said, Hagar, Sarai's maid, whence camest thou? And whither wilt thou go? And she said, I flee from the face of my mistress Sarai. And the angel of the Lord said unto her, Return to thy mistress, and submit thyself under her hands. And the angel of the Lord said unto her, I will multiply thy seed exceedingly, that it shall be not numbered for multitude."

"And the angel of the Lord said unto her, Behold, thou art

---

145. Jasher XVI:28-33, Legends I:238-239

49

with child, and shalt bear a son, and shalt call his name Ishmael; because the Lord hath heard thy affliction. And he will be a wild man; his hand will be against every man, and every man's hand against him; and he shall dwell in the presence of all his brethren."

"And she called the name of the Lord that spake unto her, Thou God seest me, for she said, Have I also here looked after him that seest me? Wherefore the well was called Beer-lahai-roi; behold it is between Kadesh and Bered."

"And Hagar bare Abram a son: and Abram called his son's name which Hagar bare, Ishmael. And Abram was fourscore and six years old, when Hagar bear Ishmael to Abram."[146]

The Masoretic text refers to Ishmael as one who would become a "wild ass of a man" as contrasted to "wild man". In either case, the metaphor here probably means a freedom loving, nomadic man.

JST Genesis declared that Beer-lahai-roi was the name of the angel who appeared unto Hagar, wherefore the well was called Beer-lahai-roi for a memorial.[147]

146. Genesis 16:7-16;KJV, MT; JST16:8-20; Legends I: 239
147. Genesis 16:14-18 JST

CHAPTER V

WALK UPRIGHTLY BEFORE ME AND BE PERFECT

Genesis records nothing of the next thirteen years of Abram's life from eighty six until he is ninety nine years of age. Much of great significance, however, is recorded about his ninety ninth and one hundredth years. The Lord appears to Abram, again, and commands him to be perfect. He reaffirms and amplifies the covenant already made, introduces the token of that covenant, foreshadows the blessings Sarai will receive, extends the covenant to Isaac, a child yet to be conceived and gives Abram and Sarai new names: Abraham and Sarah.

In addition, the Lord reaffirms his gift of the land of Canaan to Abraham and his seed, for an everlasting possession, and commands Abraham and all his seed after him to keep the covenants between them and God.

(From Genesis) "And when Abram was ninety years old and nine, the Lord appeared to Abram, and said unto him, I am the Almighty God; walk before me, and be thou perfect (whole hearted). And I will make my covenant between me and thee, and will multiply thee exceedingly. And Abram fell on his face: and God talked with him saying, As for me, behold, my covenant is with thee, and thou shalt be a father of many (a multitude of) nations."[148]

To which JST Genesis adds "walk *uprightly* before me and be perfect."[149]

(From Genesis) "Abram fell on his face, and called upon the name

---

148. Genesis 17:1-4 KJV, MT
149. Genesis 17:1 JST

of the Lord. And God talked with him, saying, my people have gone astray from my precepts, and have not kept mine ordinances, which I gave unto their fathers; and they have not observed mine anointing, and the burial or baptism wherewith I commanded them; But have turned from the commandment, and taken unto themselves the washing of children, and the blood of sprinkling; and have said that the blood of the righteous Abel was shed for sins, And have not known wherein they are accountable before me."

"But as for thee, behold, I will make my covenant with thee, and thou shalt be a father of many nations. And this covenant I make, that thy children may be known among all nations."[150]

(From KJV, MT Genesis) "Neither shall thy name anymore be called Abram, but thy name shall be Abraham; for a father of many (a multitude of) nations have I made thee. And I will make thee exceeding fruitful and I will make nations of thee, and kings shall come out of thee, and of thy seed."[151]

(From JST Genesis) "And I will establish a covenant of circumcision with thee, and it shall be my covenant between me and thee, and thy seed after thee, in their generations; that thou mayest know forever that children are not accountable before me until they are eight years old. And thou shalt observe to keep all my covenants wherein I covenanted with thy fathers, and thou shalt keep the commandments which I have given thee with mine own mouth, and I will be a God unto thee and thy seed after thee."[152]

Continuing the Lord said,

(From Genesis) "And I will give unto thee, and to thy seed after thee, the land wherein thou art a stranger (the land of thy sojournings), all the land of Canaan, for an everlasting possession; and I will be their God. And God said unto Abraham, (and, as for

---

150. Genesis 17:3-9 JST
151. Genesis 17:5-6 KJV, MT, (17:9-10) JST
152. Genesis 17:11-12 JST

thee) Thou shalt keep my covenant therefore, thou, and thy seed after thee in their generations. This is my covenant, which ye shall keep, between me and you and thy seed after thee: Every man child among you shall be circumcised. And ye shall circumcise the flesh of your foreskin; and it shall be a token of the covenant betwixt me and you."

"And he that is eight days old shall be circumcised among you, every man child in your generations, he that is born in the house, or bought with money of any stranger which is not of thy seed. He that is born in thy house, and he that is bought with thy money, must needs be circumcised: and my covenant shall be in your flesh for an everlasting covenant. And the uncircumcised man child whose flesh of his foreskin is not circumcised, that soul shall be cut off from his people; he hath broken my covenant."[153]

While the covenant was to be everlasting, the sign of the covenant was later discontinued, as far as Christians are concerned, because the Lord no longer required it.

And as if to be certain that he knew through whom the covenant was to be continued after Abraham's death, the Lord gave Sarai a new name Sarah, blessed her and prophecied she was to be the mother of nations, and that kings of (and) people would come of her. In other words, Abraham was to be the father of many nations and Sarah was to be the mother of many nations, and that, not only would their descendants be numerous as the stars in the sky or the grains of sand in the sea, but kings of (and) nations would be among their posterity. Further, that their descendants would be known among all nations.

(From Genesis) "And God said unto Abraham, As for Sarai, thy wife, thou shalt not call her name Sarai, but Sarah shall her name be. And I will bless her, and (moreover) give thee a son also of her: yea, I will bless her, and she shall be a mother of nations; kings of (and) people shall be of her. Then Abraham fell upon his face, and laughed (rejoiced), and said in his heart, Shall a child be born unto him that is an hundred years old? and shall Sarah, that is ninety years old, bear?"

---

153. Genesis 17:8-14 KJV, MT, (17:13-20)JST, Jasher XVII:16-19, Legends I:239

Thinking that might be impossible Abraham said unto God:

(From Genesis) ..."O that Ishmael might live before thee: And God said, (nay, but) Sarah thy wife shall bear thee a son indeed; and thou shalt call his name Isaac: and I will establish my covenant with him for an everlasting covenant, and with his seed after him."[154]

And as if to clarify Ishmael's role (he was just thirteen years of age at the time), the Lord said,

(From Genesis) "And as for Ishmael, I have heard thee; Behold, I have blessed him, and will make him fruitful, and will multiply him exceedingly; twelve princes shall he beget, and I will make him a great nation."[155]

The future history of the world was to see the literal fulfillment of these great prophesies given to Abraham and Sarah when she was eighty nine, passed normal child bearing age, by today's standards, and he was ninety nine years old. Pointing out through whom these blessings and covenants would continue, the Lord declared that Sarah would bare a son, that his name was to be Isaac, and that the Lord would establish His everlasting covenant with Isaac's seed or posterity after him.

Again, future history was to reveal that twelve princes were born of Ishmael and his descendants did, indeed, become a great nation in fulfillment of that prophesy. The covenant the Lord had established with Abraham, however, was to be continued through Isaac and his seed.

(From Genesis) "But my covenant will I establish with Isaac, which Sarah shall bear unto thee at this set time in the next year. And he left off talking with him, and God went up from Abraham."[156]

From the language used in these scriptures we may infer that this had been a face to face encounter between the Lord God of Heaven and

154. Genesis 17:15-18 KJV, MT (17:21-25) JST
155. Genesis 17:20 KJV, MT (17:26-27) JST
156. Genesis 17:21-22 KJV, MT

Abraham, and that the shape of the future history of the world was being formed by the great covenants entered into that day, the token or symbol of which was to be circumcision. Implied in JST Genesis is that the ordinance of baptism was introduced by the Lord as a commandment prior to Abraham's day and that the people had gone astray and had not kept the ordinances introduced to their fathers. Further, that the ordinance was being re-introduced through Abraham, that children were not accountable unto the Lord before eight years of age, and that circumcision at eight days of age was introduced as a reminder that children of God's covenant people should enter into the covenant through baptism at age eight years.[157]

Abraham moved quickly to seal his covenant with the Lord God the self same day by assembling his household. He executed the token of the covenant by circumcising the males as required.

(From Genesis) "And Abraham took Ishmael his son, and all that were born in his house and all that were bought with his money, every male among the men of Abraham's house; and circumcised the flesh of their foreskin in the selfsame day, as God had said unto him. And Abraham was ninety years old and nine, when he was circumcised in the flesh of his foreskin. And Ishmael his son was thirteen years old, when he was circumcised in the flesh of his foreskin. In the selfsame day was Abraham circumcised, and Ishmael his son. And all the men of his house, living in the house, and bought with money of the stranger (foreigner), were circumcised with him."[158]

Other important events in the life of Abraham and Sarah quickly followed: The Lord again appeared, this time with heavenly messengers. They informed Sarah, in the land of Mamre, that her body would be returned to one capable of bearing a child and that she would indeed bare a son. These representatives of God had also come to destroy the cities of Sodom and Gomorrah, whose "sin was very grievous". The Legends say that each of these three messengers assumed the form of human beings and that each had an assignment:

1. Michael brought Sarah the glad tidings that she would bear a son.

---

157. Genesis 17:11-12 JST
158. Genesis 17:23-27 KJV, MT, (17:30-33) JST

2. Gabriel would deal destruction to Sodom and Gomorrah
3. Raphael was to heal the wounds of Abraham, and assist Gabriel in the destruction of Sodom and Gomorrah.

Abraham felt confident enough to appeal to the Lord for the lives of the righteous living among the wicked in Sodom and Gomorrah. Lot and his family were spared destruction, Sodom and Gomorrah were destroyed. Abraham and Sarah moved on to Gerar in the land of the Philistines where Abimelech, the King, was encountered. Here, Abraham declared that Sarah was his sister a second time, again to spare his life, and to prevent the King from taking Sarah unto himself for a wife. Though almost ninety years of age, Sarah, whose body had been returned to child bearing age, was desired by King Abimelech. The Lord intervened and plagued the King and his people, for Sarah's sake. When Sarah was returned to Abraham, the Lord lifted the plague imposed on King Abimelech.

To reiterate, the Lord again appeared immediately following Abraham's circumcision as he sat in the tent door in the heat of the day. His tent had been pitched in the plains of Mamre. Three men referred to as angels by JST Genesis, by the Book of Jasher, and the Antiquities and Legends of the Jews (Michael, Gabriel and Raphael) came to converse with Abraham and Sarah.

(From Jasher) "And in the third day Abraham went out of his tent and sat at the door to enjoy the heat of the sun, during the pain of his flesh. And the Lord appeared to him in the plain of Mamre, and sent three of his ministering angels to visit him, and he was sitting, at the door of the tent, and he lifted his eyes and saw, and lo, three men were coming from a distance, and he rose up and ran to meet them and he bowed down to them and brought them into his house."[159]

And Abraham said to them, (From Genesis)..."My Lord (brethren) if now I have found favour in thy sight pass not away, I pray thee, from thy servant: Let a little water, I pray you, be fetched, and wash your feet, and rest (recline) yourselves under the tree: And I will fetch a morsel of bread, and comfort (stay) ye your hearts; after that ye shall pass on: for therefore are ye come to your servant. And they said, So do, as thou hast said. And

---

159. Jasher XVIII:3-6, Legends I:240

Abraham hastened into the tent unto Sarah, and said, Make ready quickly three measures of fine meal, knead it and make cakes upon the hearth. And Abraham ran unto the herd, and fetched a calf tender and good, and gave it unto a young man (the servant) (Eliezer?) and he hasted to dress it. And he took butter (curd) and milk, and the calf which he had dressed, and set it before them, and he stood by them under a tree, and they did eat."[160]

(From JST Genesis) "And they said unto him, Where is Sarah thy wife? And he said, Behold in the tent. And one of them blessed Abraham and he said, I will certainly return unto thee from my journey, and lo, according to the time of life, Sarah thy wife shall have a son. And Sarah heard him in the tent door."[161]

"now Abraham and Sarah were old and well stricken in age; and it ceased to be with Sarah after the manner of women. Therefore, Sarah laughed within herself, saying, After I am waxed old shall I have pleasure, my lord being old also? And the angel of the Lord said unto Abraham, Wherefore did Sarah laugh, saying, Shall I of a surety bear a child, which am old? Is anything too hard for the Lord?"

"At the time appointed, behold, I will return unto thee from my journey, which the Lord hath sent me; and according to the time of life thou mayest know that Sarah shall have a son. Then Sarah denied, saying, I laughed not; for she was afraid. And he said, Nay, but thou didst laugh."[162]

The Legends indicate that Abraham's friends Aner, Eshcol and Mamre were present during this event and the meal prepared was actually eaten by them. The angels therefore did not eat. In addition, Michael was the greatest of the angels and it was he who announced the birth of Isaac.[163]

Having completed the first two assignments, i.e. to inform Sarah

---

160. Genesis 18:1-8 KJV, MT, (18:1-7) JST
161. Genesis 18:8-10 JST, (18:9-10) KJV, MT
162. Genesis 18:8-15 JST (18:11-15) KJV, MT, Legends I:243-244
163. Legends I:243; Antiquities Book I Ch XI:2

that she would have a son, even at her age, and to heal Abraham, the angels of the Lord turn to their third assignment, which involved the cities of Sodom and Gomorrah, and the saving of Lot.

CHAPTER VI

SODOM AND GOMORRAH ARE DESTROYED, SOME OF LOT'S FAMILY IS SAVED

The sins of Sodom and Gomorrah were very grievious. Angels were sent by the Lord to destroy these cities and their people.

The sins of Sodom and Gomorrah included homosexuality, and other grievious sexual transgressions alluded to in Genesis Chapter 19.

(From Jasher) "In those days all the people of Sodom and Gomorrah, and of the whole five cities, were exceedingly wicked and sinful against the Lord, and they provoked the Lord with their abominations, and they strengthened in acting abominably and scornfully before the Lord, and their wickedness and crimes were in those days great before the Lord."

"And they had in their land a very extensive valley, about half a day's walk, and in it there were fountains of water and a great deal of herbage surrounding the water. And all the people of Sodom and Gomorrah went there four times in the year, with their wives and children and all belonging to them, and they rejoiced there with timbrels and dances."

"And in the time of rejoicing they would all rise and lay hold of their neighbor's wives, and some, the virgin daughters of their neighbors, and they enjoyed them, and each man saw his wife and daughter in the hands of his neighbor and did not say a word. And they did so from morning to night, and they afterward returned home each man to his house and each woman to her tent; so they always did four times in the year."[164]

---

164. Jasher XVIII:11-15; Legends I:245

In this account we see the people of Sodom and Gomorrah participated in other sexual orgies adding these grievious sins to homosexuality mentioned in Genesis. Nor were their sins limited to those of a sexual nature.

Continuing,

(From Jasher) "Also when a stranger came into their cities and brought goods which he had purchased with a view to dispose of there, the people of these cities would assemble, men, women, and children, young and old, and go to the man and take his goods by force, giving a little to each man until there was an end to all the goods of the owner which he had brought into the land."

"And if the owner of the goods quarrelled with them, saying, 'What is this work which you have done to me', then they would approach to him one by one, and each would show him the little which he took and taunt him, saying, 'I only took that little which thou didst give me', and when he heard this from all, he would arise and go from them in sorrow and bitterness of soul, when they would all arise and go after him, and drive him out of the city with great noise and tumult."[165]

Not only were they unfriendly, the people of Sodom and Gomorrah took advantage of strangers and would steal their goods. Corrupt judges were appointed meting out vicious, inhumane and sadistic sentences.

(From Jasher) "And by desire of their four judges the people of Sodom and Gomorrah had beds erected in the streets of the cities, and if a man came to these places they laid hold of him and brought him to one of their beds, and by force made him to lie in them."

"And as he lay down, three men would stand at his head and three at his feet, and measure him by the length of the bed, and if the man was less than the bed these six men would stretch him at each end, and when he cried out to them they would not answer him.

165. Ibid XVIII:16-18, Legends I:246

And if he was longer than the bed they would draw together the two sides of the bed at each end, until the man had reached the gates of death. And if he continued to cry out to them, they would answer him, saying, 'Thus shall it be done to a man that cometh into our land'."

"And when men heard all these things that the people of the cities of Sodom did, they refrained from coming there. And when a poor man came to their land they would give him silver and gold, and cause a proclamation in the whole city not to give him a morsel of bread to eat, and if the stranger should remain there some days, and die from hunger, not having been able to obtain a morsel of bread, then at his death all the people of the city would come and take their silver and gold which they had given to him."

"And those that could recognize the silver and gold which they had given him took it back, and at his death they also stripped him of his garments, and they would fight about them, and he that prevailed over his neighbor took them."[166]

Paltith, apparent daughter of Lot, born at the time Abraham recovered Lot and his family from the Kings of Elam, showed compassion upon a stranger entering Sodom, gave him bread and water contrary to the law of the land, she was burned to ashes for her acts of compassion. Another woman showed similar acts of compassion in the neighboring city of Calneh. She was covered with honey and stung to death as her punishment.[167]

(From Jasher) "And the young woman cried out on account of the bees, but no one took notice of her or pitied her, and her cries ascended to heaven. And the Lord was provoked at this and all the works of the cities of Sodom, for they had abundance of food, and had tranquility amongst them, and still would not sustain the poor and the needy, and in those days their evil doings and sins became great before the Lord. And the Lord sent for two of the angels that had come to Abraham's house, to destroy Sodom and its cities."[168]

166. Ibid XIX:3-9, Legends I:247
167. Ibid XIX:24-43, Legends I:249, V:157 Yasher Wa Yera 35b - 38a
168. Ibid XIX:43-45, Legends I:250, V:157 Yasher Wa Yera 39a - 39a

As mentioned previously, these angels had the additional assignment of notifying Sarah her body would be restored to child bearing age and that she would indeed bare a son. Having completed this assignment, "the men (angels) rose up from thence, and looked toward Sodom and Abraham went with them on the way."[169]

(From Genesis) "And the angel of the Lord, said, Shall I hide from Abraham that thing which the Lord will do for him; seeing that Abraham shall surely become a great and mighty nation, and all the nations of the earth shall be blessed of him."?

"For I know him, that he will command his children, and his household after him, and they shall keep the way of the Lord, to do justice and judgement, that the Lord may bring upon Abraham that which he has spoken of him. And the angel of the Lord said unto Abraham, The Lord said unto us, Because the cry of Sodom and Gomorrah is great, and because their sin is very grievious, I will destroy them."

"And I will send you and ye shall go down now, and see that their iniquities are rewarded unto them. And ye shall have all things done altogether according to the cry of it, which is come unto me. And if you do it not, it shall be upon your heads; for I will destroy them, and you shall know that I will do it, for it shall be before your eyes. And the angels which were holy men, and were sent forth after the order of God, turned their faces from thence and went towards Sodom."[170]

At this point the angels of the Lord left for Sodom:

(From Genesis) "But Abraham stood yet before the Lord, remembering the things which had been told him. And Abraham drew near to Sodom, and said unto the Lord, calling upon his name saying, Wilt thou destroy the righteous with the wicked? Wilt thou not spare them?

"Peradventure there may be fifty righteous within the city,

---

169. Genesis 18:16 KJV, MT, JST
170. Genesis 18:17-23 JST, (18:17-22) MT, KJV

62

wilt thou also destroy and not spare the place for the fifty righteous that may be therein? O may that be far from thee to do after this manner, to slay the righteous with the wicked; and that the righteous should be as the wicked. O God, may that be far from thee, for shall the Judge of all the earth do right? And the Lord said unto Abraham, If thou findest in Sodom fifty righteous within the city, then I will spare all the place for their sakes."

"And Abraham answered and said, Behold, now, I have taken upon me to speak unto the Lord, which is able to destroy the city, and lay all the people in dust and ashes, Will the Lord spare them peradventure there lack five of fifty righteous; wilt thou destroy all the city for their wickedness, if I find there forty and five righteous? And he said, I will not destroy, but spare them."

"And he spake unto him again, and said, Peradventure there should be forty found there? And he said, I will not destroy it for forty's sake. And he said again unto the Lord, O, let not the Lord be angry, and I will speak: Peradventure there shall be thirty found there? And he said, I will not destroy them if thou shalt find thirty there."

"And he said, Behold now, I have taken upon me to speak unto the Lord; will thou destroy them if peradventure there shall twenty be found there? And he said, I will not destroy them for twenty's sake. And Abraham said unto the Lord, O, let not the Lord be angry, and I will speak yet but this once, peradventure ten shall be found there? And the Lord said, I will not destroy them for ten's sake. And the Lord ceased speaking with Abraham. And as soon as he had left communing with the Lord, Abraham went his way. And it came to pass that Abraham returned unto his tent."[171]

In this exchange we see an unafraid Abraham defending the righteous, even in Sodom, certain the Lord God of Heaven is a God of righteousness and confident the Lord would hear him.

Not surprising that Abraham would take such a stand. He had

---

171. Genesis 18:24-42 JST, (18:22-33) KJV, MT, Legends I:250-251

declared himself a follower of righteousness nearly fifty years earlier and desiring to be an even greater follower of righteousness, had won the respect of the King of Righteousness, Melchizedek, by whom Abraham was blessed and from whom he received the priesthood.

The events that followed revealed that there were less than ten righteous in Sodom and Gomorrah, limited to his nephew Lot, his wife, and two daughters, who were counseled by angels to leave the about to be destroyed cities.

(From Genesis) "And it came to pass that there came three angels to Sodom in the evening; and Lot sat in the door of his house, in the city of Sodom. And Lot seeing the angels, rose up to meet them; and he bowed himself with his face toward the ground. And he said, Behold now, my lords, turn in, I pray you, into your servant's house, and tarry all night, and wash your feet, and ye shall rise up early, and go on your ways." (continuing)

"And they said, Nay, but we will abide in the street all night. And he pressed them greatly; and they turned in unto him, and entered into his house: and he made them a feast, and did bake unleavened bread and they did eat. But before they lay down to rest, the men of the city of Sodom compassed the house round, even men which were both old and young, even the people from every quarter; And they called unto Lot, and said unto him, where are the men which came in unto thee this night? Bring them out unto us, that we may know them." (continuing)

"And Lot went out of the door, unto them, and shut the door after him, and said, I pray you, brethren do not so wickedly. And they said unto him, Stand back. And they were angry with him. And they said among themselves, This one man came in to sojourn among us, and he will needs now make himself to be a judge: now we will deal worse with him than with them. Wherefore they said unto the man, We will have the men, and thy daughters also, and we will do with them as seemeth us good. Now this was after the wickedness of Sodom." (continuing)

"And Lot said, Behold now, I have two daughters, which have not known man; let me I pray you, plead with my brethren that I may not bring them out unto you; and ye shall not do unto them as seemeth good in your eyes. For God will not justify his servant in this thing; wherefore let me plead with my brethren this once only, that unto these men ye do nothing, that they may have peace in my house; for therefore came they under the shadow of my roof." (continuing)

"And they were angry with Lot and came near to break the door, but the angels of God, which were holy men, put forth their hand and pulled Lot into the house unto them, and shut the door. And they smote the men with blindness, both small and great, that they could not come at the door. And they were angry, so that they wearied themselves to find the door, and they could not find it." (continuing)

"And these holy men said unto Lot, Hast thou any here besides thy sons-in-law, and thy sons sons and thy daughters? And they commanded Lot, saying, Whatsoever thou hast in the city, thou shalt bring out of this place, for we will destroy this place: Because the cry of them is waxen great and their abominations have come up before the face of the Lord; and the Lord has sent us to destroy it." (continuing)

"And Lot went out and spake unto his sons-in-law which married his daughters, and said, Up, get ye out of this place, for the Lord will destroy this city. But he seemed as one that mocked unto his sons-in-law."

"And when morning came, the angels hastened Lot, saying, Arise, take thy wife, and thy two daughters which are here, lest thou be consumed in the iniquity of the city. And while he lingered the angels laid hold upon his hand, and upon the hand of his wife, and upon the hand of his two daughters; the Lord being merciful to them; and they brought them forth, and set them down without the city. And it came to pass, when they had brought them forth abroad that they said unto them, Escape for your lives; look not behind you, neither stay you in all the plain; escape to the mountain lest you be consumed."[172]

---

172. Genesis 19:1-25 JST (19:1-17) KJV, MT, Jasher XIX:44-50

But Lot didn't want to go to the mountains, fearing something evil would happen to him there. He pled with the Lord to allow him to enter the small city of Zoar, nearby and the Lord allowed him to do so.

(From Genesis) "And Lot said unto one of them, Oh, not so my Lord! Behold now, thy servant has found grace in thy sight, and thou hast magnified thy mercy which thou hast showed unto me in saving my life; and I cannot escape to the mountain, lest some evil overtake me and I die. Behold now, here is another city, and this is near to flee unto, and it is a little one; oh let me escape thither, and may the Lord not destroy it, and my soul shall live. And the angel said unto him, See, I have accepted thee concerning this thing also, that I will not overthrow this city for the which thou hast spoken; haste thee, escape thither, for I cannot do anything until thou be come thither. And the name of the city was called Zoar. Therefore, the sun was risen upon the earth when Lot entered into Zoar. And the Lord did not destroy Sodom until Lot had entered unto Zoar."[173]

Angels led Lot, his wife and two daughters to safety before raining fire and brimstone upon Sodom and Gomorrah. This act of mercy in remembering Lot and his family brought comfort to Abraham and fulfilled the Lord's promise not to destroy the righteous with the wicked. Absolute obedience to the Lord's commands in the face of imminent danger (however) was particularly important. Ado's (Lot's wife) failure to obey brought immediate tragic consequences. She disobeyed the angels command not to look back and suffered the consequences. She was turned into a pillar of salt.

(From Genesis) "And then, when Lot had entered into Zoar, the Lord rained upon Sodom, and upon Gomorrah, for the angels called upon the name of the Lord for brimstone and fire from the Lord out of heaven. And thus they overthrew those cities and all the plain, and all the inhabitants of the cities, and that which grew upon the ground. But it came to pass, when Lot fled, his wife looked back from behind him, and became a pillar of salt." (continuing)

"And Abraham got up early in the morning to the place

173. Genesis 19:26-30 JST (19:18-22) KJV, MT

where he stood before the Lord; and he looked toward Sodom and Gomorrah, and toward all the land of the plain, and behold, lo, the smoke of the country went up as the smoke of a furnace. And it came to pass, when God had destroyed the cities of the plain, that God spake unto Abraham, saying I have remembered Lot, and sent him out of the midst of the overthrow, that thy brother might not be destroyed, when I overthrew the city in which thy brother Lot dwelt. And Abraham was comforted."[174]

Genesis, Chapter 19 relates the sad ending of Lot and his two daughters and the beginning of the Moabites and the Ammonites. Moab was the son of Lot by his first born daughter and Benammi through whom the Ammonites came was the son of Lot by Lot's younger daughter. Except for a report of Lot's death, nothing more of him appears to have been written than that which follows:

(From Genesis) "And Lot went up out of Zoar, and dwelt in the mountain and his two daughters with him, for he feared to dwell in Zoar. And he dwelt in a cave (Adullam), he and his two daughters. And the first born dealt wickedly, and said unto the younger, Our father has become old, and we have not a man in the earth to come in unto us, to live with us after the manner of all that live on the earth; Therefore come, let us make our father drink wine, and we will lie with him, that we may preserve seed of our father. And they did wickedly, and made their father drink wine that night; and the first-born went in and lay with her father; and he perceived not when she lay down, nor when she arose." (continuing)

"And it came to pass on the morrow that the first-born said unto the younger, 'Behold, I lay yesternight with my father; let us make him drink wine this night also, and go thou in and lie with him, that we may preserve seed of our father. And they made their father drink wine that night also, and the younger arose, and lay with him, and he perceived not when she lay down nor when she arose. Thus were both the daughters of Lot with child by their father." (continuing)

"And the first born bare a son and called his name Moab; the

174. Genesis 19:31-36 JST (19:24-29) KJV, MT, Jasher XIX:51-56

father of the Moabites, the same which are unto this day. And the younger, she also bare a son, and called his name Benammi, the father of the children which are Ammonites, the same which are unto this day."[175]

Jasher and the Antiquities rationalize Lot's daughters behavior. They thought the whole earth was destroyed. They also report, that Lot and his daughters and two grandsons moved across the Jordan where his grandsons grew up and took wives from the idolatrous land of Canaan. There they begat children and were fruitful and multiplied.[176]

---

175. Genesis 19:36-44 JST, (19:30-38) KJV, MT, Jasher XIX:55-60
176. Jasher XIX:57-60

CHAPTER VII

RESTORE THE MAN (ABRAHAM) HIS WIFE, FOR HE IS A PROPHET

Tent dwellers in the plain of Mamre near Hebron for many years not far from the cities of Sodom and Gomorrah, now destroyed, Abraham and Sarah journeyed southward and pitched their tent between Kadesh and Shur in Gerar. Kadesh was apparently a well-watered and fruitful spot in the wilderness of Zin, while Shur was part of the Arabian desert bordering Egypt. Abraham and Sarah located themselves in between Kadesh and Shur.

Here Abraham and Sarah encountered Abimelech, King of Gerar, Gerar being the land of the Philistines.[177] The Philistines were descendants of Caphtor occupying part of Egypt, and the land between Egypt and Canaan.[178] Jasher identifies Caphtor (Chaphtor) as the son of Mitzraim, the son of Ham, with his family of descendants dwelling by the river Sihor, that is the brook of Egypt, with a city being called after his name.[179]

Sarah faced another test at the hands of a King who desired her, even at ninety years of age. Apparently Sarah had retained her beauty, or her beauty had been restored as part of the process of being returned to child bearing age, in anticipation of her conception of Isaac. And Abraham faced another threat to his life because of her, making it necessary to once again invoke his blood relationship to Sarah, his wife and niece. "She is my sister" Abraham again declared. The Lord intervened, saved his prophet and his Sarah. He directed Abimelech, the King, to restore Sarah to Abraham. Abimelech and all of his would die if he failed to do so. The Lord had promised an heir to Abraham and Sarah through whom their posterity would become as numerous

---

177. Genesis Chapters 20 & 21 KJV, MT, JST
178. Genesis Dictionary p.751 KJV
179. Jasher VII:11, X:21-22

as the sands of the sea and through whom all the earth would be blessed. Abimelech's intended action to take Sarah would frustrate the plans. The Lord intervened. The Genesis account reads:

"And Abraham journeyed from thence toward the south country, and dwelled between Kadesh and Shur, and sojourned in Gerar. And Abraham said of Sarah his wife, She is my sister: and Abimelech king of Gerar sent, and took Sarah. But God came to Abimelech in a dream by night, and said to him, Behold, thou art but a dead man, for the woman which thou hast taken; for she is a man's wife. But Abimelech had not come near her: and he said, Lord, wilt thou slay also a righteous nation? Said he not unto me, She is my sister? and she, even she herself said, He is my brother; in the integrity (simplicity) of my heart and innocency of my hands have I done this. And God said unto him in a dream, Yea, I know that thou didst this in the integrity (simplicity) of thy heart; for I also withheld thee from sinning against me: therefore suffered I thee not to touch her. Now therefore restore the man his wife; for he is a prophet, and he shall pray for thee, and thou shalt live: and if thou restore her not, know thou that thou shalt surely die, thou, and all that are thine."[180]

Jasher and the Legends amplify the event considerably.

"And at that time Abraham journeyed from the plain of Mamre, and he went to the land of the Philistines, and he dwelt in Gerar; it was in the twenty-fifth year of Abraham's being in the land of Canaan, and the hundredth year in the life of Abraham, that he came to Gerar in the land of the Philistines. And when they entered the land he said to Sarah his wife, Say thou art my sister, to any one that shall ask thee in order that we may escape the evil of the inhabitants of the land."

"And as Abraham was dwelling in the land of the Philistines, the servants of Abimelech, king of the Philistines, saw that Sarah was exceedingly beautiful, and they asked Abraham concerning her, and he said, She is my sister. And the servants of Abimelech went to Abimelech saying, A man from the land of Canaan is

---

180. Genesis 20:1-7 KJV, MT (20:1-8) JST

come to dwell in the land, and he has a sister that is exceeding fair. And Abimelech heard the words of his servants who praised Sarah to him, and Abimelech sent his officers, and they brought Sarah to the King."

..."As at evening time, before men lie down to rest, the king was sitting upon his throne, and a deep sleep fell upon him, and he lay upon the throne and slept till morning. And he dreamed that an angel of the Lord came to him with a drawn sword in his hand, and the angel stood over Abimelech, and wished to slay him with the sword, and the king was terrified in his dream, and said to the angel, In what have I sinned against thee that thou comest to slay me with thy sword?"

"And the angel answered and said to Abimelech, Behold thou diest on account of the woman which thou didst yesternight bring to thy house, for she is a married woman, the wife of Abraham who came to thy house; now therefore return that man his wife; for she is his wife; and shouldst thou not return her, know that thou wilt surely die, thou and all belonging to thee."

"And on that night there was a great outcry in the land of the Philistines, and the inhabitants of the land saw a figure of a man standing with a drawn sword in his hand, and he smote the inhabitants of the land with the sword, yea he continued to smite them. And the angel of the Lord smote the whole land of the Philistines on that night, and there was a great confusion on that night and on the following morning. And every womb was closed, and all their issues, and the hand of the Lord was upon them on account of Sarah, wife of Abraham, who Abimelech had taken."

"And in the morning Abimelech rose with terror and confusion and with a great dread, and he sent and had his servants called in, and he related his dream to them, and the people were greatly afraid. And one man standing amongst the servants of the king answered the king, saying, O sovereign king, restore this woman to her husband, for he is her husband, for the like happened to the king of Egypt when this man came to Egypt. And he said concerning his wife, She is my sister, for such is his manner of doing when he cometh to dwell in the land in which he is a stranger. And Pharaoh sent and took this woman for a wife and the Lord brought upon him grievous plagues until he returned the woman to her husband. Now therefore, O sovereign king, know what happened yesternight to the whole land, for there was a very great consternation and great pain and lamentation, and we know that it was on account of the woman which thou didst take."

"Now, therefore, restore this woman to her husband, lest it should befall us as it did to Pharaoh king of Egypt and his subjects, and that we may not die, and Abimelech hastened and called and had Sarah called for, and she came before him, and he had Abraham called for, and he came before him."[181]

Returning now to Genesis account:

"Therefore Abimelech rose early in the morning, and called all his servants, and told all these things in their ears: and the men were sore afraid. Then Abimelech called Abraham, and said unto him, What hast thou done unto us? and what have I offended thee, that thou hast brought on me and on my kingdom a great sin? thou hast done deeds unto me that ought not to be done. And Abimelech said unto Abraham, What sawest thou, that thou hast done this thing?[182]

The Jasher account:

"And Abimelech said to them, What is this work you have been doing in saying you are brother and sister, and I took this woman for a wife?"[183]

Back to Genesis:

"And Abraham said, Because I thought, Surely the fear of God is not in this place; and they will slay me for my wife's sake. And yet indeed she is my sister; she is the daughter of my father, but not the daughter of my mother; and she became my wife. And

---

181. Jasher XX:1-23, Legends I:258-259, V:190 Yashar Wa-Yera 39a - 40a, Antiquities Book I CH XII:I
182. Genesis 20:8-10 KJV, MT, (20:9-11) JST
183. Jasher XX:24

it came to pass, when God caused me to wander from my father's house, that I said unto her, This is thy kindness which thou shalt shew unto me; at every place whither we shall come, say of me, He is my brother."[184]

Abraham followed up his explanation with more history. He recounted his life explaining efforts to lead him into idolatry had not been successful. God revealed himself to him, Abraham declared, and had commanded him to leave Ur.[185]

Once again we see the hand of the Lord in the lives of Abraham and Sarah with whom the covenants had been made. The heir had not been born through whom the covenants were to be continued. The Lord prevented Sarah from being violated by Abimelech, King of the Philistines, who certainly had secular power to take her. He also had secular power to take Abraham's life. The Lord God of Heaven let King Abimelech know that taking Sarah would cost him his (the King's) life, and all his subjects as well. His actions had already brought penalties to the women of Gerar whose wombs had been closed. Other afflictions were also suffered by his people.

Recognizing at last that Abraham and Sarah were anointed servants of God, Abimelech gave them gifts and a choice of the land of Gerar in which to live. Abimelech then feared God and asked Abraham to pray for him. Though Abimelech had done him great injury, Abraham forgave. Abraham indicated that when a man is offended,

"He should be easily appeased, and slow to anger, and as soon as he who has sinned against him asks for pardon, he should forgive him with all his heart. Even if deep and serious injury has been done to him, he should not be vengeful, nor bear his brother a grudge in his heart."[186]

Abraham added that "the injured one should pray to God to forgive the injurer, even if he is not asked to do so. Thus did Abraham, who prayed for the Lord to lift the plagues inflicted upon Abimelech and his people." His prayer: "O Lord of the world! Thou hast created man that he may increase and propagate his kind. Grant that Abime-

184. Genesis 20:11-13, KJV, MT, (20:12-14) JST, Legends I:260
185. Legends I:260
186. Legends I:260-61

lech and his house may multiply and increase".[187] The Lord God answered Abraham and the Philistine women bore children again. Sarah was given a veil to cover her eyes as evidence she was Abraham's wife, a chosen vessel of the Lord.

In the language of Genesis:

"And Abimelech took sheep, and oxen, and menservants, and women-servants, and gave them unto Abraham, and restored him Sarah his wife. And Abimelech said, Behold, my land is before thee: dwell where it pleaseth thee."[188]

"And unto Sarah he said, Behold, I have given thy brother a thousand pieces of silver; behold, he shall give unto thee a covering of the eyes, and it shall be a token unto all that thou mayest not be taken again from Abraham thy husband. And thus she was reproved."[189]

"So Abraham prayed unto God: and God healed Abimelech, and his wife, and his maidservants; and they bare children. For the Lord had fast closed up all the wombs of the house of Abimelech, because of Sarah Abraham's wife."[190]

The Legends record this was the first time in the history of mankind that God fulfilled the prayer of one human being for another. Abimelech's wife was a beneficiary of this prayer for she, too, was barren and subsequently bore a child.

Abraham had pleaded for a blessing upon Abimelech and his people, even a blessing that had so far been denied Sarah; a child. The Lord answered and blessed Abimelech and his people, as Abraham desired.[191]

---

187. Ibid V:245
188. Genesis 20:14-15 KJV, MT (20:15-16) JST, Jasher XX:25-26
189. Genesis 20:17 JST (20:16) KJV, MT
190. Genesis: 17-18 KJV, MT, (20:18-19) JST, Jasher XX:29-30
191. Legends I:261, V:202

74

CHAPTER VIII

ISAAC IS BORN AT A TIME SET BY THE LORD

Abraham and Sarah, Hagar and Ishmael, apparently were living in Gerar, the land of the Philistines controlled by King Abimelech, when the "set time" for Sarah to conceive and bare a son (Isaac) arrived.

Some thirty or more years earlier, before Abraham had gone into Egypt, he learned of his own "set time" for coming to earth, that he, Abraham, existed as a spirit before coming to earth and that he, Abraham, was chosen for his role on earth before he was born in the flesh. In addition, Abraham had learned that one spirit may be more intelligent than another, both having no beginning and no end, and that He (God) is more intelligent than all of them.

Not only did Abraham learn that he had existed as a spirit before he was born in the flesh, he, Abraham, would also live after his existence on this earth, for he (Abraham) is eternal, and so is every one else who comes to earth.

The Book of Abraham reads:

"And the Lord said unto me, Abraham.....If there be two spirits, and one shall be more intelligent than the other, yet these two spirits, notwithstanding one is more intelligent than the other, have no beginning; they existed before, they shall have no end, they shall exist after, for they are gnolaum, or eternal. And the Lord said unto me: These two facts do exist, that there are two spirits, one being more intelligent than the other; there shall be another more intelligent than they; I am the Lord thy God, I am more intelligent than they all....I dwell in the midst of them all; I now, therefore, have come down unto thee to deliver unto thee the works which my hands have made, wherein my wisdom excelleth them all, for I rule in the heavens above, and in the earth beneath, in all wisdom and prudence, over all the intelligences thine eyes have seen from the beginning; I came down in the beginning in the midst of all the intelligences thou hast seen."

"Now the Lord had shown unto me, Abraham, the intelligences that were organized before the world was; and among all these there were many of the noble and great ones; And God saw these souls that they were good, and he stood in the midst of them, and he said: These I will make my rulers; for he stood among those that were spirits, and he saw that they were good; and he said unto me: Abraham, thou art one of them; thou wast chosen before thou wast born."[192]

Likewise, the Lord had revealed to Abraham and Sarah a special spirit would be born unto them at a time appointed by the Lord, a set time, and that his name was to be called Isaac, through whom the Lord would establish his covenant and through whose seed after him would the Lord's covenant be continued.[193]

Jasher reports the "set time" for this event to have been

"a year and four months of Abraham's dwelling in the land of the Philistines in Gerar; that God visited Sarah, and the Lord remembered her, and she conceived and bare a son to Abraham."[194]

The Genesis account:

"And the Lord visited Sarah as he had said, and the Lord did unto Sarah as he had spoken. For Sarah conceived, and bare Abraham a son in his old age, at the set time of which God had spoken to him. And Abraham called the name of his son that was born unto him, whom Sarah bare to him, Isaac."[195]

---

192. Book of Abraham 3:15-23
193. Genesis 17:19-21, KJV, MT, (17:25-28) JST
194. Jasher XXI:1
195. Genesis 21:1-3 KJV, MT, (21:1-2) JST

Abraham previously entered into a covenant with the Lord, to walk uprightly before Him and be perfect and to keep all the previous covenants and commandments God had made with Abraham's fathers: Eber, Shem, Noah, Enoch, Seth and Adam. God had established an additional covenant, circumcision sometimes referred to as a token of the covenant/s to symbolize all of the covenants Abraham and his seed made with the Lord, i.e. to walk uprightly before Him and to become perfect.

Other symbols of the covenants or ordinances included baptism of their children at eight years of age, when, children began to be accountible before the Lord, and the offering of plant and animal sacrifices to the Lord. Sacrifice was evidently introduced to Adam and practiced in the days of Cain and Abel. Abel's sacrifice was accepted of the Lord and Cain's was not.

Keeping the covenants and commandments required of the Lord were to bring great blessings: Abraham and Sarah were to be the father and mother of nations. Their seed was to be as numerous as the stars in the heaven and numerous as the sands of the sea, kings (and queens) and rulers were to be among their posterity, a land of promise was to be given to them and through their posterity all of the nations and families of the earth were to be blessed.

Abraham and Sarah had been taught by the Lord that they existed as spirits before coming to the earth, that this life is a second estate for those who had kept their first estate and were worthy to come to earth. They knew from their encounters with the Lord that there were two creations, the first a spiritual creation of all life followed by a natural or physical creation.

They knew that individual spirits were formed from individual intelligences which had always existed and that the spirit is gnolaum, or eternal. When each spirit unites with a physical body it becomes a living soul. Through Adam's transgression the physical body became subject to death. Separation of each spirit from his/her physical body takes place eventually. The spirit returns to God for a time and the physical body to the elements of the earth through decay.

This separation of body and spirit was not to be forever, however. Following revelation to Abraham that he Abraham was one of the great spirits who had been chosen before he was born, the Lord also revealed unto Abraham that among those spirits there was another like unto God who would participate in the creation of this earth. The name of this one like unto God is Jehovah or (Yahweh).[196] The Book of Abraham reads:

"And there stood one among them that was like unto God, and he said unto those who were with him: We will go down, for there is space there, and we will take of these materials, and we will make an earth whereon these (spirits) may dwell; and we will prove them herewith, to see if they will do all things whatsoever the Lord their God shall command them; And they who keep their first estate shall be added upon; and they who keep not their first estate shall not have glory in the same kingdom with those who keep their first estate; and they who keep their second estate shall have glory added upon their heads for ever and ever. And the Lord said: Whom shall I send? And one answered like unto the Son of Man: Here am I, send me. And another answered and said: Here am I, send me. And the Lord said, I will send the first. And the second was angry, and kept not his first estate and at that day, many followed after him."

"And then the Lord said: Let us go down, And they went down at the beginning, and they, that is the Gods, organized and formed the heavens and earth. And the earth, after it was formed, was empty and desolate, because they had not formed anything but the earth, and darkness reigned upon the face of the deep, and the Spirit of the Gods was brooding upon the face of the waters. And they (the Gods) said, Let there be light; and there was light..........."[197]

From this account we see that the Lord revealed to Abraham that all who came to earth for a physical body in which to house his/her spirit had kept their first estate, i.e. were obedient to the Lords plan and commands. Other spirits were denied bodies because they kept not their first estate and followed after him who was angry.

Who were these two great spirits in the world before this? One was like unto God and the other who became angry and rebelled? Who were the Gods spoken of by Abraham who created the earth? Abraham's account doesn't say, but he undoubtedly knew for Moses knew.

---

196. Book of Abraham 2:7-8
197. Ibid 3:24-28, 4:1-31,5:1-21

Moses had it revealed to him when the Lord also talked to him face to face on the Mount. While revealing to Moses the beginning, what is known as the first book of Moses, Genesis, the Lord God added to Abraham's account as follows:

"And I, the Lord God, spake unto Moses saying: That Satan whom thou hast commanded in the name of mine Only Begotten, is the same which was from the beginning, and he came before me, saying - Behold, here am I, send me, I will be thy son, and I will redeem all mankind, that one soul shall not be lost, and surely I will do it; wherefore give me thine honor. But behold, my Beloved Son, which was my Beloved and Chosen from the beginning, said unto me: Father, thy will be done, and the glory be thine forever. Wherefore, because that Satan rebelled against me, and sought to destroy the agency of man, which I, the Lord God, had given him, and also, that I should give unto him mine own power; by the power of mine Only Begotten, I caused that he should be cast down; And he became Satan yea, even the devil, the father of all lies, to deceive and to blind men, and to lead them captive at his will, even as many as would not hearken unto my voice."[198]

This account reveals that the two spirits, were one like unto God, a Beloved Son, one chosen from the beginning and the other as Satan who was cast out for rebelling against God, each spirit son's of their Father (Elohim). It also reveals that God's own power was given to the Beloved Son, chosen from the beginning and He, the Beloved, participated in the creation of this earth and all life therein. The Lord will prove those who come to earth to see if they will do all things whatsoever the Lord their God shall command. The plan included free agency or freedom to choose to obey. Compulsion to obey was Satan's plan. Just as the reward for keeping the first estate was growth and development through life's experiences with a physical body on earth, so would glory be added forever and ever to those who keep their second estate on earth, if they walk uprightly before God, become perfect, and keep the covenants as Abraham had been commanded to do.

With all this in mind Abraham circumcised Isaac at eight days

---

198. Genesis 3:1-5 JST, Book of Moses, Pearl of Great Price 4:1-2

old, as God had commanded him, and rejoiced with Sarah that one of God's promises to them had been fulfilled. The Genesis account reads:

"And Abraham circumcised his son Isaac being eight days old, as God had commanded him. And Abraham was an hundred years old, when his son Isaac was born unto him. And Sarah said, God hath made me to laugh (rejoice), so that all that hear will laugh (rejoice) with me. And she said, Who would have said unto Abraham, that Sarah should have given children suck? for I have born him a son in his old age."[199]

The Legends report that

"The birth of Isaac was a happy event, and not in the house of Abraham alone. The whole world rejoiced, for God remembered all barren women at the same time with Sarah. They all bore children. And all the blind were made to see, all the lame were made whole, the dumb to speak, and the mad were restored to reason....the sun shone with such splendor as had not been seen since the fall of man"...[200]

The Legends note also that Isaac was Abraham's first son borne in the covenant marked by circumcision and therefore Abraham celebrated Isaac's circumcision with much pomp and ceremony on the eighth day. Shem, Eber and Abimelech, king of the Philistines, were present on this day.[201]

"And the child grew, and was weaned: and Abraham made a great feast the same day that Isaac was weaned."[202]

Shem, Eber and Terah, Abraham's fathers, and Nehor (Abraham's brother) came to the great feast, along with Abimelech, king of the Philistines.

"And Shem and Eber and all the great people of the land, and Abimelech, king of the Philistines, and his servants and

---

199. Genesis 21:4-7 KJV, MT, (21:3-6) JST
200. Legends I:261-262, Jasher XXI:5
201. Ibid I:262, V:307 Yashar Wa-Yera 40b
202. Genesis 21:8 KJV, MT, (21:7) JST

Phicol, the captain of his host, came to eat and drink and rejoice at the feast which Abraham made upon the day of his son Isaac's being weaned. Also Terah, the father of Abraham, and Nahor his brother, came from Haran, they and all belonging to them, for they greatly rejoiced on hearing that a son had been born to Sarah. And they came to Abraham, and they ate and drank at the feast which Abraham made upon the day of Isaac's being weaned."[203]

---

203. Jasher XXI 5-8; see also Legends I:p.262, V:207 Yasher Wa-Yera 40b

Chapter IX

GOD IS WITH THEE
IN ALL THOU DOEST

(From Jasher) "...And Terah and Nahor rejoiced with Abraham, and they remained with him many days in the land of the Philistines. At that time Serug the son of Reu died, in the first year of the birth of Isaac, son of Abraham."[204]

The Genesis account of Isaac's childhood is limited to a reference to the mocking of Isaac by Ishmael. Whatever the mocking was, it motivated Sarah to insist Hagar and Ishmael be cast out.

(From Genesis) "And Sarah saw the son of Hagar the Egyptian, which she had born unto Abraham, mocking (making sport, and she was troubled). Wherefore she said unto Abraham, Cast out this bondwoman and her son: for the son of this bondwoman shall not be heir with my son, even with Isaac."[205]

The Legends report that Sarah wanted Abraham to divorce Hagar and return her to the role of bondwoman. With some reluctance Abraham complied and only after the Lord said it was agreeable with Him.[206]

Jasher claims Ishmael at nineteen years of age tried to kill Isaac (then five years of age) with a bow and arrow. Sarah witnessed the attempt and demanded Ishmael and his mother be cast out.

(From Jasher) "And Ishmael, the son of Abraham was grown up in those days, he was fourteen years old when Sarah bare Isaac to

---

204. Jasher XXI:8-9
205. Genesis 21:9-10 KJV, MT, (21:7-8) JST
206. Legends I:263-4

Abraham. And God was with Ishmael the son of Abraham, and he grew up, and he learned to use the bow and became an archer. And when Isaac was five years old he was sitting with Ishmael at the door of the tent. And Ishmael came to Isaac and seated himself opposite to him, and he took the bow and drew it and put the arrow in it; and intended to slay Isaac. And Sarah saw the act which Ishmael desired to do to her son Isaac, and it grieved her exceedingly on account of her son, and she sent for Abraham, and said to him, Cast out this bondwoman and her son, for her son shall not be heir with my son, for thus did he seek to do unto him this day."[207]

Sarah's request upset Abraham. He loved both sons. The Lord comforted Abraham and advised him to follow Sarah's counsel. He was assured that Ishmael would be the father of nations as well as Isaac. However, Isaac was to be the son through whom the covenants were to continue. Abraham subsequently took Ishmael and his mother into the wilderness of Beersheba and left them there. The Lord intervened in the life of Ishmael too, and protected him as he matured. Hagar never completely turned from the idols of her youth. She returned to Egypt where a wife for Ishmael was found.[208] Ishmaels' first wife was named Meribah and bore him four sons and two daughters.[209]

The Genesis account of Ishmael's departure from the presence of Isaac reads:

"And the thing was very grievous in Abraham's sight because of his son. And God said unto Abraham. Let it not be grievous in thy sight because of the lad, and because of thy bondwoman, in all that Sarah hath said unto thee, hearken unto her voice; for in Isaac shall thy seed be called. And also of the son of the bondwoman will I make a nation, because he is thy seed. And Abraham rose up early in the morning, and took bread, and a bottle of water, and gave it unto Hagar, putting it on her shoulder, and the child, and sent her away: and she departed, and wandered in the wilderness of Beersheba. And the water was spent in the bottle, and she cast the child under one of the shrubs.

---

207. Jasher XXI:11-15, Legends I:264-5
208. Legends I:267
209. Jasher XXI:12-18

83

And she went, and sat her down over against him a good way off, as it were a bowshot: for she said, Let me not see the death of the child. And she sat over against him, and lift up her voice, and wept."

"And God heard the voice of the lad; and the angel of God called to Hagar out of heaven, and said unto her, What aileth thee, Hagar? fear not; for God hath heard the voice of the lad where he is. Arise, lift up the lad, and hold him in thine hand; for I will make him a great nation. And God opened her eyes, and she saw a well of water; and she went, and filled the bottle with water, and gave the lad drink. And God was with the lad; and he grew, and dwelt in the wilderness, and became an archer. And he dwelt in the wilderness of Paran: and his mother took him a wife out of the land of Egypt."[210]

The Genesis account moves on to Abraham's dispute with Abimelech and Phicol's men over wells of water at this point. Jasher and the Legends elaborate on Ishmael's life. As his family grew Ishmael prospered in the wilderness increasing in flocks and herds and in cattle. Abraham visited his son Ishmael from time to time checking on his welfare learning that Meribah did not honor him. Ishmael took another wife from the land of Canaan. After many years he moved his family to the land of the Philistines near his father, Abraham.[211]

As previously mentioned, Ishmael had four sons and two daughters by his first wife from the land of Egypt, Ribah or Meribah. Their names: Nebayoth, Kedar, Adbeel, Mibsam and a sister Bosmath. A second sister is not named.[212]

Ishmael took a second wife from the land of Canaan. Her name was Malchuth and she bare Ishmael Nishma, Dumah, Masa, Chadad, Tema, Yetur, Naphish and Kedma. "These are the sons of Ishmael and these are their names, being twelve princes....according to their nations."[213]

How long Ishmael and his family stayed in the wilderness before joining his father, Abraham, again is not known. Abraham stayed in

210. Genesis 21:11-21 KJV, MT, (21:9-19) JST
211. Jasher XXI:17-48, XXII:1-3; Legends I:266-7
212. Ibid XXV:14-17; Genesis 25:13; Legends I:267-8; Antiquities BookI CH XII:3-4
213. Ibid XXV:18-19, Genesis 25:13-16; Legends I:268-9; Antiquities Book I
    CH XII:3-4

the land of the Philistines a long time, about twenty six years before returning to an area near Hebron.

During this long period Abraham and his household lived in peace and harmony with Abimelech, King of the Philistines, under an agreement whereby they would respect one another and be honest with one another. Abimelech respected Abraham as a favored servant of the Lord allowing Abraham to live in the land saying "God is with thee in all thou doest". Abraham respected Abimelech as king of the land.

Abraham and his household moved near to Hebron and dug some wells, which King Abimelech's servants violently took away. Abraham complained to King Abimelech. Abimelech asserted he was unaware of the incident. Abraham gave Abimelech seven ewe lambs as a witness that his household had actually dug the wells. The wells were restored to Abraham. Tranquility returned by covenant between them at the well. A grove of trees was planted and the place was named Beersheba. Abimelech and Phicol returned to their own places of abode in the land of the Philistines. Abraham and his household lived at Beersheba near Hebron another long period where he gained in stature and reputation.[214]

(From Jasher) "And Abraham planted a large grove in Beersheba, and he made to it four gates facing the four sides of the earth, and he planted a vineyard in it, so that if a traveler came to Abraham he entered any gate which was in his road, and remained there and ate and drank and satisfied himself and then departed."

"For the house of Abraham was always open to the sons of men that passed and repassed, who came daily to eat and drink in the house of Abraham. And any man who had hunger and came to Abraham's house, Abraham would give him bread that he might eat and drink and be satisfied and any one that came naked to his house he would clothe with garments as he might choose, and give him silver and gold and make known to him the Lord who had created him in the earth, this did Abraham all his life."

"And Abraham and his children and all belonging to him dwelt in Beersheba, and he pitched his tent as far as Hebron."[215]

214. Genesis 21:22-34; Jasher XXII:4-16; Legends I:269, V:219 Yasher Wa-Yera 42a
215. Jasher XXII:11-14; Legends I:270-271, V:223 Yashar Wa-Yera 42b

Abraham would also

"make known to passersby and the hungry, the Lord who had created him and set him on earth."

"After the wayfarers had eaten, they were in the habit of thanking Abraham for his kind entertainment of them, whereto he would reply: 'what ye give thanks to me! Rather return thanks to your host, He who alone provides food and drink for all creatures.' Then the people would ask, 'Where is He?' and Abraham would answer them and say: 'He is the Ruler of heaven and earth. He woundeth and He healeth, He formeth the embryo in the womb of the mother and bringeth it forth into the world, He causeth the plants and the trees to grow, He killeth and He maketh alive, He bringeth down to Sheol and bringeth up.' When the people heard such words, they would ask, 'How shall we return thanks to God and manifest gratitude unto Him?' And Abraham would instruct them in these words: 'Say, Blessed be the Lord who is blessed! Blessed be He that giveth bread and food unto all flesh!'"

"In this manner did Abraham teach those who had enjoyed his hospitality, how to praise and thank God. Abraham's house thus became not only a lodging place for the hungry and thirsty, but also a place of instruction where knowledge of God and His law were taught."[216]

Abraham, Sarah and Isaac were unaware of the great test they were soon to face. A test of obedience and sacrifice like no other persons in previously recorded history had been asked to face. Before reporting and discussing these tests however, an update on their relatives in Haran is in order, at the time Abraham was about 135 years old, Sarah about 125 years old, and Isaac was about 35 years old.

---

216. Legends I:271

AND THE CHILDREN OF BETHUEL
WERE SECHAR, LABAN AND THEIR
SISTER REBECCA

About the time of Terah's death when Abraham was 135 years old,

(From Genesis)..."it was told Abraham, saying, Behold Milcah, she hath also born children unto thy brother Nahor; Huz his first born, and Buz his brother, and Kemuel the father of Aram, And Chesed, and Hazo, and Pildash, and Jidlaph, and Bethuel. And Bethuel begat Rebekah: these eight Milcah did bear to Nahor, Abraham's brother. And his concubine, whose name was Reumah, she bare also Tebah, and Gaham, and Thahash, and Maachah."217

Jasher gives more information about Nahor's family and additional information about Terah's family by a third wife named Pelilah.

(From Jasher) "And Abraham's brother Nahor and his father and all belonging to them dwelt in Haran, for they did not come with Abraham to the land of Canaan. And children were born to Nahor which Milca the daughter of Haran, and sister to Sarah, Abrahams wife, bare to him. And these are the names of those that were born to him, Uz, Buz, Kemuel, Kesed, Chazo, Pildash, Tidlaf, and Bethuel, being eight sons, these are the children of Milca, which she bare to Nahor, Abrahams brother."

"And Nahor had a concubine and her name was Reumah, and she also bare to Nahor, Zebach, Gachash, Tochash, and

---

217. Genesis 22:20-24 KJV, MT, (22:24-28) JST

Maacha, being four sons. And the children that were born to Nahor were twelve sons besides his daughters, and they also had children born to them in Haran."

"And the children of Uz the first born of Nahor were Abi, Cheref, Gadin, Melus, and Deborah their sister. And the sons of Buz were Berachel, Naamath, Sheva, and Madonu. And the sons of Kemuel were Aram and Rechob. And the sons of Kesed were Anamlech, Meshai, Benon and Yifi, and the sons of Chaso were Pildash, Mechi and Opher. And the sons of Pildash were Arud, Chamum, Mered and Moloch, and the sons of Tidlaf were Mushan, Cushan, and Mutzi. And the children of Bethuel were Sechar, Laban and their sister Rebecca."

"These are the families of the children of Nahor, that were born to them in Haran; and Aram the son Kemuel and Rechob his brother went away from Haran, and they found a valley in the land by the river Euphrates. And they built a city there and they called the name of the city after the name of Pethor the son of Aram, that is Aram Naherayim* unto this day."

"And the children of Kesed also went to dwell where they could find a place, and they went and they found a valley opposite to the land of Shinar, and they dwelt there. And they there built themselves a city, and they called the name of the city Kesed after the name of their father, that is the land Kasdim** unto this day, and the Kasdim dwelt in that land and they were fruitful and multiplied exceedingly."[218]

And now for father Terah's death and the genealogy of his third family:

(From Jasher) "And Terah, father of Nahor and Abraham, went and took another wife in his old age, and her name was Pelilah, and she conceived and bare him a son and she called his name

---

218. Jasher XXII:15-30

*Mesopotamia
**Chaldea

Zoba. And Terah died in that year, that is in the thirty fifth year of the birth of Isaac, son of Abraham. And the days of Terah were two hundred and five years, and he was buried in Haran. And Zoba, the son of Terah lived thirty years and he begat Aram, Achlis and Merik."

"And Aram son of Terah, had three wives and he begat twelve sons and three daughters; and the Lord gave to Aram the son of Zoba riches and possessions, and abundance of cattle, and flocks and herds, and the man increased greatly."

"And Aram the son of Zoba and his brother and all his household journeyed from Haran, and they went to dwell where they could find a place, for their property was too great to remain in Haran together with their brethren the children of Nahor. And Aram the son of Zoba went with his brethren, and they found a valley at a distance toward the eastern country and they dwelt there. And they also built a city there, and they called the name there of Aram, after the name of their eldest brother, that is Aram Zoba to this day."[219]

---

219. Jasher XXII:31-39; Legends I:298-299

CHAPTER XI

LAY NOT THINE HAND UPON THE LAD

The Genesis account does not report Abraham's or Isaac's age at the time the Lord called on Abraham to

"Take now thy son, thine only son Isaac, whom thou lovest, and get thee into the land of Moriah, and offer him there for a burnt offering upon one of the mountains which I will tell thee of."[220]

Isaac is referred to as a lad, which by definition is a young man, or informally, a man of any age. It would appear, however, from Genesis that Isaac was less than forty years of age when he was offered by his father as a sacrifice to the Lord. Isaac married Rebekah at age forty after his mother's death.[221]

Ironically, Abraham was called upon to offer his only son born in the covenant, that son through whom the covenants were to be continued, that son who had not yet taken a wife, that son through whom Abraham's descendants were to become as numerous as the stars in the sky and as the sands of the sea, that son through whom all the families of the earth were to be blessed. Sacrificing Isaac at this point would frustrate and countermand all of Abraham's future blessings.

Abraham must have recalled his own experience as the son of Terah, and how Terah had offered him, Abraham, as a sacrifice to gods of wood and stone, gods that could neither speak, hear or deliver, and how he, Abraham, had called on the living God in mighty prayer to spare his life and how the Lord God Jehovah had broken the altar, destroyed the priest and saved him. Now this same God, the living God, Jehovah, called upon Abraham to sacrifice his only son born in

---

220. Genesis 22:2 KJV, MT, JST
221. Ibid 25:20

the covenant on an altar, seemingly negating all that God had promised Abraham and Sarah. One wonders how Abraham and Sarah felt about this unprecedented requirement of the Lord. No prior explanation is given in Genesis as to why the Lord would require this of Abraham and of Sarah and of Isaac.

Abraham, with characteristic and complete faith in the Lord, without vacillation, immediately obeyed. The Genesis account reads:

"And it came to pass after these things, that God did tempt (prove, try) Abraham, and said unto him, Abraham: and he said, Behold, here I am. And he said, Take now thy son, thine only son Isaac, whom thou lovest, and get thee into the land of Moriah; and offer him there for a burnt offering upon one of the mountains which I will tell thee of. And Abraham rose up early in the morning, and saddled his ass, and took two of his young men with him, and Isaac his son, and clave the wood for the burnt offering, and rose up, and went unto the place of which God had told him."

"Then on the third day, Abraham lifted up his eyes, and saw the place afar off. And Abraham said unto his young men, Abide ye here with the ass; and I and the lad will go yonder and worship, and come again to you."

"And Abraham took the wood of the burnt offering, and laid it upon Isaac his son; and he took the fire in his hand, and a knife, and they went both of them together. And Isaac spake unto Abraham his father, and said, My father: and he said, Here am I, my son. And he said, Behold the fire and the wood: but where is the lamb, for a burnt offering? And Abraham said, my son, God will provide himself a lamb for a burnt offering; so they went both of them together."

"And they came to the place which God had told him of; and Abraham built an altar there, and laid the wood in order, and bound Isaac his son, and laid him on the altar upon the wood. And Abraham stretched forth his hand, and took the knife to slay his son. And the angel of the Lord called unto him out of heaven, and said, Abraham, Abraham: And he said, Here am I."

"And he (the angel) said, Lay not thine hand upon the lad,

neither do thou anything unto him: for now I know that thou fearest God, seeing thou hast not withheld thy son, thine only son (Isaac) from me. And Abraham lifted up his eyes, and looked, and behold behind him a ram caught in a thicket by his horns: and Abraham went and took the ram, and offered him up for a burnt offering in the stead of his son. And Abraham called the name of that place Jehovah-jireh (Adonai-jireh): as it is said to this day, In the mount of the Lord it shall be seen."[222]

From the Genesis account it appears that Isaac didn't know he was the intended sacrifice until he was bound and laid on the altar. One wonders why Isaac did not resist being bound. Was he just a boy and too small to resist, or was he a teenager or a grown man, able to resist, but a willing sacrifice? After all, Abraham was well over a hundred years old and physically probably not strong enough to hold a teenager or young man against his will.

The account of this experience recorded in Jasher and in the Legends of the Jews, however, puts Isaac at thirty seven years of age at the time of the intended sacrifice, the same year of Sarah's death (and at twenty five years of age by Antiquities). These accounts identify the two young men that Abraham took along with Isaac to the Mount as being Ishmael his son through Hagar, and Eleazer, Abraham's long time servant.

Apparently Abraham did not tell Sarah or Isaac of the Lord's command to offer up Isaac.

Did the Lord spring this great requirement upon Abraham suddenly without provocation or motivation? The Jasher and Legend accounts claim that Abraham had not offered a sacrifice unto the Lord since Isaac's birth, thirty seven years previously. Satan claimed that Abraham had forgotten and forsaken the Lord.

The Lord countered Satan's claim by declaring,

(From Jasher)..."There is none like him (Abraham) upon the earth, a perfect and an upright man before me, one that feareth God and avoideth evil; as I live, were I to say unto him, Bring up Isaac thy son before me, he would not withhold him from me,

---

222. Genesis 22:1-14 KJV, MT (22:1-18) JST

92

much more if I told him to bring up a burnt offering before me from his flocks and herds."[223]

Satan then challenged the Lord to prove it with these words, "Speak then thou now unto Abraham as thou hast said, and thou wilt see whether he will not this day transgress and cast aside thy words."[224]

(From Jasher) "At that time the word of the Lord came to Abraham, and he said unto him, Abraham, and he said, Here I am. And he said to him, Take thou thy son, thine only son whom thou lovest, even Isaac, and go to the land of Moriah, and offer him there for a burnt offering upon one of the mountains which shall be shown to thee, for there wilt thou see a cloud and the glory of the Lord."[225]

Was Isaac prepared in any way for the experience of facing sudden death by the hand of his father, Abraham?

The Jasher and Legend accounts claim Ishmael boasted to Isaac that when he, Ishmael, was thirteen years old he had been circumcised and that he, Ishmael had given his soul to the Lord, and that he Ishmael, had not transgressed God's word.[226]

(From Jasher) "And Isaac answered Ishmael saying, Why dost thou boast to me about this, about a little bit of thy flesh which thou didst take from thy body, concerning which the Lord commanded thee? As the Lord liveth, the God of my father Abraham, if the Lord should say unto my father, Take now thy son Isaac and bring him up an offering before me, I would not refrain but I would joyfully accede to it. And the Lord heard the word that Isaac spoke to Ishmael, and it seemed good in the sight of the Lord, and he thought to try Abraham in this matter."[227]

Isaac already had agreed in his heart to joyfully accede to being a

223. Jasher XXII:54, Legends I:272-3, V:228 Yashar Wa-Yera 43b
224. Ibid XXII:55, Legends I:273, V:228 Yashar Wa-Yera 43b
225. Ibid XXIII:1-2, Legends I:273
226. Ibid XXII:41-42; Legends I:273
227. Ibid XXII:43-45

sacrifice, should the Lord require it of him. If true, this would explain why Isaac resisted not being bound to be slain by his father.

But what of Isaac's departure from his mother Sarah, whom he dearly loved and to whom he was deeply attached? And what of Sarah, did Abraham prepare her in any way for permanent separation from Isaac, her only son born in her old age, a covenant son, whose name was announced to her by an angel of God?

Again the Genesis account is silent, and the Legends and Jasher have some thing to say:

(From Jasher) "And Abraham said within himself, How shall I separate my son Isaac from Sarah his mother in order to bring him up for a burnt offering before the Lord? And Abraham came into the tent and sat before Sarah his wife, and he spoke these words to her, My son Isaac is grown up and he has not for some time studied the service of his God, now tomorrow I will go and bring him to Shem and Eber his son, and there he will learn the ways of the Lord, for they will teach him to know the Lord as well as to know that when he prayeth continually before the Lord, he will answer him, therefore there he will know the way of serving the Lord his God."

"And Sarah said, Thou hast spoken well, go my lord and do unto him as thou hast said, but remove him not at a great distance from me, neither let him remain there too long, for my soul is bound within his soul. And Abraham said unto Sarah, My daughter, let us pray to the Lord our God that he may do good with us."[228]

Thus Abraham and Sarah prayed for Isaac's well being, Abraham knowing what the Lord had asked him to do.

Knowing that Isaac was going away and wondering whether she would see him again, Sarah stayed up all that night giving him instructions, as mothers sometimes do. When Sarah finished instructing Isaac, she turned to Abraham and counseled him to take good care of her only son.

Sarah selected a fine and beautiful garment given her by Abimelech and dressed Isaac her son therewith and put a turban with a

---

228. Legends I:274-5; Jasher XXIII:3-7

precious stone in it upon his head. She gave the four of them, Abraham, Isaac, Ishmael and Eliazer provisions for the road and they departed. The servants of Sarah also arose to see them off.

Apparently Sarah couldn't say goodbye, for Isaac finally said, "Return to the tent." At the final farewell Sarah, Isaac and Abraham wept a great weeping, and Sarah said, "who knoweth if after this day I shall ever see you again?" Though Abraham told her he was taking Isaac to Shem and Eber he was really taking Isaac as an offering to the Lord as commanded.

> ..."And Abraham went with Isaac his son to bring him up as an offering before the Lord, as He had commanded him."[229]

Ishmael must have sensed what was happening. Isaac had already told Ishmael, if the Lord required it, he Isaac, would be a willing sacrifice. As the journey proceeded, Ishmael, the son of Hagar, and Eliezer, Abraham's servant, spoke among themselves and speculated as who would inherit Abraham's estate after Isaac was sacrificed, and Abraham was dead.

Ishmael asserted that he, as first born, would receive all that Abraham possessed, as an inheritance. Eliezer reminded Ishmael that Abraham had cast him away with his mother Hagar, thereby disqualifying Ishmael as the heir. Eliezer asserted he as Abraham's long time faithful servant would inherit all Abraham had. Neither anticipated that the Lord would save Isaac's life at the last minute and that Isaac would be Abraham's actual heir.[230]

The Lord's requirement was difficult enough without any other obstacles. However, Satan added to the test by tempting both Abraham and Isaac, planting doubts in their minds. Appearing to Abraham as an old man, and to Isaac as a young man, Satan tried to dissuade them.

> (From Jasher) ..."Satan came and appeared to Abraham in the figure of a very aged man, humble and of contrite spirit, and he approached Abraham and said to him, Art thou silly or brutish, that thou goest to do this thing this day to thine only son?
>
> For God gave thee a son in thy latter days, in thy old age, and

---

229. Ibid I:275-6, Jasher XXIII:8-20
230. Ibid I:276-7, Jasher XXIII:21-24

95

wilt thou go and slaughter him this day because he committed no violence, and wilt thou cause the soul of thine only son to perish from the earth? Dost thou not know and understand that this thing cannot be from the Lord? for the Lord cannot do unto man such evil upon earth to say to him, Go slaughter thy child. And Abraham heard this and knew that it was the word of Satan who endeavored to draw him aside from the way of the Lord, but Abraham would not hearken to the voice of Satan, and Abraham rebuked him so that he went away."

"And Satan returned and came unto Isaac; and he appeared unto Isaac in the figure of a young man comely and well favored. And he approached Isaac and said unto him, Dost thou not know and understand that thy old silly father bringeth thee to the slaughter this day for naught? Now therefore, my son, do not listen nor attend to him, for he is a silly old man, and let not thy precious soul and beautiful figure be lost from the earth. And Isaac heard this, and said unto Abraham, Hast thou heard, my father, that which this man has spoken? even thus he has spoken. And Abraham answered his son Isaac and said to him, Take heed of him and do not listen to his words, nor attend to him, for he is Satan, endeavoring to draw us aside this day from the commands of God."[231]

Abraham again rebuked Satan. He departed, but not for long. He returned to create a mirage of water. As Abraham, Isaac, Ishmael and Eliezer struggled to cross these waters Abraham realized it was Satan's doing, hedging up the way to draw them aside from the commands of God. Abraham again rebuked Satan a third time, this time calling on the Lord to rebuke him saying, "The Lord rebuke thee, O Satan, begone from us for we go by the commands of God."

The voice of Abraham, filled with the spirit of God terrified Satan who went away and the mirage of water disappeared. "And Abraham went with Isaac toward the place that God had told him."[232]

These two accounts add much concerning Isaac as a willing sacrifice. Both Abraham and Isaac recognized the place where the act was to take place, but Ishmael and Eliezer did not. Ishmael and Eliezer

---

231. Jasher XXIII:25-33; Legends I:276-7, V:227-230 Yashar Wa-Yera 43b - 44a
232. Ibid XXIII:34-40; Legends I:277-8, V:231-234 Yashar Wa-Yera 44a - 45a

were left behind with their beast of burden while Abraham and Isaac proceeded to the mount.

(From Jasher) "And on the third day Abraham lifted up his eyes and saw the place at a distance which God had told him of. And a pillar of fire appeared to him that reached from the earth to heaven, and a cloud of glory upon the mountain, and the glory of the Lord was seen in the cloud. And Abraham said to Isaac, My son, dost thou see in that mountain, which we perceive at a distance, that which I see upon it? And Isaac answered and said unto his father, I see and lo a pillar of fire and a cloud, and the glory of the Lord is seen upon the cloud. And Abraham knew that his son Isaac was accepted before the Lord for a burnt offering."[233]

(Continuing Jasher) "And Abraham said unto Eliezer and unto Ishmael his son, Do you also see that which we see upon the mountain which is at a distance? And they answered and said, we see nothing more than like the other mountains of the earth. And Abraham knew that they were not accepted before the Lord to go with them, and Abraham said to them, Abide ye here with the ass whilst I and Isaac my son will go to yonder mount and worship there before the Lord and then return to you. And Eliezer and Ishmael remained in that place, as Abraham had commanded. And Abraham took wood for a burnt offering and placed it upon his son Isaac, and he took fire and the knife, and they both went to that place."

"And when they were going along Isaac said to his father, Behold, I see here the fire and the wood, and where then is the lamb that is to be the burnt offering before the Lord? And Abraham answered his son Isaac, saying, The Lord has made choice of thee my son, to be a perfect burnt offering instead of the lamb. And Isaac said unto his father, I will do all that the Lord spoke to thee with joy and cheerfulness of heart. And Abraham again said unto Isaac his son, Is there in thy heart any thought or

---

233. Jasher XXIII:42-45, Legends I:278, V:234-236 Yasher Wa-Yera 45a - 45b

counsel concerning this which is not proper? tell me my son, I pray thee, O my son conceal it not from me."

"And Isaac answered his father Abraham and said unto him, O my father, as the Lord liveth and as thy soul liveth, there is nothing in my heart to cause me to deviate either to the right or to the left from the word that he has spoken to thee. Neither limb nor muscle has moved or stirred at this, nor is there in my heart any thought or evil counsel concerning this. But I am of joyful and cheerful heart in this matter, and I say, Blessed is the Lord who has this day chosen me to be a burnt offering before Him. And Abraham greatly rejoiced at the words of Isaac, and they went on and came together to that place that the Lord had spoken of."

"And Abraham approached to build the altar in that place, and Abraham was weeping, and Isaac took stones and mortar until they had finished building the altar. And Abraham took the wood and placed it in order upon the altar which he had built. And he took his son Isaac and bound him in order to place him upon the wood which was upon the altar, to slay him for a burnt offering before the Lord."

"And Isaac said to his father, Bind me securely and then place me upon the altar lest I should turn and move, and break loose from the force of the knife upon my flesh and thereby profane the burnt offering; and Abraham did so. And Isaac still said to his father, O my father, when thou shalt have slain me and burnt me for an offering, take with thee that which shall remain of my ashes to bring to Sarah my mother, and say to her, This is the sweet smelling savor of Isaac; but do not tell her this if she should sit near a well or upon a high place, lest she should cast her soul after me and die."

"And Abraham heard the words of Isaac, and he lifted up his voice and wept when Isaac spake these words; and Abraham's tears gushed down upon Isaac his son, and Isaac wept bitterly, and he said to his father, Hasten thou, O my father, and do with me the will of the Lord our God as He has commanded thee. And the hearts of Abraham and Isaac rejoiced at this thing which the Lord had commanded them; but the eye wept bitterly whilest the heart rejoiced."

"And Abraham bound his son Isaac, and placed him on the altar upon the wood, and Isaac stretched forth his neck upon the altar before his father, and Abraham stretched forth his hand to take the knife to slay his son as a burnt offering before the Lord."

"At that time the angels of mercy came before the Lord and spake to him concerning Isaac, saying, O Lord, thou art a merciful and compasionate King over all that thou hast created in heaven and in earth, and thou supportest them all; give, therefore ransom and redemption instead of thy servant Isaac, and pity and have compassion upon Abraham and Isaac his son, who are this day performing thy commands. Hast thou seen O Lord, how Isaac the son of Abraham thy servant is bound down to the slaughter like an animal? now therefore let thy pity be roused for them, O Lord."

"At that time the Lord appeared unto Abraham, and called to him, from heaven, and said unto him, Lay not thine hand upon the lad, neither do thou anything unto him, for now I know that thou fearest God in performing this act, and in not withholding thy son, thine only son, from me. And Abraham lifted up his eyes and saw, and behold, a ram was caught in a thicket by his horns; that was the ram which the Lord God had created in the earth in the day that he made earth and heaven. For the Lord had prepared this ram from that day, to be a burnt offering instead of Isaac."

"And this ram was advancing to Abraham when Satan caught hold of him and entangled his horns in the thicket, that he might not advance to Abraham, in order that Abraham might slay his son. And Abraham, seeing the ram advancing to him and Satan withholding him, fetched him and brought him before the altar, and he loosened his son Isaac from the binding, and he put the ram in his stead, and Abraham killed the ram upon the altar, and brought it up as an offering in the place of his son Isaac."

"And Abraham sprinkled some of the blood of the ram upon the altar, and he exclaimed and said, This is in the place of my son, and may this be considered this day as the blood of my son before the Lord. And all that Abraham did on this occasion by the altar, he would exclaim and say, This is in the room of my son, and may it this day be considered before the Lord in the place of my son; and Abraham finished the whole of the service by the altar, and the service was accepted before the Lord, and was accounted as if it had been Isaac, and the Lord blessed Abraham and his seed that day."[234]

The blessing Abraham and his seed received that day was a reaffirmation of the promises made to him by the Lord earlier, which were part of the covenant Abraham made with the Lord. That is, Abraham was to prove to the Lord's satisfaction that he would indeed walk uprightly before Him and be perfect. Part of Abraham's test was to wait fifty years for his heir to be born through whom the rest of the world would be blessed and through whom the covenants with God would be continued.

Another part of the Lord's test was to see how much faith and trust Abraham and Isaac had in the Lord. The final part of the Lord's test was to see if Abraham would obey without flinching which would prove beyond doubt that Abraham loved the Lord with all his heart and indeed had no other gods before him, even if it meant sacrificing his own son and all the blessings which were to follow. Abraham and Isaac passed the test and the blessings were assured.

Returning now to the Genesis account:

"And the angel of the Lord called unto Abraham out of heaven the second time. And said, By myself have I sworn, saith the Lord, for because thou hast done this thing, and hast not withheld thy son, thine only son: That in blessing I will bless thee, and in multiplying I will multiply thy seed as the stars of the heaven, and as the sand which is upon the sea shore; and thy seed

---

234. Jasher XXIII:46-75, Legends I:279-283, V:238-245 Yashar Wa-Yera 45b - 46b

shall possess the gate of his enemies; And in thy seed shall all the nations of the earth be blessed; because thou hast obeyed (hearkened to) my voice."[235]

And through him and his seed all the nations of the earth have been blessed because Abraham (and Isaac) obeyed (hearkened to) the voice of God.

The great trial and test were over:

"So Abraham returned unto his young men, and they rose up and went together to Beersheba; and Abraham dwelt at Beersheba."[236]

---

235. Genesis 22:15-18 KJV, MT (22:19-22) JST
236. Ibid 22:19 KJV, MT, (22:23) JST

CHAPTER XII

AND ABRAHAM BURIED SARAH WITH POMP AS OBSERVED AT THE INTERMENT OF KINGS

Except for a brief genealogy of Abraham's brother Nahor and his posterity, Genesis moves directly from a description of Abraham's offering of Isaac as a sacrifice, to Sarah's death without indicating how much time had lapsed or what else might have transpired between these two events. It gives no indication of how Sarah died, saying only she died in Kirjatharba or Hebron in Canaan some distance from Beersheba. Abraham came there to mourn and weep for Sarah and eventually to arrange for her burial, implying he was not present at her death. She died at 127 years of age or in Isaac's 37th year, the year Jasher and the Legends claim Isaac had been offered as a sacrifice.

These accounts tie the two events, Isaac's offer as a sacrifice and Sarah's death, inextricably together. Satan, according to this account, lied to Sarah, told her Abraham sacrificed Isaac without showing any compassion, and that Isaac was dead. Sarah wept bitterly, then acknowledged the Lord, offered a prayer of thanksgiving, rose up and searched for Abraham. The search took her to Kireath Arba (Kirjatharba) or Hebron. Satan appeared to her again there, and changed his story and told her Isaac was alive.

The shock of all this was too great for Sarah. She got so excited that her heart failed and she died on the spot in Kirjatharba.

(From Jasher) "And Satan went to Sarah, and he appeared to her in the figure of an old man very humble and meek, and Abraham was yet engaged in the burnt offering before the Lord. And he said unto her, Dost thou not know all the work that Abraham has made with thine only son this day? for he took Isaac and built an altar, and killed him, and brought him up as a sacrifice upon the altar, and Isaac cried and wept before his father, but he looked not at him, neither did he have compassion over him. And Satan repeated these words and he went away from her, and Sarah heard all the words of Satan, and she imagined him to be an old man from amongst the sons of men, who had been with her son, and had come and told her these things."

"And Sarah lifted up her voice and wept and cried out bitterly on account of her son, and she threw herself on the ground and she cast dust upon her head, and she said, O my son, Isaac my son, O that I had this day died instead of thee. And she continued to weep and said, It grieves me for thee, O my son, my son Isaac. O that I had died this day in thy stead. And she continued to weep, and said, It grieves me for thee after that I have reared thee and have brought thee up, now my joy is turned to mourning over thee. I that had a longing for thee, and cried and prayed to God till I bare thee at ninety years old; and now hast thou served this day for the knife and the fire, to be made an offering."

"But I console myself with thee, my son, in its being the word of the Lord, for thou didst perform the command of thy God; for who can transgress the word of our God, in whose hands is the soul of every living creature? Thou art just O Lord our God, for all thy works are good and righteous: for I also am rejoiced with thy word which thou didst command, and whilst mine eye weepeth bitterly my heart rejoiceth. And Sarah laid her head upon the bosom of one of her handmaids, and she became as still as a stone."

"She afterward rose up and went about making enquiries till she came to Hebron, and she inquired of all those whom she met walking in the road, and no one could tell her what had happened to her son. And she came with her maid servants and men servants to Kireath Arba, which is Hebron, and she asked concerning her son, and she remained there while she sent some of her servants to seek where Abraham had gone with Isaac; they went to seek him in the house of Shem and Eber, and they could not find him, and they sought throughout the land and he was not there."

"And behold, Satan came to Sarah in the shape of an old man, and he came and stood before her, and he said unto her, I spoke falsely unto thee, for Abraham did not kill his son and he is not dead; and when she heard the word her joy was so exceedingly violent on account of her son, that her soul went out through joy; she died and was gathered to her people."

"And when Abraham had finished his service and he returned with his son Isaac to his young men, and they rose up and went together to Beersheba and they came home. And Abraham sought for Sarah, and could not find her, and he made inquiries concerning her, and they said unto him, She went as far as Hebron to seek you both where you had gone, for thus she was informed. And Abraham and Isaac went to her to Hebron, and when they found that she was dead they lifted up their voices and wept bitterly over her; and Isaac fell upon his mother's face and wept over her, and he said, O my mother, my mother, how hast thou left me, and where hast thou gone? O how, how hast thou left me! And Abraham and Isaac wept greatly, and all their servants wept with them on account of Sarah, and they mourned over her a great and heavy mourning."[237]

Returning now to the Genesis account:

"And (the life of) Sarah was an hundred; and seven and twenty years old; these were the years of the life of Sarah. And Sarah died in Kirjath - arba; the same is Hebron in the land of Canaan: And Abraham came to mourn for Sarah, and to weep for her. And Abraham stood up from before his dead and spake unto the sons of Heth, saying, I am a stranger and a sojourner with you: give me a possession of a burying place with you, that I may bury my dead out of my sight."

"And the children of Heth answered Abraham, saying unto him, Hear us, my lord: thou art a mighty prince (of God) among

---

237. Jasher XXIII:76-90; Legends I:286-87, V:256 Yashar Wa-Yera 46a - 47a

us: in the choice of our sepulchres bury thy dead; none of us shall withhold from thee his sepulchre, but that thou mayest bury thy dead. And Abraham stood up, and bowed himself to the people of the land, even to the children of Heth. And he communed with them, saying, If it be your mind that I should bury my dead out of my sight; hear me, and intreat for me (i.e. speak for me) to Ephron the son of Zohar, that he may give me the cave of Machpelah, which he hath, which is in the end of his field; for as much money as it is worth he shall give it to me for a possession of a burying place amongst you."

"And Ephron dwelt among the children of Heth: and Ephron the Hittite answered Abraham in the audience of the children of Heth, even of all that went in at the gate of his city, saying, Nay, my lord, hear me: the field give I thee, and the cave that is therein, I give it thee; in the presence of the sons of my people give I it (to) thee: bury thy dead. And Abraham bowed down himself before the people of the land. And he spake unto Ephron in the audience of the people of the land, saying But if thou wilt give it, I pray thee, hear me: I will give thee money for the field; take it of me, and I will bury my dead there. And Ephron answered Abraham, saying unto him, My lord, hearken unto me: the land is worth four hundred shekels of silver; what is that betwixt me and thee? bury therefore thy dead."

"And Abraham hearkened unto Ephron: And Abraham weighed to Ephron the silver, which he had named in the audience of the sons of Heth, four hundred sheckels of silver, current money with the merchant. And the field of Ephron which was in Mach-pelah, which was before Mamre, the field, and the cave which was therein, and all the trees that were in the field, that were in all the borders round about, were made sure unto Abraham for a possession in the presence of the children of Heth, before all that went in at the gate of his city."[238]

The Jasher and Legends accounts add that Abraham wrote the transaction down, obtained four witnesses and kept the book of purchase in his possession. The book of purchase also contained a more complete description of the transaction which was to last forever.

238. Genesis 23:1-18 KJV, MT (23:1-16) JST

Jasher reads:

"And Ephron and all his brethren heard this and Abraham weighed to Ephron four hundred shekels of silver in the hands of Ephron and in the hands of all his brethren; and Abraham wrote this transaction, and he wrote it and testified it with four witnesses. And these are the names of the witnesses, Amigal son of Abishma the Hittite, Adichorom, son of Ashunach, the Hivite, Abdon son of Achiram the Gomerite, Bakdil the son of Abudish the Zidonite."

"And Abraham took the book of purchase, and placed it in his treasures, and these are the words that Abraham wrote in the book, namely: That the cave and the field Abraham bought from Ephron the Hittite, and from his seed, and from those that go out of his city, and from their seed forever, are to be a purchase to Abraham and to his seed and to those that go forth from his loins, for a possession of a burial place forever; and he put a signet to it and testified it with witnesses. And the field and the cave that was in it and all that place were made sure unto Abraham and to his seed after him, from the children of Heth; behold it is before Mamre in Hebron, which is in the land of Canaan. And after this Abraham buried his wife Sarah there. And that place and all its boundary became to Abraham and unto his seed for a possession of a burial place."[239]

These accounts conclude Sarah's death and burial with this description.

"And Abraham buried Sarah with pomp as observed at the interment of kings, and she was buried in very fine and beautiful garments. And at her bier was Shem, his sons Eber and Abimelech, together with Anar, Ashcol and Mamre, and all the grandees of the land followed her bier. And the days of Sarah were one hundred and twenty-seven years and she died, and Abraham made a great and heavy mourning, and he performed the rites of mourning for seven days. And all the inhabitants of the land comforted Abraham and Isaac his son on account of Sarah. And

---

239. Jasher XXIV:7-12, Legends I:289-90, Genesis 23:19-20 KJV, MT, JST

when the days of their mourning passed by Abraham sent away his son Isaac, and he went to the house of Shem and Eber, to learn the ways of the Lord and his instructions, and Abraham remained there three years."[240]

Apparently "there" meant at or near the cave of Machpelah where Sarah was buried.

Sarah's Qualities and Contributions

Sarah was an extraordinary person in her own right. She, like Abraham, has few peers in history. Blessed with breath taking beauty, she attracted the immediate attention of men of the highest secular rank, even kings and pharaohs. She remained loyal and true to Abra ham under all circumstances. Her love for the mighty God, Jehovah (Yahweh) and His program matched Abraham's. She prayed often. Her prayers were answered by angels sent from the presence of God to protect her from the highest officers of the land. They had sought her body.

Two experiences more than fifteen years apart, the first with the Pharaoh of Egypt and the second with Abimelech, King of the Philistines, illustrate divine interevention in her life, where her physical and spiritual safety was at stake. The Lord God plagued the Pharaoh with disease in the first instance and closed the wombs of the Philistine women for a period until her safety was assured, in the second.

The Legends of the Jews contain at least six different references to her prophetic gifts. Sarah was known as Iscah, the Seer. Some say Sarah foresaw in vision Israel's history to come, and that she prayed to God to assist Israel in her future tribulations.

A missionary equal in rank with Abraham, Sarah converted the women of her day to the teachings of God.

Some say she is the only woman of her day with whom God directly spoke. It was the Lord who counseled her to give Hagar to Abraham as a wife. Sarah obeyed. She had many tests and trials of her own, living as a stranger in the land of Canaan. Hagar conceived almost immediately and used her conception as evidence she was superior to Sarah. Sarah's character was severely tested as she suffered barreness for fourteen more years while Abraham's son via Hagar grew to maturity.

---

240. Jasher XXIV:13-17, Legends I:290, V:268 Yasher Hay ye Sarah 47a - 48b

Sarah bore her afflictions well. When she had given up hope for a child of her own the Lord God intervened, restored her body to child bearing age and blessed her with a son whose name was given by the Lord God Himself, and whose date of birth He also set.

It has been said that Rachel's beauty was akin to Sarah's beauty and that Joseph inherited the beauty of his mother and great grandmother. It has also been said that Rebekah was Sarah's counterpart in her relationship to Isaac.

Abraham laid Sarah to rest with pomp and ceremony burying her in the Cave of Mach-Pelah. He and all who knew her greatly mourned her death, looking forward however, with faith and hope in the mighty God Yahweh who had promised her body would be quickened and restored to life again sometime in the future.

CHAPTER XIII

AND TAKE A WIFE UNTO MY SON ISAAC

Sarah's life came to an end in Abraham's 137th year and Isaac's 37th year. The Jasher account claims Isaac went with Shem and Eber leaving Abraham alone to mourn for Sarah and to recover from her death. It was during this three year period that Abraham concluded that his son Isaac should not take a wife from among the Canaanites, but from among his own people who lived in Haran.

Other events took place which are not recorded in Genesis. Abimelech, King of the Philistines, died and was succeeded by his son Benmalich who was twelve years old at the time. He took his father's name as king. Lot died and his posterity were identified. Nahor, Abraham's brother, also died. The deaths of Sarah, Lot, Nahor and Abimelech undoubtedly shocked Abraham.

After noting that Abraham stayed by Sarah's burial place three years the Jasher account reads:

"At that time Abraham rose up with all his servants, and they went and returned homeward to Beersheba, and Abraham and all his servants remained in Beersheba. And at the revolution of the year, Abimelech king of the Philistines died in that year; he was one hundred and ninety three years old at his death; and Abraham went with his people to the land of the Philistines, and they comforted the whole household and all his servants, and he then turned and went home. And it was after the death of Abimelech that the people of Gerar took Benmalich his son, and he was only twelve years old, and they made him king in the place of is father. And they called his name Abimelech after the name of his father, for thus was it their custom to do in Gerar, and Abimelech reigned instead of Abimelech his father, and he sat upon his throne."

"And Lot the son of Haran also died in those days in the thirty ninth year of the life of Isaac, and all the days that Lot lived were one hundred and forty years and he died. And these are the children of Lot that were born to him by his daughters, the name of the first born was Moab, and the name of the second was Benami. And the two sons of Lot went and took themselves wives from the land of Canaan, and they bare children to them, and the children of Moab were Ed, Mayon, Tarsus, and Kanvil, four sons, these are the fathers to the children of Moab unto this day. And all the families of the children of Lot went to dwell wherever they should light upon, for they were fruitful and increased abundantly. And they went and built themselves cities in the land where they dwelt, and they called the names of the cities which they built after there own names."

"And Nahor the son of Terah, brother to Abraham died in those days in the fortieth year of the life of Isaac, and all the days of Nahor were one hundred and seventytwo years and he died and was buried in Haran. And when Abraham heard that his brother was dead he grieved sadly, and he mourned over his brother many days."[241]

With four of his dear friends and relatives now dead, Abraham worried about Isaac's future. Rather than send Isaac directly, Abraham sent his eldest servant, Eliezer, to fetch a wife for Isaac from his kinfolk in Haran.

The Genesis account declared that Abraham wanted Isaac to remain in Canaan as the Lord commanded. Abraham used his servant instead. Jasher and the Legends explained that Isaac was not with Abraham at this time, rather Isaac was in the house of Shem and Eber obtaining religious instruction. Shem was king of Salem, (Adonizedek) (Melchizedek). Abraham therefore sent Eliezer to obtain a wife for Isaac.

(From Jasher) "And Abraham called for Eliezer his head servant,

241. Jasher XXIV:18-28, Legends I:290-291, V:270 Yashar Hay ye Sarah 48a

to give him orders concerning his house, and he came and stood before him. And Abraham said to him, Behold I am old, I do not know the day of my death; for I am advanced in days; now therefore rise up, go forth and do not take a wife for my son from this place and from this land, from the daughters of the Canaanites amongst whom we dwell. But go to my land and to my birthplace, and take from thence a wife for my son, and the Lord God of Heaven and earth who took me from my father's house and brought me to this place, and said unto me, to thy seed will I give this land for an inheritance forever, he will send his angel before thee and prosper thy way, that thou mayest obtain a wife for my son from my family, and from my father's house."[242]

To assure that Eliezer agreed to carry out Abraham's instructions, Eliezer was to seal his committment by placing his hand under Abraham's thigh, a gesture in those days akin to raising the right hand to be sworn in, in our day.

Returning to the Genesis account of the assignment:

"And Abraham said unto his eldest servant of his house, that ruled over all that he had, Put I pray thee, thy hand under my thigh: And I will make thee swear by the Lord, the God of heaven, and the God of the earth, that thou shalt not take a wife unto my son of the daughters of the Canaanites, among whom I dwell: But thou shalt go unto my country, and to my kindred, and take a wife unto my son Isaac."[243]

Abraham was confident that the Lord would prosper the way of his servant via an angel but released Eliezer from the oath in the event a wife for Isaac will not follow him back. Eliezer was also instructed not to take Isaac out of Canaan.

Genesis continues:

"And the servant said unto him, Peradventure the woman will not be willing to follow me unto this land: must I needs bring

242. Ibid XXIV:29-31, Legends I:292-293, V:278 Yashar Hay ye 48b
243. Genesis 24:2-4 KJV, MT, (24:2) JST

thy son again unto the land from whence thou camest? And Abraham said unto him, Beware thou that thou bring not my son thither again. The Lord God of Heaven, which took me from my father's house, and from the land of my kindred, and which spake unto me, and that sware unto me, saying, Unto thy seed will I give this land; he shall send his angel before thee; and thou shalt take a wife unto my son from thence. And if the woman will not be willing to follow thee, then thou shalt be clear from this my oath: only bring not my son thither again. And the servant (Eliezer) put his hand under the thigh of Abraham his master, and sware to him concerning that matter."[244]

Eliezer said to his master "Peradventure no woman will be willing to follow me unto this land. May I then marry my own daughter to Isaac?" "No" replied Abraham, "Thou art of the accursed race, and my son is of the blessed race, and cursing and blessing cannot be united". So say the Legends.[245] On the other hand Eliezer, though of the accursed race (Canaanites), was blessed on account of his faithful service to Abraham.[246]

Eliezer took ten camels and ten of Abraham's servants and departed for the city of Nahor. Simultaneously, or nearly so, Jasher reports, Abraham sent other servants to bring Isaac from the house of Shem and Eber where Isaac had been since his mother Sarah's death.

From Genesis:

"And the servant took ten camels of the camels of his master, and departed; for all the goods of his master were in his hand and he arose and went to Mesopotamia unto the City of Nahor. And he made his camels to kneel down without the city by a well of water at the time of the evening, even the time that women go out to draw water."[247]

---

244. Genesis 24:5-9; Legends I:293-94
245. Legends I:293-294
246. Ibid IV:282
247. Genesis 24:10-11 KJV, MT, (24:9-11) JST

The Jasher account of Eliezer's departure, his prayer and the answer:

"And Eliezer rose up and took ten camels of the camels of his master, and ten men from his master's servants with him, and they rose up and went to Haran, the city of Abraham and Nahor, in order to fetch a wife for Isaac the son of Abraham; and whilst they were gone Abraham sent to the house of Shem and Eber, and they brought from thence his son Isaac. And Isaac came home to his father's house to Beersheba whilst Eliazer and his men came to Haran: and they stopped in the city by the watering place, and he made his camels to kneel down by the water and they remained there."

"And Eliezer, Abraham's servant prayed and said, O God of Abraham my master; send me I pray thee good speed this day and show kindness unto my master, that thou shalt appoint this day a wife for my master's son from his family. And the Lord hearkened to the voice of Eliezer, for the sake of his servant Abraham, and he happened to meet with the daughter of Bethuel, the son of Milcah, the wife of Nahor, brother to Abraham, and Eliezer came to her house."[248]

The Genesis account of Abraham's servant's (Eliazer) departure, his prayer and the answer is in much greater detail.

"And he said, O Lord God of my master Abraham, I pray thee, send me good speed this day, and shew kindness unto my master Abraham. Behold, I stand here by the well of water; and the daughters of men of the city come out to draw water: And let it come to pass, that the damsel to whom I shall say, Let down thy pitcher, I pray thee, that I may drink; and she shall say, Drink, and I will give thy camels drink also: let the same be she that thou hast appointed for thy servant Isaac; and thereby shall I know that thou hast shewed kindness unto my master."

"And it came to pass before he had done speaking, that, behold, Rebekah came out, who was born to Bethuel, son of

---

248. Jasher XXIV:34-37

Milcah, the wife of Nahor, Abrahams brother, with her pitcher upon her shoulder. And the damsel was very fair to look upon, a virgin, neither had any man known her: and she went down to the well, and filled her pitcher, and came up. And the servant (Eliezer) ran to meet her, and said, Let me, I pray thee, drink a little water of thy pitcher. And she said, Drink my lord: and she hasted, and let down her pitcher upon her hand, and gave him drink. And when she had done giving him drink, she said, I will draw water for thy camels also, until they have done drinking. And she hasted and emptied her pitcher into the trough, and ran again unto the well to draw water, and drew for all his camels."

"And the man wondering at her held his peace, to wit whether the Lord had made his journey properous or not. And it came to pass, as the camels had done drinking, that the man took a golden earring of half a shekel weight, And two bracelets for her hands of ten sheckels weight of gold; and said, Whose daughter art thou? tell me, I pray thee: is there room in thy father's house for us to lodge in? And she said unto him, I am the daughter of Bethuel the son of Milcah, whom she bare unto Nahor. She said moreover unto him, We have both straw and provender enough, and room to lodge in. And the man (Eliezer) bowed down his head and worshipped the Lord."[249]

Eliezer thanked the Lord for answering his prayer. Rebecca ran to tell her mother and brother Laban what happened.

(From Genesis) "And he said, Blessed be the Lord God of my master Abraham, who hath not left destitute my master of his mercy and his truth: I being in the way, the Lord led me to the house of my master's brethren. And the damsel ran, and told them of her mother's house these things."[250]

Laban, Rebecca's brother, returned with her to the well where Eliezer and Abraham's other servants had waited. Laban invited Eliezer and the others with him to abide with Rebecca's household. The camels were fed, the men's feet were washed and a meal was spread

---

249. Genesis 24:12-26 KJV, MT, (24:12-25) JST
250. Ibid 24:27-28

for Eliezer and those with him. Eliezer declined to eat until he has conveyed the purpose of his journey. He reiterated his prayer and the answer he felt he had received, that is, that Rebecca was the Lord's anointed and chosen wife for Isaac. Eliezer asked of Rebecca's family for permission to take her back to Beersheba for Isaac. The family agreed, then had second thoughts and asked for more time. Later they concurred that Rebecca was free to go immediately, if she agreed. Rebecca was asked, and she agreed to leave immediately. Before the departure Rebecca's family gave her a blessing. Eliezer must have told the family of Abraham's and Sarah's and subsequently, Isaac's promise of the Lord that his posterity was to be as numerous as the stars in the sky and the sands of the seashore, for Rebekah's family blessed her to be the mother of thousands of millions. Eliezer took up his return journey to Beersheba. Rebekah brought her nurse, later identified by Genesis as Deborah, and by Jasher as Deborah the daughter of Uz, Bethuel's brother and thereby, Rebekah's first cousin. Isaac, out in the field, saw them coming afar off, greeted them and was told all that had transpired. Isaac then brought Rebekah into his mother Sarah's tent. Rebecca became Isaac's wife whom he loved and by whom he was comforted after his mother's death. Isaac was forty years of age. Rebekah's age at this time is unknown. Jasher's account placed her between 10 and 13 years of age. A damsel is a young woman, a girl by definition.

The Genesis account reads:

"And Rebekah had a brother, and his name was Laban: And Laban ran out unto the man, unto the well. And it came to pass, when he saw the earring and bracelets upon his sister's hands, and when he heard the words of Rebekah his sister, saying, Thus spake the man unto me; that he came unto the man; and, behold, he stood by the camels at the well. And he said, Come in, thou blessed of the Lord; wherefore standest thou without? for I have prepared the house, and room for the camels. And the man came into the house: and he ungirded his camels, and gave straw and provender for the camels, and water to wash his feet, and the men's feet that were with him."

"And there was set meat before him to eat: but he said, I will not eat, until I have told mine errand. And he said, Speak on. And he said, I am Abraham's servant. And the Lord hath blessed my master greatly; and he is become great: and he hath given him flocks, and herds, and silver, and gold, and menservants, and maidservants, and camels, and asses. And Sarah my master's wife bare a son to my master when she was old: and unto him hath he given all that he hath. And my master made me swear, saying, Thou shalt not take a wife to my son of the daughters of the Canaanites, in whose land I dwell: But thou shalt go unto my father's house, and to my kindred, and take a wife unto my son."[251]

Eliezer rehearsed with Laban and Bethuel his prayer and the answer through Rebekah which, he felt, confirmed the correctness of his impressions.[252]

(From Genesis) "And now if ye will deal kindly and truly with my master, tell me: and if not, tell me; that I may turn to the right hand, or to the left. Then Laban and Bethuel answered and said, The thing proceedeth from the Lord: we cannot speak unto thee bad or good. Behold, Rebekah is before thee, take her, and go, and let her be thy master's son's wife, as the Lord hath spoken. And it came to pass, that when Abraham's servant heard their words, he worshipped the Lord, bowing himself to the earth. And the servant brought forth jewels of silver, and jewels of gold, and raiment, and gave them to Rebekah: he gave also to her brother and to her mother precious things. And they did eat and drink, he and the men that were with him, and tarried all night; and they rose up in the morning, and he said, Send me away unto my master."

"And her brother and her mother said, Let the damsel abide with us a few days, at the least ten; after that she shall go. And he said unto them, Hinder me not, seeing the Lord hath prospered my way; send me away that I may go to my master. And they said, We will call the damsel, and enquire at her mouth. And they called Rebekah, and said unto her, Wilt thou go with this man? And she said, I will go. And they sent away Rebekah their sister, and her

---

251. Genesis 24:29-38 KJV, MT, JST
252. Ibid 24:39-48

nurse (Deborah), and Abraham's servant, and his men. And they blessed Rebekah, and said unto her, Thou art our sister, be thou the mother of thousands of millions, and let thy seed possess the gates of those which hate them."

"And Rebekah arose and her damsels, and they rode upon the camels and followed the man: and the servant took Rebekah and went his way. And Isaac came from the way of the well Lahai-roi; for he dwelt in the south country. And Isaac went out to meditate in the field at the eventide: and he lifted up his eyes, and saw, and, behold, the camels were coming. And Rebekah lifted up her eyes, and when she saw Isaac, she lighted off the camel. For she had said unto the servant, What man is this that walketh in the field to meet us? And the servant had said, It is my master: therefore she took a vail, and covered herself. And the servant told Isaac all things that he had done. And Isaac brought her into his mother Sarah's tent, and took Rebekah, and she became his wife; and he loved her: and Isaac was comforted after his mother's death."[253]

Veil's in the case of Sarah and Rebekah, no doubt had special significance.

---

253. Genesis 24:49-67 KJV, MT, (24:53-73) JST

CHAPTER XIV

ABRAHAM AGAIN TOOK A WIFE
IN HIS OLD AGE

Genesis shifts its focus from Abraham to Isaac at this point covering the final thirtyfive years of Abraham's life in ten verses. Four of the ten verses report his taking Keturah to wife and identifies six sons, and ten grand and great grandsons born to them. Another two verses declares Abraham gave all that he had to Isaac, and that he gave his sons by Keturah and Hagar gifts and sent them into the east country. A seventh verse mentions Abraham lived one hundred seventy five years and the eighth verse declares Abraham gave up the ghost and died in a good old age, an old man, full of years, and was gathered to his people. The ninth and tenth verses report that Isaac and Ishmael, his sons, buried him in the cave of Machpelah next to Sarah. The cave was located in the field Abraham had purchased from the Sons of Heth.[254] Abraham had eight sons, one through Hagar, one through Sarah, and six through Keturah.

Obviously, much transpired during the evening of Abraham's life (the last 35 years) not reported in Genesis. His six sons through Keturah grew up and began to have families during this period. Ishmael took at least five wives, and had twelve sons through whom many grandchildren were born to Abraham. Rebekah, Isaac's wife, bore two sons, Esau and Jacob, before Abraham's death.

Rebekah was barren during most of this thirty five year period. She did, however, give birth to Esau and Jacob when Abraham was 160 years old. His twin grandsons, were therefore born in the covenant and were fifteen years old when Abraham died.

Abraham's descendants by Hagar, the Egyptian, through Ishmael and his twelve sons, and Abraham's descendants by Keturah, of the land of Canaan, through Zimran, Jokshan, Medan, Median, Ishbak

---

254. Genesis 25:1-10 KJV, MT, JST

and Shuak, rapidly multiplied. Abraham's descendants through his son Isaac were none until help was sought from the Lord through prayer, some twenty years after Rebekah had become Isaac's wife.

(From Genesis) "And these are the names of the sons of Ishmael, by their names, according to their generations: the first born of Ishmael, Nebajoth; and Kedar, and Adbeel, and Mibsam, And Mishma, and Dumah, and Massa, Hadar, and Tema, Jetur, Naphish, and Kedemah: These are the sons of Ishmael, and these are their names, by their towns, and by their castles; twelve princes according to their nations.[255]

Jasher adds that Ishmael's first wife was named Ribah, the same is Meribah, and that in addition to bearing Nebayoth, Kedar, Adbeel and Mibsam, she bare Ishmael a daughter Bosmath. Ribah, or Meribah, was from the land of Egypt. Her behavior was unbecoming or bad in the sight of Ishmael and his father Abraham. Ishmael cast her away or was divorced. She returned to Egypt. Ishmael took a second wife from the land of Canaan named Malchuth. Ishmael's eight other sons, Nishma, Dumah, Masa, Chadad, Tema, Yetur, Naphish and Kedma were born unto him by Malchuth.[256]

Jasher lists the children of Ishmael's sons and thereby the names of Abraham's grandsons and great grandsons through Ishmael. These great grandsons of Abraham through Ishmael were the contemporaries of Abraham's greatgrandsons through Isaac and Jacob i.e. the twelve sons of Israel, one generation removed.

The Jasher account:

These are the sons of Ishmael, and these are their names, being twelve princes according to their nations; and the families of Ishmael afterward spread forth, and Ishmael took his children and all the property that he had gained, together with the souls of his household and all belonging to him, and they went to dwell where they should find a place. And they went and dwelt near the wilderness of Paran, and their dwelling was from Havilah unto Shur, that is before Egypt as thou comest toward Assyria, And

255. Genesis 25:13-17 see also I Chron 1:29-31
256. Jasher XXV:14-18

Ishmael and his sons dwelt in the land, and they had children born to them, and they were fruitful and increased abundantly."[257]

Jasher continues:

"And these are the names of the sons of Nebayoth the first born of Ishmael; Mend, Send, Mayon; and the sons of Kedar were Alym, Kezem, Chamad, and Eli. And the sons of Adbeel were Chamad and Jabin; and the sons of Mibsam were Obadiah, Ebedmelech and Yeush; these are the families of the children of Ribah, the wife of Ishmael."

"And the sons of Mishma the son of Ishmael were Shamua, Zecaryon and Obed; and the sons of Dumah were Kezed, Eli, Machmad and Amed. And the sons of Masa were Melon, Mula, and Ebidadon, and the sons of Chadad were Azur, Minzar and Ebedmelech; and the sons of Tema were Seir, Sadon and Yakol. And the sons of Yetur were Merith, Yaish, Alyo, and Pachoth; and the sons of Naphish were Ebed-Tamed, Abiyasaph, and Mir; and the sons of Kedma were Calip, Tachti and Omir, these were the children of Malchuth the wife of Ishmael according to their families. All these are the families of Ishmael according to their generations, and they dwelt in those lands wherein they had built themselves cities unto this day."[258]

Keturah, Abraham's wife or concubine during his final thirty five years, is identified as being from the land of Canaan. She may not have been a descendant of Canaan, however, The Legends indicate that Keturah was a descendant of Japhet or Japheth. If this is true, Abraham had descendants through all three of Noahs sons, Shem through himself and Sarah, Ham through Hagar and Japheth through Keturah.[259]

Genesis names the six sons of Abraham through Keturah as Zimran, Jokshan, Medan, Midian, Ishabah and Shuah. In addition two grandsons through Jokshan, Sheba and Dedan: Three great grandsons are identified: Asshurin, Letushim and Leummim, the sons

---

257. See also Genesis 25:18
258. Jasher XXV:19-27
259. Legends I:314

120

of Dedan, grandson of Abraham through Jokshan. Five other grandsons through Midian are identified: Ephah, Epher, Hanoch, Abidah and Eldaah. In other words, Genesis identifies six sons, seven grandsons and three great grandsons of Abraham through Keturah.[260]

Jasher, on the other hand, lists Abrahams six sons, twentyone grandsons, and twenty one great grandsons through Keturah. Jasher does not list the three great grandchildren of Abraham through Dedan, however, when these three are added, twenty four great grandchildren of Abraham are identified.

The Jasher account identifying Abrahams' grandchildren through Keturah reads:

"And it was at that time that Abraham again took a wife in his old age, and her name was Keturah from the land of Canaan. And she bare unto him Zimran, Jokshan, Medan, Midian, Ishbak and Shuach being six sons. And the children of Zimran were Abihen, Molich and Narim. And the sons of Jokshan were Sheba and Dedan, and the sons of Medan were Amida, Joab, Gochi, Elisha and Nothach; and the sons of Midian were Ephah, Epher, Chanoch, Abida and Eldaah. And the sons of Ishbak were Makiro, Beyodua, and Tator. And the sons of Shuach were Bildad, Mamdad, Munan, and Meban; all these are the families of the children of Keturah the Canaanitish woman which she bare unto Abraham the Hebrew."[261]

Abraham's twentyone great grandchildren through Keturah listed by Jasher are all grandchildren of Midian, son of Abraham.

"And Abraham sent all these away, and he gave them gifts, and they went away from his son Isaac to dwell wherever they should find a place. And all these went to the mountains at the east, and they built themselves six cities in which they dwelt unto this day. But the children of Sheba and Dedan, children of Jokshan, with their children, did not dwell with their brethren in their cities, and they journeyed and encamped in the countries and wildernesses unto this day. And the children of Midian, son of Abraham, went to the east of the land of Cush, and they there

260. Genesis 25:1-4 see also I Chronicles 1:32-33
261. Jasher XXV:1-5

found a large valley in the eastern country, and they remained there and built a city, and they dwelt therein that is the land of Midian unto this day."

"And Midian dwelt in the city which he built, he and his five sons and all belonging to him. And these are the names of the sons of Midian according to their names in their cities, Ephah, Epher, Chanoch, Abida and Eldaah. And the sons of Ephah were Methach, Meshar, Avi and Tzanua, and the sons of Epher were Ephron, Zur, Alirun, Medin, and the sons of Chanoch were Reuel, Rekem, Azi, Alyoshub and Alad. And the sons of Abida were Chur, Melud, Kerury, Molchi; and the sons of Eldaah were Miker, and Reba and Malchiyah and Gabol; these are the names of the Midianites according to their families; and afterward the families of Midian spread throughout the land of Midian."[262]

Reuel or Jethro the Midianite, father in law to Moses, most likely is a descendant of one of these great grandchildren of Abraham. There is remote possiblity that Reuel son of Chanoch, son of Midian, son of Abraham, is Moses' father-in-law. From Abraham to Moses is seven generations, from Abraham to Reuel through Midian via Chanoch is four generations. Midian was 40 to 60 years younger than Isaac, one generation at least. Jethro was theoretically at least, one generation older than Moses, narrowing the gap to one generation difference between Jethro in the Exodus account and Reuel the great grandson of Abraham through Midian referred to above.

---

262. Jasher XXV:6-13

Chapter XV

I HAVE BECOME OLD...
BUT MY DAYS ARE FULL

As the final days of Abraham approached, he called all his family together including Ishmael and his twelve sons, Isaac and his two sons, Zimran, Jokshan, Medan, Midian, Ishbah and Shuah and their sons. Ishmael and his sons and Zimran, Jokshan, Medan, Midian, Ishbak and Shuah and their sons, were commanded to follow the path of Lord, to live righteously. They were each to love his neighbor and to act in love toward all men.[263] Abraham gave them gifts and "sent them away eastward into the east country".[264]

To Isaac, Abraham gave all that he had, probably meaning his herds, flocks, tents, silver and gold, etc. and the land of Canaan. More importantly he gave Isaac a blessing and additional instruction in the ways and commandments of the Lord. Abraham retold of his departure from Ur at the command of the Lord and admonished Isaac to live His commandments. He admonished Isaac to teach his children these commandments and to walk uprightly before the Lord and be perfect.

Abraham said:

(From Jubilees) "I have become old but I do not know the day of my death but my days are full; behold, I am one hundred and seventy five years old and all throughout my life I have been mindful of the Lord and have tried to do his will all my days and to walk righteously before him. I have hated idols and I have followed the will of him who has created me. He is the living God and he is holy and faithful, and he is righteous beyond anyone and he is no respector of persons and does not accept bribes..."[265]

---

263. Jubilees 20:1-2
264. Genesis 25:6 KJV, MT, JST
265. Jubilees 21:1-4

(From Jasher) "And Abraham gave all that he had to his son Isaac, and he also gave him all his treasures. And he commanded him saying, Dost thou not know and understand the Lord is God in heaven and in earth, and there is no other beside him? And it was he who took me from my fathers house, and from my birth-place, and gave me all the delights upon earth; who delivered me from the counsel of the wicked, for in him did I trust. And he brought me to this place, and he delivered me from Ur Casdim, and he said unto me, To thy seed will I give all these lands, and they shall inherit them when they keep my commandments, my statutes and my judgments that I have commanded thee and which I shall command them."

"Now therefore my son, hearken to my voice and keep the commandments of the Lord thy God, which I commanded thee, do not turn from the right way either to the right or to the left in order that it may be well with thee and thy children after thee forever. And remember the wonderful works of the Lord, and his kindness that he has shown toward us, in having delivered us from the hands of our enemies, and the Lord our God caused them to fall into our hands, and now therefore keep all that I have commanded thee, and turn not away from the commandments of thy God, and serve none beside him, in order that it may be well with thee and thy seed after thee."

Isaac was admonished to teach his children the instructions of the Lord.

The Jasher account continues:

"And teach thou thy children and thy seed the instructions of the Lord and his commandments, and teach them the upright way in which they should go, in order that it may be well with them forever. And Isaac answered his father and said unto him, That which my Lord has commanded that will I do, and I will not depart from the commands of the Lord my God, I will keep all that he commanded me, and Abraham blessed his son Isaac, and also his children; and Abraham taught Jacob the instruction of the Lord and his ways."[266]

266. Jasher XXVI:21-29

Having completed the blessing of his family and having completed his instructions to his heir Isaac and to Isaac's heir apparent Jacob, Abraham died. Isaac and Ishmael buried him next to Sarah in the cave of Machpelah. However, before his burial, a grand funeral was conducted.[267] The small and the great of the land (including Shem), and all the families of the house of Abraham from Haran to Canaan, his children by Hagar, Keturah, and Sarah came to pay tribute to Abraham, prophet of the most high God, patriarch of a great and valiant household, and a leader with few peers in history. Abraham's life, his accomplishments and his legacy are recounted before he is laid to rest.

The Jasher account relates:

"And it was at that time that Abraham died in the fifteenth year of the life of Jacob and Esau, the sons of Isaac, and all the days of Abraham were one hundred seventyfive years, and he died and was gathered to his people in good old age, old and satisfied with days, and Isaac, and Ishmael his sons buried him. And when the inhabitants of Canaan heard that Abraham was dead, they all came with their kings and princes and all their men to bury Abraham. And all the inhabitants of the land of Haran, and all the families of the house of Abraham, and all the princes and grandees, and the sons of Abraham by the concubines, all came when they heard of Abraham's death, and they requited Abraham's kindness, and comforted Isaac, his son, and they buried Abraham in the cave which he bought from Ephron the Hittite and his children, for the possession of a burial place."[268]

Continuing:

"And all the inhabitants of Canaan, and all those who had known Abraham, wept for Abraham a whole year, and men and women mourned over him. And all the little children, and all the inhabitants of the land wept on account of Abraham, for Abraham had been good to them all, and because he had been upright with God and men. And there arose not a man who feared God

---

267. Legends I:299, V:257
268. Jasher XXVI:29-31

125

like unto Abraham, for he had feared his God from his youth, and had served the Lord, and had gone in all his ways during his life, from his childhood to the day of his death. And the Lord was with him and delivered him from the counsel of Nimrod and his people, and when he made war with the four kings of Elam he conquered them. And he brought all the children of the earth to the service of God, and he taught them the ways of the Lord, and caused them to know the Lord. And he formed a grove and he planted a vineyard therein, and he had always prepared in his tent meat and drink to those that passed through the land, that they might satisfy themselves in his house. And the Lord God delivered the whole earth on account of Abraham."[269]

Thus we see that Abraham loved the Lord his God, walked in His ways and served Him with all his heart and soul, foreshadowing the command of the Lord to all Israel through Moses, as preparations were being made to enter the promised land.

"And now, Israel, what doth the Lord require of thee, but to fear the Lord thy God, to walk in all his ways, and to love him, and to serve the Lord thy God with all thy heart and with all thy soul..."[270]

Abraham loved his neighbor as himself, endured to the end, and turned not to the right or to the left from the commands of God. He walked uprightly before the Lord from his childhood until his death and he taught his children to pray and walk uprightly before the Lord.

Abraham has few peers in the history of mankind. It is written of him that Abraham:
- was chosen for his role on earth before he was born.
- was one of the members of the Messiah's counsel in the premortal world.
- was one of the elect of God and received revelations from Him.
- was a friend, servant, and prophet of God.
- was obedient to the commands of the Lord.
- received the reward of the generations before him.
- received the priesthood or power to act for God and so did some of his descendants

---

269. Ibid XXVI:30-38
270. Deuteronomy 10:12 KJV, MT, JST

- had a foretaste of the world to come.
- would have all his blessings fulfilled in the world to come.
- was the father of proscelytes/missionaries
- was the progenitor of thirty nations.
- glorified the name of God.
- loved the Lord God Jehovah with all his heart, offered sacrifices often and had no other gods before Him.
- loved his neighbor as himself.
- honored his father and mother.
- did not kill, commit adultery, steal, covet, bear false witness, or take the name of the Lord in vain.

In summary, Abraham lived a righteous life, kept the covenants he had made with God, passed all the tests put to him, including the Akedah, and strived to walk uprightly before Him and be perfect. For his efforts Abraham was granted his exaltation and he, Abraham sitteth upon his celestial throne.

"Abraham received all things, whatsoever he received, by revelation and commandment, by my word, saith the Lord, and hath entered into his exaltation and sitteth upon his throne."[270A]

270A. Doctrine & Convenants 132:29

CHAPTER XVI

AND THE LORD WAS INTREATED OF HIM (ISAAC) AND REBEKAH HIS WIFE CONCEIVED

Isaac was born in the 500th year of the life of Shem, 390th year of the life of Arphaxad, 355th year of Salah, 325th year of Eber, the 170th year of Terah and the 100th and 90th years respectively of Abraham and Sarah. Shem, Arphaxad, Salah, Eber, Terah, Sarah and Abraham all preceded Isaac in death.

The first thirty seven years of Isaac's life is covered in two chapters of Genesis (Chapters 21 & 22). His birth and weaning is covered in verses 1-8 inclusive of Chapter 21. Isaac's test of sacrifice (Akedah) along with Abraham's is covered in verses 1-18 inclusive of Chapter 22. Chapter 23 records his mother's death and burial. Chapter 24 contains the account of Eleaser's journey to obtain a wife for Isaac. Isaac enters the picture again after Eleaser returns with Rebekah and they meet (verses 62-67). Isaac takes her into his mother's tent.

The record in Genesis Chapter 25 rehearses the posterity of Abraham through Keturah and Hagar, covers Rebekah's barrenness and Isaac's request of the Lord to relieve it. This account plus the account covering the birth of Esau and Jacob is recorded in six verses. Chapter 25 moves on to the selling of Esau's birthright to Jacob. Chapter 26 mentions Isaac's and Rebekah's life in Gerar where they went to escape the famine and where they prosper. Isaac reopens the well of Beersheba. By the closing of Chapter 26 Esau is 40 years old and Isaac is 100 years old. All previous ancestors living at Isaac's birth are dead by this time except Eber.

Isaac's desire to bless Esau before he, Isaac, dies, and Jacob's supplanting of Esau with the help of his mother, who initiated a scheme to do so, are contained in Genesis Chapter 27. Jacob was sent away to preserve his life from the threats of Esau. In addition, Jacob was to obtain a wife from the house of Bethuel his mother's father. Genesis

128

shifts the focus to Jacob at this point, saying virtually nothing more about Isaac except to report that he died at one hundred eighty years of age and that Esau and Jacob buried him. No report of Rebekah's death or burial is given in Genesis.

At one hundred eighty years of age, the year of Isaac's death, Esau and Jacob were 120 years old. Jacob had but 27 years remaining in his life, 17 of which were to be lived out in Egypt, and 10 other years in Canaan prior to his family's move into Egypt at the invitation of Joseph. Joseph was 29 years old and in Egypt, placing his ten older brother's between the ages of 30 and 40 years at Isaac's death, with Benjamin being about 18 years of age.

What else do we know about Isaac and Rebekah through whom all the families and nations of the earth were to be blessed? Did Isaac bless his grandsons? i.e. the house of Israel. Where were Isaac and Rebekah during all these years? Is Isaac indeed the least distinguished of the three great patriarchs Abraham, Isaac and Jacob, as claimed by a prominent encyclopedia, or is it simply a matter of the least information being extant about him?

Reconstruction of the life of Isaac requires help from other writings not contained in the Holy Scriptures.

Isaac's birth was forecast and his name was given to Abraham and Sarah by the Lord himself. Isaac was circumsized by his father Abraham, as the Lord commanded. Shem was present as this token of the covenant was executed. Abraham and Sarah rejoiced as the promises of the Lord were fulfilled. The child, Isaac, grew and was weaned. A great feast was held on the day of his weaning. And on that day Shem, Eber, Abimelech, Terah and Nahor all came to rejoice with Abraham and Sarah.

While Isaac was yet a child, Sarah saw Ishmael mocking and arranged for Ishmael and his mother Hagar to be sent away. Some writers claim Ishmael tried to kill Isaac and that incident motivated Sarah to demand that Abraham send Ishmael and his mother away. Isaac was about five and Ishmael was about 19 years of age. See Chapter IX.

See Chapter XI for the account of Isaac's test of sacrifice. Isaac undoubtedly knew he was the sacrifice, and he voluntarily and bravely acceded to it. His attitude toward the impending sacrifice is most touching. Isaac may have been thirty seven years of age just before his mother died when this took place.

After his mother's death, he was sent to the house of Shem and

Eber for three years of instruction and to learn the ways of the Lord, returning home to Beersheba in time to meet Rebekah.

No explanation is given in Genesis as to why Abraham sent his servant (Eleaser) to get a wife for Isaac, instead of sending Isaac directly. Years later Isaac and Rebekah sent Jacob directly to Haran to get a wife from the house of Bethuel. If Isaac were away at Shem and Eber's house, this would explain why Abraham sent Eleaser instead of Isaac directly.

Rebekah was most likely many years Isaac's junior, perhaps 25 years or more. Isaac was 59 years of age before Rebekah conceived, Rebekah having been barren for 20 years. In the meantime, Ishmael and his six half brothers by Keturah took several wives each and multiplied their posterity rapidly.

Finally, Rebekah asked Isaac to inquire of the Lord, concerning her barrenness. At first Isaac blamed Rebekah for her barrenness, then relented upon Rebecca's insistence and faith. He inquired of and entreated the Lord. The Lord answered through Rebecca's conception. Genesis reads:

"And Isaac intreated the Lord for his wife, because she was barren and the Lord was intreated of him, and Rebekah his wife conceived."[271]

(From Jasher) "And Rebecca the daughter of Bethuel, the wife of Abraham's son Isaac, was barren in those days, she had no offspring; and Isaac dwelt with his father in the land of Canaan; and the Lord was with Isaac; and Arpachshad the son of Shem the son of Noah died in those days, in the forty eighth year of the life of Isaac, and all the days that Arpachshad lived were four hundred and thirty-eight years, and he died."

"And in the fifty ninth year of the life of Isaac the son of Abraham, Rebecca his wife was still barren in those days. And Rebecca said unto Isaac, Truly I have heard, my lord, that thy mother Sarah was barren in her days until my Lord Abraham, thy father, prayed for her and she conceived by him. Now therefore stand up, pray thou also to God and he will hear thy prayer and remember us through his mercies. And Isaac answered his wife

---

271. Genesis 25:21 KJV, MT, JST

Rebecca, saying, Abraham has already prayed for me to God to multiply his seed, now therefore this barreness must proceed to us from thee. And Rebecca said unto him, But arise now thou also and pray, that the Lord may hear thy prayer and grant me children, and Isaac hearkened to the words of his wife, and Isaac and his wife rose up and went to the land of Moriah to pray there and to seek the Lord, and when they had reached that place Isaac stood up and prayed to the Lord on account of his wife because she was barren."[272]

Isaac uttered a mighty prayer of thanksgiving for his blessings and requested the Lord give Rebecca and him seed of man.

(From Jasher) "And Isaac said, O Lord God of heaven and earth, whose goodness and mercies fill the earth, thou who didst take my father from his father's house and from his birthplace, and didst bring him unto this land, and didst say unto him, To thy seed will I give the land, and thou didst promise him and didst declare unto him, I will multiply thy seed as the stars of heaven and as the sand of the sea, now may thy words be verified which thou didst speak unto my father. For thou art the Lord our God, our eyes are toward thee to give us seed of men, as thou didst promise us, for thou art the Lord our God and our eyes are directed toward thee only. And the Lord heard the prayer of Isaac the son of Abraham, and the Lord was entreated of him and Rebecca his wife conceived."[273]

From Genesis:

".....And Rebekah his wife conceived, and the children struggled together within her, and she said, If it be so, why I am I thus? And she went to enquire of the Lord. And the Lord said unto her, Two nations are in thy womb, and two manner of people shall be separated from thy bowels; and the one people shall be stronger than the other people; and the elder shall serve the younger. And when her days to be delivered were fulfilled, behold, there were twins in her womb."[274]

272. Jasher XXV:28, XXVI:1-5; Legends I:312
273. Ibid XXVI:6-8, Legends I:312, V:8 Yashar Toledet 50a - 50b
274. Genesis 25:21-24 KJV, MT, JST

Jasher and Legends record that Rebecca went to inquire of the Lord through Shem, Eber and Abraham, and it was they, the priesthood bearers, who received the answer and reported it to her.

(From Jasher)..."And Rebecca his wife conceived. And in about seven months after the children struggled together within her, and it pained her greatly that she was wearied on account of them, and she said to all the women who were then in the land, Did such a thing happen to you as it has to me? And they said unto her, No. And she said unto them, Why am I alone in this amongst all the women that were upon the earth? and she went to the land of Moriah to seek the Lord on account of this; and she went to Shem and Eber his son to make inquiries of them in this matter, and that they should seek the Lord in this thing respecting her. And she also asked Abraham to seek and inquire of the Lord about all that had befallen her."

"And they all inquired of the Lord concerning this matter, and they brought her word from the Lord and told her, Two children are in thy womb; and two nations shall rise from them; and one nation shall be stronger than the other, and the greater shall serve the younger. And when her days to be delivered were completed, she knelt down, and behold there were twins in her womb, as the Lord had spoken to her."[275]

Thus Esau and Jacob were born, from whom two nations have come into existence, and who struggled with another then and who are still struggling with one another, even today.

Once again we read a prophecy concerning the future seed of Isaac and Rebecca made before their children were born, even to foretelling the relationship of two yet unborn children who were to be born in the covenant.

We return to the Genesis account for the actual birth.

"And when her days to be delivered were fulfilled, behold, there were twins in her womb. And the first came out red, all over like an hairy garment; and they called his name Esau. And after that came his brother out and his hand took hold on Esau's heel;

---

275. Jasher XXVI:8-13 see also Legends I:314, V:17 Yashar Toledet 50b

and his name was called Jacob; and Isaac was three score years when she bare them."[276]

The Legends indicate that Esau was not circumcised at eight days due to poor circulation of his blood. Isaac decided to wait until Esau was thirteen the age when Ishmael received the sign of the covenant. When Esau grew up he refused to give heed to his father's wish and so he was left uncircumcised. By contrast, the Legends say Jacob was born with this sign of the covenant upon his body already, and so were Adam, Seth, Enoch, Noah, Shem, Moses, David, Isaiah, Jeremiah and Zerubbabel.[277]

The boys grew up, Esau became a hunter, an expert and cunning hunter, designing and deceitful. Jacob was a plain man, dwelling in tents, feeding flocks and learning the instructions of the Lord and the commandments of his father and mother. Isaac, Rebekah and their children continued to dwell with Abraham in the land of Canaan, as God had commanded them.

Isaac loved Esau because he did eat of his venison, but Rebekah loved Jacob. After reporting the birth of Esau and Jacob, Genesis next gives the account of Jacob's purchase of Esau's birthright. No mention of their ages at the time of this transaction is made in Genesis. Jasher and the Legends report their ages to be 15 years old just prior to Abraham's death. Jacob was instructed in the ways of the Lord by his grandfather before Abraham died.

Abraham's blessing of Jacob (age 15):

"Jacob, my beloved son, whom my soul loveth, may God bless thee from above the firmament, and may He give thee all the blessing wherewith He blessed Adam, and Enoch, and Noah and Shem, and all the things of which He told me, and all the things which He promised to give me may He cause to cleave to thee and to thy seed forever according to the days of the heavens and the earth. And the spirit of Mastema shall not rule over thee or over thy seed, to turn thee from the Lord, who is thy God from henceforth and forever. And may the Lord God be a father to

---

276. Genesis 25:24-26 KJV, MT, JST
277. Legends I:315, V:273

thee, and mayest thou be His first born son, and may He be a father to thy people always. Go in peace my son."[278]

"Abraham knew that his end was approaching, and he thanked the Lord for all the good He had granted him during the days of his life, and blessed Jacob and bade him walk in the ways of the Lord, especially he was not to marry a daughter of the Canaanites."[279]

With reference to the sale of the birthright Genesis reports only that Esau said he was faint and at the point of death, and that he, Esau, saw no value in his birthright, and that he, Esau, sold his birthright unto Jacob who gave him bread and a pottage of lentils in exchange for it.

Jasher and the Legends, on the other hand, add much to the story. They record that while hunting in the field Esau killed Nimrod, king of Babel, that is Amraphel, and two of his men in a desperate fight. Further that Esau stripped Nimrod of the valuable garments which came down from Adam to Noah, which were stolen by Ham from Noah and were handed down from Ham to Cush to Nimrod who began to wear them when he was 20 years old.

Nimrod's host or guards were in hot pursuit of Esau who managed to elude them and return to his father Isaac's house. The fight with Nimrod's men nearly cost Esau his life, and the chase that followed before Esau eluded them completely wearied and exhausted him to the point he was ready to die.

These records indicate that Jacob acted wisely in the matter and bought the birthright from Esau for value given and that the exchange was brought about by the Lord, implying the garments were part of the transaction. Further, that the exchange included Esau's portion in the cave of the field of Machpelah for a burying place, the place in which Jacob was later buried along side Abraham and Isaac. Further, that Jacob recorded the whole transaction in a book and that there were witnesses to the transaction, which, when completed, was sealed and remained in the possession of Jacob.[280]

The Legends record that Jacob was lying down next to Abraham

---

278. Ibid I:317, V:34, Jubilees 19:16-30, Yashar Toledet 51a
279. Ibid I:317
280. Jasher XXVII:1-14; Legends I:318-321, V:38 Yashar Toledet 51b - 52a

134

on the day of his death and did not know his grandfather had died until the next morning. The pottage or lentils he was cooking the next day was part of a mourning ceremony for Abraham. By contrast Esau was guilty of five crimes on the day of Abraham's death. (1) He ravished a betrothed maiden, (2) He committed murder (i.e. killed Nimrod) (3) He doubted the resurrection of the dead, (4) He scorned the birthright and (5) He denied God.

Esau reportedly accosted Jacob thus, "Why art thou preparing lentils?" Jacob: "Because our grandfather passed away; they shall be a sign of my grief and mourning, that he may love me in the days to come".

Esau: "Thou fool! Dost thou really think it possible that man should come to life again after he has been dead and has mouldered in his grave?" Jacob answered that God will right the deeds of man in the future."

Esau: "Is there a future world? Or will the dead be called back to life? If it were so, why hath not Adam returned? Hast thou heard that Noah, through whom the world was raised anew, hath reappeared? Yea Abraham, the friend of God, more beloved of Him than any man, hath he come to life again?"

Jacob: "If thou art of opinion that there is no future world, and that the dead do not rise to new life, then why dost thou want thy birthright? Sell it to me, now, while it is yet possible to do so... Verily there is a future world, in which the righteous receive their reward. I tell thee this lest thou say later I deceived thee."[281]

Jacob was little concerned about the double share of the inheritance that went with the birthright. What he thought of was priestly service, which was the prerogative of the first born in ancient times, and Jacob was loth to have his impious brother Esau play the priest, he who despised all divine service. The scorn manifested by Esau for the resurrection of the dead he felt also for the promise of God to give the Holy Land to the seed of Abraham. He (Esau) did not believe it, and therefore was willing to cede his birthright, and the blessing attached thereto, in exchange for a mess of pottage.[281]

---

281. Legends 318-320

Jasher completes the description of this event by stating Nimrod was 215 years old at his death having reigned over his people 185 years, or during the entire life of Abraham. Nimrod had died by the sword of Esau in shame and contempt and at the hand of the seed of Abraham as he had seen in his dream at the time of Abraham's birth.

Nimrod's kingdom fell apart at his death and was divided into many divisions and the house of Nimrod became enslaved to other kings of the land.[282]

---

282. Jasher XXVII:15-17

CHAPTER XVII

AND ISAAC DWELT IN GERAR

A famine was in the land of Canaan soon after Abraham's death. Isaac, Rebekah and their two sons, now young men, plan to go to Egypt to escape it as Abraham had done earlier. The Lord appeared to Isaac and redirected him into Gerar, the land of the Philistines, under the reign of Abimelech, the son of Abimelech, with whom Abraham had earlier dealt. The Lord confirmed the blessings of Abraham unto Isaac. Isaac was a little more than 75 years old at the time and Rebekah was probably about 50 years old.

The Genesis account reads:

"And there was a famine in the land, beside the first famine that was in the days of Abraham. And Isaac went unto Abimelech king of the Philistines unto Gerar. And the Lord appeared unto him, and said, Go not down into Egypt, dwell in the land which I shall tell thee of. Sojourn in this land and I will be with thee, and will bless thee; for unto thee, and unto thy seed, I will give all these countries, and I will perform the oath which I sware unto Abraham thy father; And I will make thy seed to multiply as the stars of heaven, and will give unto thy seed all these countries; and in thy seed shall all the nations of the earth be blessed; Because that Abraham obeyed my voice, and kept my charge, my commandments, my statutes, and my laws. And Isaac dwelt in Gerar."[283]

The Legends describe God's conversations with Isaac on this matter as follows:

"but God appeared unto him (Isaac), and spake: Thou are a perfect sacrifice, without a blemish, and as a burnt offering is

---

283. Genesis 26:1-6 KJV, MT, JST

made unfit if it is taken outside of the Sanctuary, so thou wouldst be profaned if thou shouldst happen outside the Holy Land. Remain in the land and endeavor to cultivate it. In this land dwells the Shekinah, (God) and in days to come I will give unto thy children the realms possessed by mighty rulers, first a part thereof, and the whole in the Messianic time."[284]

Shortly after their arrival in Gerar, the king of the Philistines, Abimelech, lusts after Rebekah, as his father had lusted after Sarah and sought to lay with her. Isaac repeated what his father Abraham did in the situation, he called Rebekah his sister, being afraid that if she was identified as his wife, he would be killed and Rebekah taken anyway. Rebekah, by today's definition was actually Isaac's cousin.

The Jasher account reads:

"And Isaac rose up and went to Gerar, as the Lord commanded him, and he remained there a full year. And when Isaac came to Gerar, the people of the land saw that Rebecca his wife was of a beautiful appearance, and the people of Gerar asked Isaac concerning his wife, and he said, She is my sister, for he was afraid to say she was his wife lest the people of the land should slay him on account of her."[285]

Returning to Genesis:

"And it came to pass, when he had been there a long time, that Abimelech king of the Philistines looked out at a window, and saw, and behold, Isaac was sporting with Rebekah his wife. And Abimelech called Isaac, and said, Behold, of a surety she is thy wife; and how sayest thou she is my sister? And Isaac said unto him, Because I said, Lest I die for her. And Abimelech said, What is this thou hast done unto us? One of the people might lightly have lien with thy wife, and thou shouldest have brought guiltness upon us. And Abimelech charged all his people saying. He that toucheth this man or his wife shall surely be put to death."[286]

---

284. Legends I:322
285. Jasher XXVIII:3-4
286. Genesis 26:8-11 KJV, MT, JST

Apparently Abimelech had remembered the covenant which had existed between his father, Abimelech and, Isaac's father, Abraham, in charging his people to leave Isaac and Rebekah alone at the penalty of death. It will be recalled that the wombs of the Philistine women were closed because of Abimelech's father who tried to sleep with Sarah. They were opened only after Abraham had prayed for it. The memory of this situation was undoubtedly on Abimelech, Junior's mind when he charged his people to leave Isaac and Rebekah alone or surely be put to death.

Jasher and the Legends accounts elaborate:

"At that time Abimelech gave orders to all his princes and great men, and they took Isaac and Rebecca his wife and brought them before the king. And the king commanded that they should dress them in princely garments and make them ride through the streets of the city, and proclaim before them throughout the land, saying, This is the man and this is his wife; whosoever toucheth this man or his wife shall surely die. And Isaac returned with his wife to the king's house, and the Lord was with Isaac and he continued to wax great and lacked nothing...."

"And Abimelech said unto Isaac, Behold the whole earth is before thee; dwell wherever it may seem good in thy sight until thou shalt return to thy land, and Abimelech gave Isaac fields and vineyards and the best part of the land of Gerar, to sow and reap and eat the fruits of the ground until the days of the famine have passed away."[287]

And back to Genesis:

"Then Isaac sowed in that land and received in the same year, an hundredfold; and the Lord blessed him. And the man waxed great and went forward, and grew until he became very great. For he had possession of flocks and possession of herds and great store of servants: and the Philistines envied him. For all the wells which his father's servants had digged in the days of Abraham his father, the Philistines had stopped them, and filled them

---

287. Jasher XXVIII:10-13, Legends I:322-323, V:59 Yashar Toledet 53a

with earth. And Abimelech said unto Isaac, Go from us; for thou art much mightier than we. And Isaac departed thence, and pitched his tent in the valley of Gerar, and dwelt there. And Isaac digged again the wells of water, which they had digged in the days of Abraham his father; for the Philistines had stopped them after the death of Abraham: and he called their names after the names by which his father had called them. And Isaac's servants digged in the valley, and found there a well of springing water."

"And the herdman of Gerar did strive with Isaac's herdmen, saying, The water is ours: and he called the name of the well Esek; because they strove with him. And they digged another well, and strove for that also: and he called the name of it Sitnah. And he removed from thence, and digged another well; and for that they strove not: and he called the name of it Rehoboth; and he said, For now the Lord hath made room for us, and we shall be fruitful in the land."[288]

It was at Beersheba the Lord appeared and reaffirmed his promises, here Isaac built an altar, here that Isaac made a peace agreement with Abimelech. And here water was also found.

From Genesis:

"And he went up from thence to Beersheba. And the Lord appeared unto him the same night, and said, I am the God of Abraham thy father: fear not, for I am with thee, and will bless thee, and multiply thy seed for my servant Abraham's sake. And he builded an altar there, and called upon the name of the Lord, and pitched his tent there and there Isaac's servants digged a well. Then Abimelech went to him from Gerar, and Ahuzzath, one of his friends, and Phichol the chief captain of his army. And Isaac said unto them, Wherefore came ye to me, seeing ye hate me, and have sent me away from you?"

"And they said, We saw certainly that the Lord was with thee: and we said, Let there be now an oath betwixt us, even betwixt us and thee, and let us make a covenant with thee; That

---

288. Genesis 26:12-22 KJV, MT, JST, Legends I:323

thou wilt do us no hurt, as we have not touched thee, and as we have done unto thee nothing but good,and have sent thee away in peace: thou art now the blessed of the Lord. And he made them a feast, and they did eat and drink. And they rose up betimes in the morning, and sware one to another; and Isaac sent them away, and they departed from him in peace. And it came to pass the same day, that Isaac's servants came, and told him concerning the well which they had digged, and said unto him, We have found water. And he called it Shebah: therefore the name of the city is Beersheba unto this day."[289]

The Legends report that Isaac tithed of all he possessed and gave to the poor of Gerar during those years.[290]

289. Ibid 26:23-33 KJV, MT, JST
290. Legends I:323

CHAPTER XVIII

I AM WEARY OF MY LIFE BECAUSE OF THE DAUGHTERS OF HETH

The famine lasted about three years. When it was over the Lord directed Isaac and Rebecca to return to the land of Canaan. The next entry in Genesis refers to Esau. At forty years of age he took a wife which brought grief of mind to Isaac and Rebekah. Isaac would have been 100 years old as Esau took a wife. Do we know anything about Isaac's life between ages 75 and 100 other than his life in Gerar and Beersheba just described? And where was Jacob during these years?

Jasher and the Legends pick up the story:

"And when the days of the famine had passed away the Lord appeared to Isaac and said unto him, Rise up, go forth from this place and return to thy land, to the land of Canaan; and Isaac rose up and returned to Hebron which is in the land of Canaan, he and all belonging to him as the Lord had commanded him. And after this Shelach the son of Arpachshad died in that year, which is the eighteenth year of the lives of Jacob and Esau, and all the days that Shelach lived were four hundred and thirty-three years and he died. At that time Isaac sent his younger son Jacob to the house of Shem and Eber, and he learned the instructions of the Lord, and Jacob remained in the house of Shem and Eber for thirty-two years, and Esau his brother did not go, for he was not willing to go, and he remained in his fathers house in the land of Canaan."[291]

We see that Abraham learned the ways of the Lord from Noah

---

291. Jasher XXVIII:16-18 see also Legends I:316,326,341,350, V274, 289

and Shem, Isaac learned the ways of the Lord from Shem and Eber, and Jacob learned the ways of the Lord, also from Shem and Eber.

Esau, on the other hand, was not willing to go to learn the ways of the Lord. He remained in his father's house in the land of Canaan where he hunted continually. Eventually the hunt extended into Seir. It was in Seir that Esau met and took Judith the daughter of Beeri, the Hittite, to wife. He brought her back to live with him near Issac and Rebecca. Esau later returned to Seir where he took a second wife Bashemath the daughter of Elon the Hittite to wife. He married first at age forty and second at about sixty three years of age. That Esau's marriages to Canaanite women displeased Isaac and Rebecca is evident from this passage.

(From Genesis) "And Esau was forty years old when he took to wife Judith the daughter of Beeri the Hittite, and Bashemath, the daughter of Elon the Hittite: Which was a grief of mind (a bitterness of spirit) unto Isaac and to Rebekah."[292]

And from this passage:

(From Genesis) "And Rebekah said to Isaac, I am weary of my life because of the daughters of Heth, if Jacob take a wife of the daughters of Heth, such as these which are of the daughters of the land, what good shall my life be to me."[293]

Rebekah, no doubt, remembered that she left her home and family to be Isaac's wife because Abraham didn't want Isaac to marry the daughters of Canaan.

The Jasher account elaborates:

"And the wives of Esau vexed and provoked Isaac and Rebecca with their works, for they walked not in the ways of the Lord, but served their father's gods of wood and stone as their father had taught them, and they were more wicked than their father. And they went according to the evil desires of their hearts, and they sacrificed and burnt incense to the Baalim, and Isaac and

---

292. Genesis 26:34-35 KJV, MT, JST
293. Ibid 27:46 KJV, MT, JST

Rebecca became weary of them. And Rebecca said, I am weary of my life because of the daughters of Heth; if Jacob take a wife of the daughters of Heth, such as these which are of the daughters of the land, what good then is life unto me."[294]

Esau's wives (daughters of Canaan) worshipped false gods, one of the reasons why Jacob wasn't to marry a Canaanite.

The Legends:

"Rebekah, weary of her life on account of the woman chosen by her older son, exhorted Jacob not to marry one of the daughters of Canaan, but a maiden of the family of Abraham. He (Jacob) assured his mother that the words of Abraham, bidding him to marry no woman of the Canannites, were graven upon his memory, and for this reason he was still unmarried, though he had attained the age of sixty two, and Esau had been urging him for twenty-two years past to follow his example and wed a daughter of the people of the land in which they lived...Deeply moved by the words of her son, Rebekah thanked him and gave praise unto God with these words: Blessed be the Lord God, and may His Holy Name be blessed forever and ever,...And when the spirit of the Lord came over her, she laid her hands upon the head of Jacob and gave him her maternal blessing. It ended with the words: May the Lord of the world love thee, as the heart of thy affectionate mother rejoices in thee and may He bless thee."[295]

Jacob was still at Shem and Eber's household when Esau took his first wife. Jacob continued there until age fifty, at which time Shem died. Jacob returned to his father Isaac's house where he resided for about thirteen more years. Esau had one wife, Jacob has none. During this period both of Isaac's sons were living with him or nearby. Word was received that Laban's wife conceived and bare twin daughters Leah and Rachel.

(From Jasher) "And it came to pass in those days, in the hundred and tenth year of the life of Isaac, that is in the fiftieth year of the

---

294. Jasher XXIX:14-16, Legends I:341, V:107 Yashar Toledet 53a - 53b
295. Legends I:327-28

144

life of Jacob, in that year died Shem the son of Noah; Shem was six hundred years old at his death. And when Shem died Jacob returned to his father to Hebron which is in the land of Canaan. And in the fifty-sixth year of the life of Jacob, people came from Haran, and Rebecca was told concerning her brother Laban the son of Bethuel. For the wife of Laban was barren in those days, and bare no children, and also all his handmaids bare none to him. And the Lord afterward remembered Adinah the wife of Laban, and she conceived and bare twin daughters, and Laban called the names of his daughters, the name of the elder Leah, and the name of the younger Rachel. And those people came and told these things to Rebecca and Rebecca rejoiced greatly that the Lord had visited her brother and that he had got children."[296]

Genesis follows its report of Esau's marriage with its account of Jacob's blessing, which Isaac intended for Esau, followed by Isaac's admonition to Jacob to go take a wife from the daughters of Laban. Isaac lived another eighty years after Esau's first marriage. It was during these eighty years that Jacob received his blessing and was sent to obtain a wife from the daughters of Laban. The Jasher and Legend accounts puts Jacob's age at fifty six when Leah and Rachel were born.

Jacob was apparently sixty three when he received his blessing and Isaac was one hundred twenty three years of age. Jacob fled to Eber's house following the blessing because he feared Esau would kill him. Jacob stayed with Eber another fourteen years continuing to learn the ways of the Lord and His commandments, before returning to live near Isaac. During these 14 years Esau took another wife, Bosmath, the daughter of Elon and called her Adah. Adah conceived and bore a son to Esau, Eliphaz: Judith bore Esau daughters.

Esau's wrath subsided during these years. However, it was quickly rekindled upon Jacob's return. Esau plotted to kill Jacob,-thinking he would do so after Isaac's death, which was thought to be eminent. Upon hearing Esau's plans, Rebecca counseled Jacob to go to her brother Laban's, to prevent Esau from killing him. Still single at seventy seven years, Jacob was a worry to Rebecca and to Isaac. Jacob departed at age seventy seven, when Isaac was one hundred thirty seven. Twenty years later Jacob returned home with four wives and

---

296. Jasher XXVIII:24-29, Legends I:327, V:71 Yashar Toledet 431 - 43b

twelve children. Genesis leaves off any further mention of Isaac's life at this point reporting only that he died at 180 years of age, and that Esau and Jacob buried him.[297]

297. Genesis 35:27-29 KJV, MT, JST

CHAPTER XIX

NOW HE HATH TAKEN AWAY MY BLESSING

Isaac was essentially incapacitated with his blindness. This may explain why the biblical account shifts its emphasis, as Jacob departs for a wife. However, Isaac was still able to give counsel, bless others and pray.

Returning now to the Genesis account of Jacob's blessing at the hand of Isaac and the deception used to get it.

(From Genesis) "And it came to pass, that when Isaac was old, and his eyes were dim, so that he could not see, he called Esau his eldest son, and said unto him, My son: and he said unto him, Behold, here am I. And he said, Behold now, I am old, I know not the day of my death: Now therefore take, I pray thee, thy weapons, thy quiver and thy bow, and go out to the field, and take me some venison; And make me savoury meat, such as I love, and bring it to me, that I may eat; that my soul may bless thee before I die."

"And Rebekah heard when Isaac spake to Esau his son, And Esau went to the field to hunt for venison, and to bring it. And Rebekah spake unto Jacob her son, saying Behold, I heard thy father speak unto Esau thy brother saying, Bring me venison, and make me savoury meat, that I may eat, and bless thee before the Lord before my death."[298]

The reported deception which followed has puzzled readers for centuries. Was it soley because Rebekah favored Jacob and maneuvered to see that he got the blessing? Is there more to the story than

---

298. Genesis 27:1-7 KJV, MT, JST

reported? In the absence of further information one may speculate that, first, Rebekah may well have remembered how Abraham had sought a wife for Isaac, not among the Canaanites, but from his own kindred and that she was very much the mother through whom all the families and nations of the earth were to be blessed. Rebecca had not forgotten what the Lord revealed to her through Shem, Eber, Abraham and Isaac just before the birth of her two son's, Esau and Jacob i.e. that the elder son Esau and his posterity would serve the younger son, Jacob and his posterity. Second, Esau had already sold his birthright to Jacob, after he had killed Nimrod, the sale being brought about by the Lord.[299] Third, Esau had taken a wife, Judith, daughter of Beeri, a Hittite, descendent of Canaan and a worshipper of Baalim, and other false gods.[300] Esau's wife/wives were a grief of mind to Isaac and Rebekah, understandably so, since all the nations and families of the earth were to be blessed in the future by Isaac's posterity. Isaac reportedly suffered even more than Rebekah through the idolatrous practices of his daughters-in-law.[301] How could all the nations and families of the earth be blessed by the posterity of Esau who showed no interest in the ways of the living God, and who had already taken idol worshippers for wives?

With these things in mind Rebekah maneuvered to see that Isaac's blessing would go to Jacob, her son, who had the birthright and her son, who had spent thirty two years in the house of Shem and Eber learning the ways of the Lord.[302]

Antiquities indicates that the meal of venison was much more than savoury meat being prepared for Isaac. Isaac was the ranking spiritual leader and a priest before God.

(From Antiquities) "The supper of savoury meat, as we call it (Genesis 27:4) to be caught by hunting, was intended plainly for a festival or a sacrifice; and upon the prayers that were frequent at sacrifices, Isaac expected, as was then usual in such, eminant cases, that a divine impulse would come upon him, in order to the solemn blessing of his son there present, and his foretelling his future behavior and fortune."[303]

---

299. Jasher XXVII:12
300. Ibid XXIX:14-16
301. Legends I:328
302. Jasher XXVIII:18
303. Antiquities Book I Ch XVIII:p.39

...."the blessing being delivered as a prediction of future events, by divine impulse, and foretelling things to befall to the posterity of Jacob and Esau in future ages, was for certain providential."[304]

The Legends also refer to the meal as a sacrifice or festival meal.[305]

Genesis continues with Rebekah's counsel to Jacob:

"Now therefore, my son, obey my voice according to that which I command thee. Go now to the flock, and fetch me from thence two good kids of the goats; and I will make them savoury meat for thy father, such as he loveth: And thou shalt bring it to thy father, that he may eat, and that he may bless thee before his death."[306]

Jacob was reluctant to follow through with the deception fearing it would be discovered by Isaac and bring him a curse rather than a blessing. Rebekah assumed responsibility for the deception and called for any curse to befall her rather than Jacob. She exhorted Jacob to obey her and do as she had commanded. Jacob complied.

(From Genesis) "And Jacob said to Rebekah his mother, Behold, Esau my brother is a hairy man, and I am a smooth man: My father peradventure will feel me, and I shall seem to him as a deceiver (mocker); and I shall bring a curse upon me, and not a blessing. And his mother said unto him, Upon me be thy curse, my son: only obey my voice, and go and fetch me them. And he went, and fetched, and brought them to his mother: and his mother made savoury meat, such as his father loved. And Rebekah took goodly raiment of her eldest son Esau, which were with her in the house, and put them upon Jacob her younger son: And she put the skins of the kids of the goats upon his hands, and upon the smooth of his neck. And she gave the savoury meat and the bread, which she had prepared, into the hand of her son Jacob."

304. Ibid Book I Ch XVIII, p.39
305. Legends I:321
306. Genesis 27:8-10 KJV, MT, JST

"And he (Jacob) came unto his father, and said, My father: and he said, Here am I; who art thou, my son? And Jacob said unto his father, I am Esau thy firstborn; I have done according as thou badest me: arise, I pray thee, sit and eat of my venison, that thy soul may bless me. And Isaac said unto his son, How is it that thou hast found it so quickly, my son? And he said, Because the Lord thy God brought it to me."

"And Isaac said unto Jacob, Come near, I pray thee, that I may feel thee, my son, whether thou be my very son Esau or not. And Jacob went near unto Isaac his father; and he felt him, and said, The voice is Jacob's voice, but the hands are the hands of Esau. And he discerned him not, because his hands were hairy, as his brother Esau's hands: so he blessed him."

"And he (Isaac) said, Art thou my very own son Esau? And he said, I am. And he said, Bring it near to me, and I will eat of my son's venison, that my soul may bless thee. And he brought it near to him, and he did eat: and he brought him wine, and he drank. And his father Isaac said unto him, Come near now, and kiss me, my son. And he came near, and kissed him: and he smelled the smell of his raiment, and blessed him, and said, See the smell of my son is as the smell of a field which the Lord hath blessed: Therefore God give thee of the dew of heaven, and the fatness of the earth, and plenty of corn and wine: Let people serve thee, and nations bow down to thee: be lord over thy brethren, and let thy mother's sons bow down to thee: cursed be every one that curseth thee, and blessed be he that blesseth thee."

"And it came to pass, as soon as Isaac had made an end of blessing Jacob, and Jacob was yet scarce gone out from the presence of Isaac his father, that Esau his brother came in from his hunting."[307]

The Legends add that Jacob put on the garment of the priesthood which he had bought from Esau with the birthright and that he wore it in addition to the goat skins when he went to receive Isaac's blessing.

---

307. Genesis 27:11-30 KJV, MT, JST

"They were the high priestly raiment in which God had clothed Adam, the first born of the world."[308]

(From Legends) "The holy spirit filled Isaac, and he gave Jacob his ten fold blessing...To which Rebekah joins hers...which was joined by the holy spirit...and Jacob left the presence of his father Isaac bathed in celestial dew."[309]

(From Genesis) "And he (Esau) also had made savoury meat, and brought it unto his father, and said unto his father, Let my father arise, and eat of his son's venison, and thy soul bless me. And Isaac his father said unto him, Who art thou? And he said, I am thy son, thy firstborn Esau. And Isaac trembled very exceedingly, and said, Who? where is he that hath taken venison, and brought it to me, and I have eaten of all before thou camest, and have blessed him? yea, and he shall be blessed."

"And when Esau heard the words of his father, he cried with a great and exceeding bitter cry, and said unto his father, Bless me, even me also, O my father. And he said, Thy brother came with subtilty (guiles), and hath taken away thy blessing. And he said, Is not he rightly named Jacob? for he hath supplanted me these two times: he took away my birthright; and behold, now he hath taken away my blessing. And he said, Hast thou not reserved a blessing for me? And Isaac answered and said unto Esau, Behold, I have made him thy Lord, and all his brethren have I given to him for servants; and with corn and wine have I sustained him: and what shall I do now unto thee: my son?"

"And Esau said unto his father, Hast thou but one blessing, my father? bless me, even me also, O my father. And Esau lifted up his voice and wept."

"And Isaac his father answered and said unto him, Behold, thy dwelling shall be the fatness of the earth, and the dew of heaven, from above, And by thy sword shalt thou live, and shalt serve thy brother; and it shall come to pass when thou shalt have

---

308. Legends I:332
309. Ibid I:334-336

151

the dominion that thou shalt break his yoke from off thy neck."[310]

Antiquities adds:

"....when Isaac had unwittingly blessed Jacob, and was afterwards made sensible of his mistake, yet did he not attempt to alter it, how earnestly soever his affection for Esau might incline him to wish it might be altered, because he knew that the blessing came not from himself, but from God, and that an alteration was out of his power. A second afflatus (inspiration) came upon him, and enabled him to foretell Esau's future behaviour and fortune also."[311]

Isaac had sought inspiration from the Lord in order to give his son a blessing. That inspiration was confirmed upon him in the blessing he gave Jacob. Even though he may have wanted to, Isaac, dared not change it, for he knew the blessing he gave was the Lord's blessing intended for Jacob. It reaffirmed the Lord's prophecy concerning the future of these two given to Rebecca before they were born.

Isaac, however, gave Esau a different blessing. Esau was to excel in hunting and strength of body, in arms, and all sorts of work, and should attain glory forever on those accounts, he and his posterity after him, but still should serve his brother.[312]

The Legends indicate that Isaac was unaware that Esau sold his birthright to Jacob. When so informed by the anguished Esau at this blessing, Isaac declared, 'I gave my blessing to the right one', only then did he say yea, and he (Jacob) shall be blessed.[313]

(From Jasher)..."And Esau hated his brother Jacob on account of the blessing that his father had given him, and his anger was greatly aroused against him. And Jacob was very much afraid of his brother Esau, and he rose up and fled to the house of Eber the son of Shem and he concealed himself there on account of his brother, and Jacob was sixty - three years old when he went forth from the land of Canaan from Hebron, and Jacob was concealed

---

310. Genesis 27:31-40 KJV, MT, JST
311. Antiquities Book I Ch XVIII p. 39
312. Ibid Book I Ch XVIII p. 40
313. Legends I:337

in Eber's house fourteen years on account of his brother Esau, and he there continued to learn the ways of the Lord and his commandments.[314]

Jacob had spent thirty two of his first fifty years in the house of Shem and Eber learning the instructions of the Lord, and another fourteen years from age sixty three to seventy seven in the house of Eber where, again, he learned the ways of the Lord and His commandments. Put another way, Jacob, whose name was later changed to Israel, spent the first two thirds of his life, i.e. fifty two of his first seventy seven years, in the house of Eber, that person from whom the word Hebrew is derived, learning the ways, the instructions and commandments of the Lord God Jehovah (Yahweh).

Esau, on the other hand, stayed in his father Isaac's house, having the opportunity to learn the ways of the Lord from Eber, but was not willing to go. He is described as a designing and deceitful man, and as having ravaged a betrothed woman at age fifteen, one who committed murder, one who doubted the resurrection of the dead, one who scorned his birthright, and one who denied God. During his hunting escapades Esau entered into Seir or Edom, and there met and married Jehudith, the daughter of Beeri, son of Epher, from the families of Heth, the son of Canaan.

While Jacob was in his twenty second year in the house of Eber or at age forty, Esau also age forty, took Jehudith for a wife and brought her back to Hebron, the land of his father Isaac's dwelling place, and he dwelt here. Judith gave birth to some of Esau's children, all daughters.

(From Jasher) "And when Esau saw that Jacob had fled and escaped from him and that Jacob had cunningly obtained the blessing, then Esau grieved exceedingly, and he also was vexed at his father and mother (Isaac and Rebecca); and he also rose up and took his wife and went away from his father and mother to the land of Seir; and he dwelt there and Esau saw there a woman from amongst the daughters of Heth whose name was Bosmath, the daughter of Elon the Hittite, and he took her for a wife in addition to his first wife, and Esau called her name Adah, saying the blessing had in that time passed from him. And Esau dwelt in the land of Seir six months without seeing his father and mother,

314. Jasher XXIX:10-11, Legends I:340, V:107 Yashar Toledet 53a - 53b

153

and afterward Esau took his wives and rose up and returned to the land of Canaan, and Esau placed his two wives in his father's house in Hebron."[315]

Upon Esau's return to his father Isaac's house with his two wives Judith and Bosmath (Adah), Adah conceived and bore a son to Esau who was given the name of Eliphaz. Esau reportedly was sixty five years old when Eliphaz was born.[316]

Ishmael, Isaac's older half brother died during this period at age 137 in Isaac's 124th year. Isaac mourned the loss of his half-brother.[317]

Isaac's and Rebecca's fourteen year experience with Esau's wives brought grief of mind unto them.

Rebecca had given up her family to come and marry Isaac because he, Isaac, was under command of the Lord to not take a wife from the daughters of Canaan. Jacob was living in the house of Eber and remained unmarried because he was not to marry the daughters of Canaan. Her other son Esau, had married the daughters of Heth, and had become wicked continuing to worship gods of wood and stone. This caused Rebecca to despair of her life, since the covenants of the Lord could not be continued through posterity who worshipped false gods.

The fourteen year period between the time of Jacob's blessings by Isaac and Jacob's return home from the house of Eber came to a close. Jacob's return rekindled in Esau hurt feelings, wrath and anger. Esau, observed the deteriorating condition of Isaac's health, and said in his heart:

(From Genesis) "The days of mourning for my father are at hand; then I will slay my brother Jacob. And these words of Esau her elder son were told to Rebekah: and she sent and called Jacob her younger son, and said unto him. Behold thy brother Esau, as touching thee, doth comfort himself, purposing to kill thee. Now therefore, my son, obey my voice; and arise, flee thou to Laban my brother to Haran. And tarry with him a few days until thy brother's fury turn away; Until thy brother's anger turn away from thee, and he forget that which thou hast done to him, then I

---

315. Jasher XXIX:12-13; Legends I:340-41
316. Ibid XXIX:17
317. Ibid XXIX:18-19

will send, and fetch thee from thence: why should I be deprived also of you both in one day? And Rebekah said to Isaac, I am weary of my life because of the daughters of Heth: if Jacob take a wife of the daughters of Heth; such as these which are the daughters of the land, what good shall my life do me?"[318]

Rebekah had prophesied Esau's intentions and had hoped that Esau's wrath would again subside. Esau's hatred for Jacob,however, persisted all his life. Jacob didn't want to run away. He told his mother he (Jacob) would kill Esau instead, to which Rebekah replied, 'Let me not be bereaved of both of my sons in one day'. By those words Rebekah showed her prophetic gift. As she spoke so it happened - when their time came, Esau was slain while the burial of Jacob was taking place, - so say the Legends.[319] Jacob still didn't want to go, but said he would if Isaac sent him.[320]

Rebekah's appeal to Isaac was heeded. Isaac called Jacob to him and counselled him not to take a wife of the daughters of Canaan but to go to Padanaram and take a wife of the daughters of Laban, his mother's brother. Isaac then gave Jacob and his seed (children) the blessing of Abraham and sent him on his way.

The Genesis account reads:

"And Isaac called Jacob and blessed him, and charged him, and said unto him, Thou shalt not take a wife of the daughters of Canaan. Arise, go to Padan-aram, to the house of Bethuel thy mother's father; and take thee a wife from thence of the daughters of Laban thy mother's brother."

"And God Almighty bless thee, and make thee fruitful and multiply thee, that thou mayest be a multitude of people; And give thee the blessing of Abraham, to thee, and to thy seed with thee; that thou mayest inherit the land wherein thou art a stranger, which God gave unto Abraham."

"And Isaac sent away Jacob: And he went to Padan-aram

318. Genesis 27:41-46; Legends I 341-42
319. Legends I:342
320. Ibid I:342

155

unto Laban, son of Bethuel the Syrian, the brother of Rebekah, Jacob's and Esau's mother."[321]

To which the Legends add as part of Jacob's blessing by Isaac.

"Take heed lest thou shouldst forget the Lord thy God and all his ways in the land to which thou goest, and shouldst join thyself to the people of the land and pursue vanity, and forsake the Lord thy God. But when thou comest to the land, serve the Lord, do not turn to the right or to the left from the way which I command thee, and which thou didst learn. And may the Almighty God grant thee favor before the people of the land, that thou mayest take a wife there according to thy choice, one who is good and upright in the ways of the Lord. And may God give unto thee and thy seed the blessing of thy father Abraham, and make thee fruitful and multiply thee, and mayest thou become a multitude of people in the land whither thou goest, and may God cause thee to return to thy land, the land of thy fathers dwelling, with children and with great riches with joy and with pleasure."[322]

Thus we see in Jacob's blessing a prophecy of his own future and the future of his posterity, provided Jacob would serve the Lord and live righteously.

---

321. Genesis 28:1-5, Legends I:342
322. Jasher XXIX 24-30, Legends I:343, V:114 Yashar Toledet 54b - 55a

CHAPTER XX

SURELY THE LORD BE IN THIS PLACE (BETHEL)

"Scarcely had Jacob left his father's house when Rebekah began to weep, for she was sorely distressed about him. Isaac comforted her saying: weep not for Jacob! In peace doth he depart, and in peace will he return. The Lord, God Most High, will guard him against all evil and be with him. He will not forsake him all the days of his life. Have no fear for him, for he walketh in the right path, he is a perfect man and he hath faith in God - he will not perish."[323]

Isaac had given Jacob silver, gold and other gifts and sent him out of Canaan from Beersheba to Haran.[324]

No reference of Isaac's gifts to Jacob is made in Genesis. The Jasher and Legends accounts report that Esau sent his son, Eliphaz, and ten of his mother's brothers to kill him (Jacob). Instead, Jacob bargained for his life, and gave Eliphaz everything he (Jacob) had received as gifts from his father Isaac in exchange. Jacob arrived in Haran with nothing to give Laban and therefore had to work seven years for his wife."[325]

Esau was angry with Eliphaz, for failing to kill Jacob as he had been instructed, so Esau took the gold and silver Eliphaz had stolen from Jacob and put it in his own house.[326]

Failing in his attempt to have Jacob killed, knowing that his father had given Jacob the blessing of Abraham, knowing Isaac had counselled Jacob not to take a wife of the daughters of Canaan, and that the daughters of Canaan were bad in the sight of Isaac and

---

323. Legends I:345, V:123, Jubilees 27:13-18
324. Jasher XXIX:24-30, Legends I:345-7, V:124 Yashar Toledet 55a - 55b
325. Ibid 31-39; Legends I:346-7
326. Ibid 40-41

Rebecca; Esau went to the house of Ishmael, his uncle, and, in addition to his other wives, took Malchlath the daughter of Ishmael and sister of Nebayoth for a wife.[327]

The Jasher account reports Jacob's age was seventy seven years as he departed Beersheba for Haran to obtain a wife and to get away from Esau. That age can be cooborated from Genesis through extrapolation as follows:

Joseph was thirty nine years of age when Jacob arrived in Egypt at age 130 making Jacob 91 years old at Joseph's birth. Joseph was the last of Jacob's children to be born in Haran, born about six years before Jacob's departure. Since he was twenty years with Laban, that would make Jacob 97 years old at his departure from Laban, 91 years old at Joseph's birth and 77 years old at his arrival in Haran.[328]

Jacob's experience enroute to Haran from Beersheba:

(From Genesis) "And Jacob went out from Beersheba and went toward Haran. And he lighted upon a certain place, and tarried there all night because the sun was set; and he took (one) of the stones of that place, and put them for his pillows and lay down in that place to sleep. And he dreamed and behold a ladder set up on the earth, and the top of it reached to heaven, and behold the angels of God ascending and descending on it. And behold the Lord stood above it, and said, I am the Lord God of Abraham thy father, and the God of Isaac, the land where on thou liest, to thee will I give it, and to thy seed; And thy seed shall be as the dust of the earth, and thou shalt spread abroad to the west, and to the east, and to the north, and to the south: and in thee and in thy seed shall all the families of the earth be blessed."

"And behold I am with thee, and will keep thee in all places whither thou goest, and will bring thee again into this land; for I will not leave thee, until I have done that which I have spoken to thee of."

"And Jacob awaked out of his sleep, and he said, Surely the Lord be in this place: and I knew it not. And he was afraid, and

---

327. Jasher XXIX:42-43; Genesis 28:6-9
328. See Genesis 31:38-41, 41:46-57, 45:6, 47:8-9; see also Legends I:415, II 4, V 296

said, How dreadful (full of awe) is this place! this is none other but the house of God, and this is the gate of heaven. And Jacob rose up early in the morning, and took the stone that he had put for his pillows, and set it up for a pillar, and poured oil upon the top of it. And he called the name of that place Bethel (House of God): but the name of that city was called Luz at the first. And Jacob vowed a vow, saying, If God will be with me, and will keep me in this way that I go, and will give me bread to eat, and raiment to put on, So that I come again to my father's house in peace; then shall the Lord be my God: And this stone, which I have set for a pillar, shall be God's house: and all that thou shalt give me I will surely give the tenth unto thee."[329]

The Lord reaffirmed Isaac's blessing on Jacob, confirmed Abraham's blessings also on him and reiterated all the families of the earth shall be blessed through Jacob and his seed (children). They will yet be born from his upcoming marriages to wives he had not yet met and whose names he probably did not yet know. Jacob promised the stone which he had set for a pillar would become God's house and that he (Jacob) would give back a (tenth) tithe of all that God should give him.

The certain place where Jacob lighted upon, where he spent the night and dreamed his dream of the ladder, where the Lord God of Abraham and Isaac appeared to him and reconfirmed those blessings and promises previously made to Abraham and Isaac, upon him (Jacob) and his seed, was none other than Mount Moriah near the city of Luz, according to Jasher. Jacob then called the name of that place where he had the vision of the Lord God, Bethel.[331]

Traditionally Josephus named Moriah as the hill upon which the Temple of Jerusalem was built.[332] If this is true, such a construction was a fulfillment of Jacob's covenant that God's house would be built on that spot.

Jasher called the place where Jacob received this vision and blessing of God, Mount Moriah. Jacob named it Bethel which means in the Greek, House of God. Thus Jacob (Israel) marked the spot where the House of the Lord (Temple) was to be built. Years later that

329. Genesis 28:10-22 KJV, MT,
330. Antiquities Book I Ch XIX:2-3
331. Jasher XXX:1-3
332. Brittanica Vol 15 P. 803

house of the Lord (Temple) was built. The design was given by the Lord through David, and it was constructed by Solomon.

(From Jasher) "And Jacob rose up from that place quite rejoiced, and when he walked his feet felt light to him for joy, and he went from there to the land of the children of the East, and he returned to Haran and he sat by the shepherd's well. And he there found some men going from Haran to feed their flocks, and Jacob made inquiries of them and they said, We are from Haran."[333]

Returning to the Genesis account:

"Then Jacob went on his journey, and came into the land of the people of the east. And he looked, and behold a well in the field, and lo, there were three flocks of sheep lying by it; for out of that well they watered the flocks: and a great stone was upon the well's mouth. And thither were all the flocks gathered: and they rolled the stone from the wells mouth, and watered the sheep, and put the stone again upon the well's mouth in his place. And Jacob said unto them, my brethren, whence be ye? And they said, of Haran are we. And he said unto them, Know ye Laban son of Nahor? And they said, We know him, And he said unto them, Is he well? And they said, He is well: and, behold, Rachel his daughter cometh with the sheep. And he said, Lo, it is yet high day, neither is it time that the cattle should be gathered together; water ye the sheep, and go and feed them. And they said. We cannot, until all the flocks be gathered together, and till they role the stone from the well's mouth; then we water the sheep."

"And while they yet spake with them Rachel came with her father's sheep, for she kept them. And it came to pass, when Jacob saw Rachel the daughter of Laban his mother's brother, and the sheep of Laban his mother's brother, then Jacob went near, and rolled the stone from the well's mouth. And watered the flock of Laban her mother's brother. And Jacob kissed Rachel, and lifted up his voice and wept."[334]

---

333. Jasher XXX:4-5
334. Genesis 29:1-11; see also Jasher XXX:5-8

Undoubtedly Jacob wept for joy. Isaac had counseled him to take not a wife of the daughters of Canaan, but to go to Haran and take a wife of the daughters of his mother's brother Laban. While obeying this counsel Jacob was subsequently robbed and had his life threatened by Eliphaz and ten men. His experience with God at Bethel heartened him, however. Rachel's confirmation of her lineage assured Jacob that the promises God had made to him at Bethel were already in the process of fulfillment. He had now made contact with Laban's family even one of his daughter's, Rachel. Nothing is said in Genesis of Rachel's age. Jacob was about seventy seven years old on his arrival in Haran, as previously noted. The Jasher and Legends accounts, indicate that word came from Haran to Rebecca concerning Laban, her brother and the son of Bethuel declaring that the previously barren wife of Laban, Adinah, had borne twin daughters Leah and Rachel in the fifty sixth year of the life of Jacob.[335]

Leah and Rachel would both have been twenty one years old when Jacob arrived in Haran.

(From Genesis) "And Jacob told Rachel that he was her father's brother, and that he was Rebekah's son and she ran and told her father. And it came to pass, when Laban heard the tidings of Jacob his sister's son, that he ran to meet him, and embraced him, and kissed him, and brought him to his house. And he told Laban all these things. And Laban said to him, Surely thou art my bone and my flesh. And he abode with him for the space of one month."[336]

(From Jasher) "And Jacob related to Laban what his brother Esau had done to him, and what his son Eliphaz had done to him in the road. And Jacob resided in Laban's house for one month, and Jacob ate and drank in the house of Laban, and afterward Laban said unto Jacob. Tell me what shall be thy wages, for how canst thou serve me for naught?[337]

(From Jasher) "And Laban had no sons but only daughters, and his other wives and handmaids were still barren in those days; and

---

335. Jasher XXVIII:26-28; see also Legends V 318
336. Genesis 29:12-14 KJV, MT, JST
337. Jasher XXX:11-12

these are the names of Laban's daughters which his wife Adinah had borne him; the name of the elder was Leah and the name of the younger was Rachel; and Leah was the tender eyed, but Rachel was beautiful, and well favored and Jacob loved her."[338]

Laban declared Jacob to be his brother and asks, "tell me, what shall thy wages be."[339]

---

338. Ibid XXX:13 Genesis 29:16-17 KJV, MT, JST
339. Genesis 29:15

AND JACOB SERVED SEVEN YEARS FOR RACHEL, AND THEY SEEMED UNTO HIM BUT A FEW DAYS FOR THE LOVE HE HAD TO HER

Jacob, having been robbed by Eliphaz, son of Esau, of all the gifts he planned to give to Laban for a wife, offered, instead, to serve Laban seven years for the younger twin daughter Rachel. Laban agreed saying, "it is better that I give her to thee, than that I should give her to another man: abide with me"[340]

The next seven years of Jacob's life and his feelings about them are reported by Genesis in these words:

"And Jacob served seven years for Rachel; and they seemed unto him but a few days, for the love he had to her."[341]

Jasher reports some other events which took place during those years: the death of Eber at age 464 years in the second year of Jacob's dwelling in Haran (in Jacob's 79th year), and the birth of Reuel, the son of Esau and Basmath, in his third year there. During the fourth year, the first of Laban's three sons, Beor, was born followed by Alib and Chorash. The Lord had blessed Laban on account of Jacob, giving him more sons and daughters. In the fifth year of Jacob's life in Haran, Jehudith, the daughter of Beeri, the wife of Esau, died. She left two daughters Marzith and Puith. After Jehudith died, Esau left Canaan and went hunting in the land of Seir. He took another wife, Ahli-bamah, the daughter of Zebeon, the Hivite and brought her back to

---

340. Genesis 29:18-19 KJV, MT, JST
341. Ibid 29:20 KJV, MT, JST

Canaan. It was Ahlibamah who bore Esau three more sons Yeush, Yaalar and Korah.

Esau's cattle and goods were now abundant. They were the source of quarrels with the people of Canaan. He took all his cattle, possessions, wives, and children and moved to the land of Seir where his descendants intermarried with the Horites and the sons of Seir. He gave Marzith to Anah the son of Zebeon and Puith to Azar the son of Bilhan the Horite.[342]

The seven years of service Jacob gave Laban for Rachel's hand, during which he worked in the house and in the field, came to an end.

(From Genesis) "And Jacob said unto Laban, Give me my wife, for my days are fulfilled, that I may go in unto her. And Laban gathered together all the men of the place, and made a feast."[343]

To which is added:

(From Jasher) "And in the evening Laban came to the house and afterward Jacob came there with the people of the feast, and Laban extinquished all the lights that were in the house. And Jacob said unto Laban, Wherefore dost thou do this thing unto us? And Laban answered, such is our custom to act in this land."[344]

Back to Genesis:

"And it came to pass in the evening, that he took Leah his daughter, and brought her to him, and he went in unto her And Laban gave unto his daughter Leah Zilpah her maid for a hand maid."[345]

Apparently Jacob didn't realize he had been deceived until the next morning. Jasher embellished the account with descriptions of eating and drinking, the playing of timbrels, dancing and the crowd singing out Heleah, Heleah meaning "she is Leah" which Jacob did not then understand.[346]

---

342. Jasher XXX:15-29
343. Genesis 29:21-22
344. Jasher XXXI:2-3; Legends I:360-61
345. Genesis 29:23-24
346. Jasher XXXI:6-9; Legends I:360

Continuing Genesis:

"And it came to pass that in the morning, behold, it was Leah: and he said to Laban, What is this thou hast done unto me? did not I serve with thee for Rachel? wherefore then hast thou beguiled me? And Laban said, It must not be so done in our country, to give the younger before the firstborn. Fulfill her week, and we will give thee this also for the service which thou shalt give serve with me yet seven other years. And Jacob did so, and fulfilled her week: and he gave him Rachel, his daughter to wife also. And Laban gave to Rachel his daughter Bilhah his hand-maid to be her maid. And he went in also unto Rachel and he loved also Rachel more than Leah, and served with him yet seven other years."[347]

Jacob married late in life, an old man by todays standards. When he did marry he took two wives within a week, Leah and Rachel, and two more within the second seven year period he worked for Rachel's hand. Within a seven year period Jacob married four wives and had twelve children, eleven sons and a daughter. His thirteenth child of record, Benjamin, was not born in Haran, but in Canaan.

Leah apparently had four sons about a year apart, Reuben, Simeon, Levi and Judah, and left bearing temporarily. Rachel could not conceive during this period. She gave Bilhah, her handmaid, to Jacob to wife. Leah followed suit and gave Jacob, her maid Zilpah, to Jacob to wife. Bilhah conceived twice giving birth to Dan and Naphtali. Zilpah conceived twice giving birth to Gad and Asher. Leah again conceived thrice more giving birth to Issachar, Zebulun and Dinah.

Joseph was the twelfth child of record to be born to Jacob. Rachel had, at last, conceived after seven years of barrenness.

Actually, Jacob only sought one wife, Rachel. He was given three others, Leah by deception of his father in law, Bilhah was given to him by Rachel who thought she couldn't have children (just like Sara gave to Abraham, Hagar) and Leah gave to Jacob, Zilpah, because Leah had finished bearing children. (She thought)

347. Genesis 29:25-30; Legends I:361

The Genesis account reads:

"And when the Lord saw that Leah was hated, he opened her womb: but Rachel was barren. And Leah conceived, and bare a son, and she called his name Reuben: for she said, Surely the Lord hath looked upon my affliction; now therefore my husband will love me. And she conceived again, and bare a son; and said, Because the Lord hath heard that I was hated, he hath therefore given me this son also: and she called his name Simeon. And she conceived again and bare a son; and said, Now this time will my husband be joined unto me, because I have born him three sons, therefore was his name called Levi. And she conceived again, and bare a son: and she said, Now will I praise the Lord: therefore she called his name Judah: and left bearing."[348]

The name of Leah's third son, Levi, say the Legends, was given by God Himself, not by his mother.[349]

(From Genesis) "And when Rachel saw that she bare Jacob no children, Rachel envied her sister; and said unto Jacob, Give me children, or else I die. And Jacob's anger was kindled against Rachel: and he said, Am I in God's stead, who hath withheld from thee the fruit of the womb? And she said, Behold my maid Bilhah, go in unto her; and she shall bear upon my knees, that I may also have children by her. And she gave him Bilhah her handmaid to wife: and Jacob went in unto her. And Bilhah conceived, and bare Jacob a son. And Rachel said, God hath judged me, and hath also heard my voice, and hath given me a son: therefore called she his name, Dan. And Bilhah, Rachel's maid conceived again, and bare Jacob a second son. And Rachel said, With great wrestlings have I wrestled with my sister, and I have prevailed: and she called his name Naphtali."[350]

"When Leah saw that she had left bearing, she took Zilpah her maid, and gave her Jacob to wife. And Zilpah Leah's maid bare Jacob a son. And Leah said, A troop cometh: and she called

---

348. Genesis 29:31-35; Legends I:361-63
349. Legends I:363
350. Genesis 30:1-8; Legends I:364-65

his name Gad. And Zilpah Leah's maid bare a second son. And Leah said, Happy am I, for the daughters will call me blessed: and she called his name Asher."

"And Reuben went in the days of wheat harvest, and found mandrakes in the field, and brought them unto his mother Leah. Then Rachel said to Leah, Give me, I pray thee, of thy son's mandrakes. And she said unto her, Is it a small matter that thou has taken my husband? and wouldest thou take away my son's mandrakes also? And Rachel said, Therefore he shall lie with thee tonight for thy son's mandrakes. And Jacob came out of the field in the evening, and Leah went out to meet him, and said, Thou must come in unto me; for surely I have hired thee with my son's mandrakes. And he lay with her that night. And God hearkened unto Leah, and she conceived, and bare Jacob the fifth son. And Leah said, God hath given me my hire, because I have given my maiden to my husband: and she called his name Issachar. And Leah conceived again, and bare Jacob the sixth son. And Leah said, God hath endued me with a good dowry; now will my husband dwell with me, because I have born him six son's: and she called his name Zebulun. And afterwards she bare a daughter, and called her name Dinah."[351]

That Zilpah and Bilhah were sisters is stated in Jubilees 28:9. They were reportedly the daughters of Rotheus, a brother of Deborah, Rebekah's nurse.[352]

The opinion that the prophet Elijah belonged to the tribe of Gad is widespread.[353]

Rachel prayed for children and beseeched Him that He take away her reproach.

The Legends report that Leah, Zilpah and Bilhah united their prayers with Jacob and Rachel, together they sought to remove the curse of barrenness from Rachel.[354]

(From Genesis) "And God remembered Rachel and God hearkened unto her, and opened her womb. And she conceived, and

351. Ibid 30:9-21; Legends I:365
352. Legends V:295
353. Ibid II:144-145, V:297
354. Legends I:368

bare a son; And said, God hath taken away my reproach. And she called his name Joseph; and said, The Lord shall add to me another son."[355]

The holy spirit had revealed to Jacob that the house of his newly born son Joseph would work the destruction of Esau, causing Jacob to declare, "Now I need not fear Esau or his legions," so say the Legends.[356]

As previously mentioned Jacob was ninety one years old at Joseph's birth and Rachel was about thirty five. Fourteen years earlier when Rebekah had counseled Jacob to flee from Esau, she said she would send for him, after his brother Esau's fury had turned away.[357]

Rebekah sent her nurse Deborah, the daughter of Uz, and two of Isaac's servants unto Jacob after Joseph was born. She beckoned Jacob to return to his father's house in the land of Canaan.[358]

Jacob implored Laban to send him back to Canaan with his wives and children, since he had completed the second seven year term of service for Laban or fourteen years altogether. Jacob was persuaded to stay. They negotiated his wages again. They were changed again, this time Jacob worked for the speckled and spotted cattle. Jacob stayed with Laban another six years. During this time the two servants of Isaac returned to Canaan but Deborah stayed with Jacob and served as a maid to his wives and 12 children.[359]

The Lord prospered Jacob and his family these six years with an abundance of speckled and spotted cattle and sheep of large size, of beautiful appearance and very productive. The Lord then implored Jacob to return to the land of His fathers in Canaan. Jacob gathered his family together and then left for Canaan.

The Genesis account of this six year period reads:

"And it came to pass, when Rachel had born Joseph, that Jacob said unto Laban, Send me away, that I may go unto mine own place, and to my country. Give me my wives and my children, for whom I have served thee, and let me go: for thou knowest my

---

355. Genesis 30:22-24; Legends I:368-69
356. Legends I:369
357. Genesis 27:43-45 KJV, MT, JST
358. Jasher XXXI:22-23; Legends I:369
359. Ibid XXXI:29-30

service which I have done thee. And Laban said unto him, I pray thee, if I have found favour in thine eyes, tarry: for I have learned by experience that the Lord hath blessed me for thy sake. And he said, Appoint me thy wages, and I will give it. And he said to him, Thou knowest how I have served thee, and how thy cattle was with me. For it was little which thou hadst before I came, and it is now increased unto a multitude; and the Lord hath blessed thee since my coming: and now when shall I provide for mine own house also?"

"And he said, What shall I give thee? And Jacob said, Thou shalt not give me anything if thou wilt do this thing for me, I will again feed and keep thy flock. I will pass through all thy flock today, removing from thence all the speckled and spotted cattle, and all the brown cattle among the sheep, and the spotted and speckled among the goats: and of such shall be my hire. So shall my righteousness answer for me in time to come, when it shall come for my hire before thy face: every one that is not speckled and spotted among the goats, and brown among the sheep, that shall bc counted stolen with me. And Laban said, Behold, I would it might be according to thy word."[360]

"And he removed that day the he goats, that were ring straked and spotted, and all the she goats that were speckled and spotted, and every one that had some white in it, and all the brown among the sheep, and gave them into the hand of his sons. And he set three days journey betwixt himself and Jacob: and Jacob fed the rest of Laban's flocks. And Jacob took him rods of green poplar, and of the hazel and chestnut tree: and pilled white strakes in them, and made the white appear which was in the rods. And he set the rods which he had pilled before the flocks in the gutters in the watering troughs when the flocks came to drink, that they should conceive when they came to drink."

"And the flocks conceived before the rods, and brought forth cattle ringstraked, speckled and spotted. And Jacob did separate the lambs, and set the faces of the flocks toward the ringstraked, and all the brown in the flock of Laban; and he put

---

360. Genesis 30:25-34 KJV, MT, JST

his own flocks by themselves, and put them not unto Laban's cattle. And it came to pass, whensoever the stronger cattle did conceive, that Jacob laid the rods before the eyes of the cattle in the gutters, that they might conceive among the rods. But when the cattle were feeble he put them not in; so the feebler were Laban's, and the stronger Jacob's. And the man increased exceedingly, and had much cattle, and maidservants and manservants and camels and asses. And he heard the words of Laban's sons, saying Jacob hath taken away all that was our father's; and of that which was our father's hath he gotten all his glory. And Jacob beheld the countenance of Laban, and, behold, it was not toward him as before."[361]

Jacob's sheep and cattle were highly sought after by the sons of men, who traded maidservants and manservants, and camels and asses for them, thus explaining how Jacob acquired servants and camels and asses as well as sheep and cattle, though he himself had so recently been a servant of Laban.[362]

The Lord commanded Jacob to return to the land of his fathers and kindred. He identified Himself as the God of Bethel where Jacob had anointed the pillar twenty years before. The place was where Jacob had vowed a vow saying:

(From Genesis) "If God will be with me, and will keep me in this way that I go and will give me bread to eat, and raiment to put on, So that I come again to my father's house in peace; then shall the Lord be my God: And this stone, which I have set for a pillar, shall be God's house: and of all that thou shalt give me I will surely give the tenth unto thee."[363]

Jacob informed Rachel and Leah of the Lord's command. They agreed to go with him and take Bilhah and Zilpah and all twelve children with them; a small sized exodus in itself which included Jacob's 200 drove of cattle. Rachel took with her the images or idols of her father, Laban. Apparently these images were felt to have astrologic value. Rachel was afraid her father would consult them to ascertain

---

361. Genesis 30:35-43, 31:1-2; Legends I:371
362. Jasher XXXI:31-34
363. Genesis 28:20-22 KJV, MT, JST

where they had gone. These images were described as skulls of first born in which candles were placed, and when lighted were worshipped and consulted.[364]

The journey was begun from Padan-aram enroute to Isaac's abode in Canaan by way of Mount Gilead, without informing Laban. He had gone to shear sheep. Laban was later told. He set out and overtook Jacob's family seven days later. Laban was warned by God in a dream to speak neither good nor bad of Jacob thus tempering his wrath.

The Genesis account reads:

"And the Lord said unto Jacob, Return unto the land of thy fathers, and to thy kindred; and I will be with thee. And Jacob sent and called Rachel and Leah to the field unto his flock. And said unto them, I see your father's countenance, that it its not toward me as before; but the God of my father hath been with me. And ye know that with all my power I have served your father. And your father hath deceived me, and changed my wages ten times; but God suffered him not to hurt me."

"If he said thus, The speckled shall by thy wages, then all the cattle bare speckled: and if he said thus, The ringstraked shall be thy hire; then bare all the cattle ringstraked. Thus God hath taken away the cattle of your father, and given them to me. And it came to pass at the time that the cattle conceived, that I lifted up mine eyes, and saw in a dream, and behold, the rams which leaped upon the cattle were ringstraked, speckled and grisled."

"And the angel of God spake unto me in a dream, saying, Jacob, and I said, Here am I. And he said, Lift up now thine eyes, and see, all the rams which leap upon the cattle are ringstraked, speckled, and grisled: for I have seen all that Laban doeth unto thee. I am the God of Beth-el, where thou anointest the pillar, and where thou vowedst a vow unto me: now arise, get thee out from this land, and return unto the land of thy kindred."

---

364. Jasher XXXl:40-44; Legends I:371

171

"And Rachel and Leah answered and said unto him, Is there yet any portion or inheritance for us in our father's house? Are we not counted of him, strangers? for he hath sold us, and hath quite devoured also our money. For all the riches which God hath taken from our father, that is ours, and our children's; now then, whatsoever, God hath said unto thee, do."[365]

365. Genesis 31:3-16 KJV, MT, JST

CHAPTER XXII

THEN JACOB ROSE UP...FOR TO GO TO ISAAC HIS FATHER

(From Genesis) "Then Jacob rose up, and set his sons and his wives upon camels; And he carried away all his cattle and all his goods which he had gotten, the cattle of his getting, which he had gotten in Padam-aram, for to go to Isaac his father in the land of Canaan. And Laban went to shear sheep: and Rachel had stolen the images that were her father's. And Jacob stole away unawares to Laban the Syrian, in that he told him not that he fled. So he fled with all that he had; and he rose up, and passed over the river, and set his face toward mount Gilead. And it was told Laban on the third day that Jacob was fled. And he took his brethren with him, and pursued after him seven day's journey; and they over took him in the mount Gilead. And God came to Laban the Syrian in a dream by night, and said unto him. Take heed that thou speak not to Jacob either good or bad."[366]

After Laban, his brothers, and servants had overtaken Jacob and his family, there were words of disagreement, a review of their twenty years together and eventual reconciliation with Laban kissing his daughters and grandchildren good-bye. Jacob and Laban had entered into a covenant with one another marked by a heap of stones as a witness of that covenant; known to Laban as Jegarsahadutha and to Jacob as Galeed.

The Genesis account reads:

"Then Laban overtook Jacob. Now Jacob had pitched his tent in the mount: And Laban with his brethren pitched in the

---

366. Genesis 31:17-24; Legends I:372-73

173

mount of Gilead. And Laban said to Jacob, What hast thou done, that thou hast stolen away unawares to me, and carried away my daughters, as captives taken with the sword? Wherefore didst thou flee away secretly, and steal away from me; and didst not tell me, that I might have sent thee away with mirth, and with songs, with tabret, and with harp? And hast not suffered me to kiss my sons, and my daughters? thou hast now done foolishly in so doing. It is in the power of my hand to do you hurt: but the God of your father spake unto me yesternight, saying, Take thou heed that thou speak not to Jacob either good or bad."[367]

"And now though thou wouldest needs be gone, because thou sore longest after thy father's house, yet wherefore hast thou stolen my gods? And Jacob answered and said to Laban, Because I was afraid: for I said, Peradventure thou wouldest take by force thy daughters from me. With whomsoever thou findest thy gods, let him not live: before our brethren discern thou what is thine with me, and take it to thee, For Jacob knew not that Rachel had stolen them."

"And Laban went into Jacob's tent, and into Leah's tent, and into the two maid servants' tents; but he found them not. Then went he out of Leah's tent, and entered into Rachel's tent. Now Rachel had taken the images (teraphim), and put them in the camel's furniture, and sat upon them. And Laban searched all the tent, but found them not. And she said to her father, Let it not displease my lord that I cannot rise up before thee; for the custom of women is upon me. And he searched but found not the images (teraphim)."[368]

The images Laban was trying to locate are described:

(From Jasher) "And this is the manner of the images; in taking a man who is the firstborn and slaying him and taking the hair off his head, and taking salt and salting the head and anointing it in oil, then taking a small tablet of copper or a tablet of gold and writing the name upon it, and placing the tablet under his tongue,

---

367. Ibid 31:25-29; Legends I:373
368. Genesis 31:30-35 KJV, MT, JST

174

and taking the head with the tablet under the tongue and putting it in the house, and lighting up lights before it and bowing down to it. And at the time when they bow down to it, it speaketh to them in all matters that they ask of it, through the power of the name which is written in it.....and the figures receive the influence of the stars, and tell them future things, and in this manner were the images which Rachel stole from her father. And Rachel stole these images which were her father's, in order that Laban might not know through them where Jacob had gone."[369]

As a worshipper of idols Laban sought the influence of false gods and of the stars through those idols (skulls of slain first born lighted up with candles) to foretell the future and to guide him. Even though Laban had just experienced a dream in which the Lord God of Jacob had warned him to "Take heed that thou speak not to Jacob either good or bad", Laban called Jacob to task for stealing his images. Instead, Rachel had taken them, and hid them in the camels' furniture. She remained seated on her camel to successfully conceal the images from detection. In so doing she spared her own life, for Jacob had already promised that "with whomsoever thou findest thy gods, let him not live." Laban failed to make good his accusation that Jacob had stolen his gods. Jacob was wroth and unloaded twenty years of frustration on Laban thusly:

(From Genesis) "And Jacob was wroth, and chode with Laban: and Jacob answered and said to Laban, What is my trespass? what is my sin, that thou hast so hotly pursued after me? Whereas thou has searched all my stuff, what hast thou found of all thy household stuff? set it before my brethren and thy brethren, that they may judge betwixt us both. This twenty years have I been with thee; thy ewes and thy she goats have not cast their young, and the rams of thy flock have I not eaten. That which was torn of beasts I brought not unto thee: I bare the loss of it; of my hand didst thou require it, whether stolen by day, or stolen by night. Thus I was, in the day the drought consumed me, and the frost by night; and my sleep departed from mine eyes. Thus have I been twenty years in thy house, I served thee fourteen years for thy two daughters, and six years for thy cattle: and thou has changed my

---

369. Jasher XXXI:41-44; Legends 371-72

wages ten times. Except the God of my father, the God of Abraham, and the fear of Isaac, had been with me, surely thou hadst sent me away now empty. God hath seen mine affliction and the labour of my hands, and rebuked thee yesternight."[370]

Jacob's defense of his own actions brought Laban to reconciliation. A covenant between them resulted. Laban asked that Jacob not afflict his daughters and not to take any more wives. Laban and Jacob agreed not to pursue one another past a heap of stones. Jacob offered sacrifice, and broke bread with his brethren. Laban left for his home the next morning after kissing his daughters and grandchildren goodbye.

(From Genesis) "And Laban answered and said unto Jacob, These daughters are my daughters, and these children are my children, and these cattle are my cattle, and all that thou seest is mine. and what can I do this day unto these my daughters, or unto their children which they have born?"

"Now therefore come thou, let us make a covenant, I and thou; and let it be for a witness between me and thee. And Jacob took a stone, and set it up for a pillar. And Jacob said unto his brethren, Gather stones; and they took stones, and made an heap: and they did eat there upon the heap. And Laban called it Jegar-sahadutha; but Jacob called it Galeed. And Laban said, This heap is a witness between me and thee this day. Therefore was the name of it called Galeed; And Mizpah; for he said, The Lord watch between me and thee, when we are absent one from another. If thou shalt afflict my daughters, or if thou shalt take other wives beside my daughters; no man is with us, see, God is witness betwixt me and thee."

"And Laban said to Jacob, Behold this heap, and behold this pillar, which I have cast betwixt me and thee; This heap be witness, and this pillar be witness, that I will not pass over this heap to thee, and that thou shalt not pass over this heap and this pillar unto me, for harm. The God of Abraham and the God of Nahor, the God of their father, judge betwixt us. And Jacob sware by the fear of his father Isaac."

---

370. Genesis 31:36-42; Legends I:374

"Then Jacob offered sacrifice upon the mount, and called his brethren to eat bread: and they did eat bread, and tarried all night in the mount. And early in the morning Laban rose up and kissed his sons and his daughters, and blessed them: and Laban departed, and returned unto his place."[371]

---

371. Genesis 31:43-55; Legends I 374-75

CHAPTER XXIII

THY NAME SHALL BE CALLED NO MORE JACOB, BUT ISRAEL

As Jacob and his family continued their journey toward Canaan and his father Isaac, angels of God met him at a place he named Mahanaim. Jacob sent messengers ahead of his party to his brother Esau who was living in the land of Seir, the country of Edom. Jacob apparently sought safe passage of his family, oxen, asses, flocks, menservants and maidservants. The messengers returned shortly with the news that Esau was coming to meet Jacob, and he had 400 men with him.

Jasher and the Legends report that Laban alerted Esau, exciting his anger and hatred toward Jacob. Hence, Esau put together his band of 400 men.[372]

Fearing Esau was coming to destroy his family and his possessions, Jacob divided them up (his family) into companies to increase the chances part of them would escape Esau's wrath. Jacob then prayed mightily unto the Lord for delivery from the hand of Esau. Finishing his prayer, Jacob felt impressed to prepare a gift for his brother Esau, a gift of 200 she goats, 20 he goats, 200 Ewes and 20 rams, 30 milk camels and colts, 40 kine(cows), 10 bulls, 20 she asses, and 10 foals. The present for Esau having been prepared and placed ahead of his family in the procession, Jacob took Leah, Rachel, Zilhah and Bilhah, his eleven sons and a daughter across the ford, Jabbok. The rest of the evening Jacob wrestled a man until the breaking of the next day. The man he wrestled was a messenger of God. Jacob's thigh was thrown out of joint in the process, (at 97 years of age). The messenger of God gave Jacob a blessing, and changed his name to Israel. The blessing declared Jacob, now named Israel, a prince who has power with God and with men. Apparently Jacob/Israel saw God

---

372. Jasher XXXII:9-12, Legends I:377

face to face while there. Israel named the place Peniel. In memory of the occasion, future generations of Israel were not to eat of the sinew which is upon the hollow of the thigh, because it was the hollow of Jacob's thigh in the sinew that shrank as a result of events of that night.

Jacob met Esau. His gifts were accepted. Jacob and his family were allowed safe passage on to Shalem, a city of Sheckem in the land of Canaan. Here Jacob and his family bought a parcel of a field, spred his tent, erected an altar, which he called El-elohe-Israel and made his family a home for awhile. Ages of family members as they settled here were Jacob, about 97 years, Leah and Rachel about 41 years. The children ranged in age from about 13 years to Joseph, at about 6 years of age.

The Genesis account reads:

"And Jacob went on his way, and the angels of God met him. And when Jacob saw them, he said. This is God's host: And he called the name of that place Mahanaim. And Jacob sent messengers before him to Esau his brother unto the land of Seir, the country of Edom. And he commanded them, saying, Thus shall ye speak unto my lord Esau: Thy servant Jacob saith thus, I have sojourned with Laban, and stayed there until now: And I have oxen and asses, flocks and menservants and womenservants: And I have sent to tell my lord, that I may find grace in thy sight."

"And the messengers returned to Jacob saying We came to thy brother Esau and also he cometh forth to meet thee and four hundred men with him. Then Jacob was greatly afraid and distressed. And he divided the people that was with him and the flocks and herds and the camels into two bands; And said If Esau come to the one company and smite it, then the other company which is left shall escape."[372A]

Jacob then prays for deliverance.

Genesis	Jasher
"And Jacob said, O God of my	"And Jacob prayed to the

372A. Genesis 32:1-8 KJV, MT, JST

father Abraham, and God of my father Isaac, the Lord which saidst unto me, Return unto thy country, and to thy kindred, and I will deal well with thee: I am not worthy of the least of all the mercies, and of all the truth which thou hast shewed unto thy servant; for with my staff I passed over this Jordan; and now I am become two bands.

Deliver me, I pray thee, from the hand of my brother, from the hand of Esau: for I fear him, lest he will come and smite me, and the mother with the children.

And thou saidst, I will surely do thee good, and make thy seed as the sand of the sea, which cannot be numbered for multitude.[372]

Lord his God, and he said, O Lord God of my fathers, Abraham and Isaac, thou didst say unto me when I went away from my father's house saying, I am the Lord God of thy father Abraham and the God of Isaac, unto thee do I give this land and thy seed after thee, and I will make thy seed as the stars of heaven and thou shalt spread forth to the four sides of heaven and in thee and in thy seed shall all the families of the earth be blessed.

And thou didst establish thy words, and didst give unto me riches and children and cattle, as the utmost wishes of my heart didst thou give unto thy servant, thou didst give unto me all I asked from thee so that I lacked nothing.

And thou didst afterward say unto me, Return to thy parents and to thy birth place and I will still do well with thee.

And now that I have come, and thous didst deliver me from Laban, I shall fall in the hands of Esau who will slay me, yea together with the mothers of my children.

Now, therefore O Lord God, deliver me, I pray thee, also from

---

372. Genesis 32:9-12

the hands of my brother Esau, for I am greatly afraid of him.

And if there is no righteousness in me, do it for the sake of Abraham and my father Isaac.

For I know that through kindness and mercy have I acquired this wealth; now therefore I beseech thee to deliver me this day with thy kindness and to answer me."[373]

After praying for deliverance from his brother Esau, Jacob proceeded to prepare a present for him and to protect his wives and children from attack, so that some might escape death.

<table>
<tr><td>Genesis</td><td>Jasher</td></tr>
</table>

Genesis	Jasher
"And he lodged there that same night; and took of that which came to his hand a present for Esau his brother; Two hundred she goats, and twenty he goats, two hundred ewes, and twenty rams, Thirty milch camels with their colts, forty kine, and ten bulls, twenty she asses and ten foals. And he delivered them into the hand of his servants, every drove by themselves; and said unto his servants, Pass over before me, and put a space betwixt drove and drove. And he commanded the foremost, saying, When Esau my brother meeteth thee, and asketh thee, saying, Whose art	"And Jacob ceased praying to the Lord, and he divided the people that were with him with the flocks and cattle into two camps, and he gave the half to the care of Damesek, the son of Eliezer, Abrahams servant, for a camp with his children, and the other half he gave to the care of his brother Elianus the son of Eliezer, to be a camp with his children ...and put a space between the droves, and when Esau and those who are with him shall meet you and ask you, saying, Whose are you, and whither do you go, and to whom belongeth all this before you, you shall say unto them, We

373. Jasher XXXII:16-23; Legends I:381

thou? and whither goest thou? and whose are these before thee? Then thou shalt say, Theybe thy servant Jacob's; it is a present sent unto my lord Esau: and, behold, he is behind us. And so commanded he the second, and the third, and all that followed the droves, saying, On this manner shall ye speak unto Esau, when ye find him. And say ye morever, Behold, thy servant Jacob is behind us. For he said, I will appease him with the present that goeth before me, and afterward I will see his face; per adventure he will accept of me. So went the present over before him: and himself lodged that night in the company. And he rose up that night, and took his two wives, and histwo women servants, and his eleven sons, and passed over the ford Jabbok. And he took them, and sent them over the wives and his maid servants, and brook, and he sent over that he had."[374]

are the servants of Jacob, and we come to meet Esau in peace, and behold Jacob cometh behind us. And that which is before us is a present sent from Jacob to his brother Esau. And if they shall say unto you, Why doth he delay behind you, from coming to meet his brother and to see his face, then you shall say unto them, Surely he cometh joyfully behind us to meet his brother, for he said, I will appease him with the present that goeth to him, and after this I will see his face, per adventure he will accept me. So the whole present passed on in the hands of his servants, and went before him on that day, and he lodged that night with his camps by the border of the brook Jabuk, and he rose up in the midst of the night, and he took his wives and his maid servants, and all belonging to him, and he that night passed them over the ford Jabuk.[375]

With the present for Esau prepared and his wives, children and possessions safely across the brook Jabbok, Jacob was left alone for the evening, but not for long.

Jacob wrestled with a man until the breaking of the day. As a result Jacob's thigh was thrown out of joint. One may improperly infer from the Genesis account that the man with whom Jacob wrestled was the Lord God, although He was present that night. With whom Jacob wrestled is not known. The Legends say Jacob wrestled with the angel Michael. Jacob sought and received a blessing. It was during this

---

374. Genesis 32:13-23 KJV, MT, JST
375. Jasher XXXII:24, 44-47; Legends I:383, V:244 Yashar Wa-Yeshlah 61a - 61b

encounter that Jacob's name was changed to Israel. Israel received strength from this experience and confidence that his family would survive an encounter with Esau and his men which he expected the following day.

"And Jacob was left alone; and there wrestled a man with him until the breaking of day. And when he saw that he prevailed not against him, he touched the hollow of his thigh; and the hollow of Jacob's thigh was out of joint, as he wrestled with him. And he said, Let me go, for the day breaketh, And he said, I will not let thee go, except thou bless me. And he said unto him, What is thy name? And he said, Jacob. And he said, Thy name shall be called no more Jacob, but Israel: for as a prince hast thou power with God and with men, and hast prevailed.

"And Jacob asked him, and said, Tell me I pray thee, thy name And he said, Wherefore is it that thou dost ask after my name? And he blessed him there. And Jacob called the name of the place Peniel, for I have seen God face to face, and my life is preserved. And as he passed over Penuel the sun rose upon him, and he halted upon his thigh. Therefore, the children of Israel eat not of the sinew which shrank, which is upon the hollow of the thigh, unto this day: because he touched the hollow of Jacob's thigh in the sinew that shrank."376

The following morning the ten droves of presents were placed in front of the caravan, followed by Bilhah and Zilpah and their children, followed by Leah and her children, (Dinah, he put in a chest). Rachel and Joseph were the hindermost or last in the caravan.

As Esau and his four hundred men approached Jacob's caravan, Jacob ran forward, bowed himself seven times before his twin brother Esau who was his elder by a few minutes. Such deference may have been suggested.

Esau also ran to meet Jacob (Israel). They kissed each other and wept. Esau was presented with a gift, which he at first declined then accepted. Esau offered to provide escort for Jacob to Seir. They eventually parted company. Esau went back to Seir and Israel moved on to the borders of Canaan.

---

376. Genesis 32:24-32; Legends I:384-87

Genesis	Jasher

"And Jacob lifted up his eyes, and looked, and behold, Esau came, and with him four hundred men. And he divided the children unto Leah, and unto Rachel, and unto the two handmaids. And he put the handmaids and their children foremost, and Leah and her children after, and Rachel and Joseph hindermost. And he passed over before them, and bowed himself to the ground seven times, until he came near to his brother. And Esau ran to meet him, and embraced him, and fell on his neck, and kissed him: and they wept.

And he lifted up his eyes, and saw the women and the children; and said, Who are those with thee? And he said, The children which God hath graciously given thy servant.

Then the handmaidens came near, they and their children, and they bowed themselves. And Leah also with her children came near, and bowed themselves: and after came Joseph near and Rachel, and they bowed themselves.

And he said, What meanest thou by all this drove which I met? And he said, These are to find grace in the sight of my lord. And

"And Jacob lifted up his eyes and looked, and behold Esau was at a distance, coming along with many men, about four hundred, and Jacob was greatly afraid of his brother. And Jacob hastened and divided his children unto his wives and his handmaids, and his daughter Dinah he put in a chest, and delivered her unto the hands of his servants. And he passed before his children and wives to meet his brother and he bowed down to the ground, and yea he bowed down seven times until he approached his brother, and God caused Jacob to find grace and favor in the sight of Esau and his men, for God had heard the prayer of Jacob.

And the fear of Jacob and his terror fell upon his brother Esau, for Esau was greatly afraid of Jacob for what the angels of God had done to Esau and Esau's anger against Jacob was turned into kindness.

And when Esau saw Jacob running toward him, he also ran toward him and embraced him, and he fell upon his neck, and they kissed and they wept.

And God put fear and kindness toward Jacob in the hearts of

Esau said, I have enough, my brother; keep that thou hast unto thyself. And Jacob said, Nay, I pray thee, if now I have found grace in thy sight, then receive my present at my hand: for therefore I have seen thy face, as though I has seen the face of God, and thou wast pleased with me. Take I pray thee, my blessing that is brought to thee; because God has dealt graciously with me, because I have enough. And he urged him, and he took it. And he said, Let us take our journey, and let us go, and I will go before thee. And he said unto him, My lord knoweth that the children are tender, and the flocks and herds with young are with me: And if men should overdrive them one day, all the flock will die.

Let my lord, I pray thee, pass over before his servant; and I will lead on softly, according as the cattle that goeth before me and the children be able to endure, until I come unto my lord unto Seir.

And Esau said, Let me now leave with thee some of the folk that are with me. And he said, What needeth it? let me find grace in the sight of my lord. So Esau returned that day on his way unto Seir.

the men that came with Esau, and they also kissed Jacob and embraced him.

And also Eliphaz the son of Esau, with his four brothers, sons of Esau, wept with Jacob, and they kissed him and embraced him, for the fear of Jacob had fallen upon them all.

And he and Esau lifted up his eyes and saw the women with their offspring, the children of Jacob, walking behind Jacob and bowing along the road to Esau.

And Esau said unto Jacob, Who are these with thee, my brother? are they thy children or thy servants? and Jacob answered Esau and said, They are my children which God hath graciously given to thy servant.

And whilst Jacob was speaking to Esau and his men, Esau beheld the whole camp, and he said unto Jacob, Whence didst thou get the whole of the camp that I met yesternight? and Jacob said, To find favor in the sight of my lord it is that which God graciously gave to thy servant.

And the present came before Esau, and Jacob pressed Esau, saying, Take I pray thee the present that I have brought to my

And Jacob journeyed to Succoth and built them an house, and made booths for his cattle; therefore the name of the place is called Succoth."[377]

lord, and Esau said, Wherefore is this my purpose? keep that which thou hast unto thyself. And Jacob said, It is incumbent upon me to give all this, since I have seen thy face, that thou livest in peace.

And Esau refused to take the present, and Jacob said unto him, I beseech thee my lord, if now I have found favor in thy sight, thou receive my present at my hand, for I have therefore seen thy face, as though I had seen a god like face, because thou wast pleased with me. And Esau took the present, and Jacob also gave unto Esau silver and gold and bdellium,for he pressed him so much that he took them.

And Esau divided the cattle that were in the camp, and he gave the half to the men who had come with him, for they had come on hire, and the other half he delivered unto the hands of his children.

And the silver and gold and bdellium he gave in the hands of Elijhaz his eldest son, and Esau said unto Jacob, Let us remain with thee, and we will go slowly along with thee until thou comest to my place with me, that we may dwell there together.

---

377. Genesis 33:1-17

And Jacob answered his brother and said, I would do as my lord speaketh unto me, but my lord knoweth that the children are tender, and the flocks and herds with their young who are with me, go but slowly, for if they went swiftly they would all die, for thou knowest their burdens and their fatigue.

Therefore let my lord pass on before his servant, and I will go on slowly for the sake of the children and the flock, until I come to my lord's place to Seir.

And Esau said unto Jacob, I will place with thee some of the people that are with me to take care of thee in the road, and to bear thy fatgue and burden, and he said, What needeth it my lord, if I may find grace in thy sight?

Behold I will come unto thee to Seir to dwell there together as thou hast spoken, go thou then with thy people for I will follow thee.

And Jacob said this to Esau in order to remove Esau and his men from him, so that Jacob might afterward go to his father's house to the land of Canaan.

And Esau hearkened to the voice of Jacob, and Esau returned with the four hundred men that were with him on their road to Seir, and Jacob and all belonging to him went that day as far as the extremity of the land of Canaan in its border and he remained there some time."[378]

So Jacob, Leah, Rachel, Zilpah, Bilhah and their eleven sons and Dinah their daughter arrive at the borders of Canaan at the behest of the Lord when Jacob was approximately 97/8 years old. His wives were much younger, most of his children were probably teenagers. Joseph, however, was about six or seven years old. The arduous journey just completed saw Jacob successfully extricate himself from the bondage imposed by his cousin, Laban and from the pent up wrath and anger of his brother Esau. Jacob was able to forgive and make peace with them both with the help of the Lord. Jacob was at last free to settle his family in Canaan as the Lord commanded.

Shem had died in Isaac's 110th year and Jacob's 50th year, leaving Eber as patriarch of the earth, with Isaac the head of the Lord God's covenant people in Canaan. By the time of Isaac's 139th and Jacob's 79th birthday's Eber had died. Jacob was two years into his service with Laban when Eber died. Unknown to Jacob, the Lord had groomed him twenty years for his future role as prophet and patriarch of the covenant people. Jacob, with a new name, and his house, the house of Israel, arrived in Canaan in Isaac's 159th year. Israel was to replace Isaac as prophet and patriarch of the Lord's covenant people. The covenant people would soon come to be known as the house of Israel.

---

378. Jasher XXXII:52-73; Legends I:388-395

ISRAEL SETTLES IN CANAAN, RACHEL, REBEKAH, AND ISAAC DIE JOSEPH IS SOLD INTO EGYPT

Jacob's trials were not over, however, neither were his blessings from the Lord at an end.

The next ten years of his life, from age 98 to 108 years of age, were difficult for Jacob. He dealt with the defiling of his daughter Dinah, and the consequent rage and actions of his son's. He moved his family back to Bethel at the Lord God's request, and built an altar there as he had done more than twenty years before, as he fled from Esau enroute to PadanAram. The Lord reiterated the promises He made to Jacob, and his posterity, and reminded him again that his new name under the covenant is Israel.

Israel moved his family to Ephrath (also known as Bethlehem) where his wife Rachel gave birth to Benjamin. She died in childbirth at age forty five. Dearly beloved Rachel was buried here, and a pillar was erected upon her grave.

Rachel, the younger twin sister of Leah, was afraid Laban would give her to Esau. Her inability to have children for a long time was a great frustration to her. Her great beauty didn't matter. She wanted children. Eventually she bore Joseph, later recognized as the greatest of the twelve sons of Israel. Joseph was destined to inherit the birthright blessings through Reuben's forfeiture of them. His posterity was/is to carry the blessings of the Torah (law of God) or gospel to all the world thereby fulfilling Jehovah's promise to Abraham that through his posterity all the families of the earth would be blessed. Rachel gave her life in the birth of Benjamin. She had foretold the Lord would give her a second son. She prayed often and was a devoted follower of the God of Abraham, Isaac and Jacob. Like Rebekah and Sarah she possessed the gift of prophecy and lived a righteous life.

Israel's first born son Reuben, heir to the priestly, kingly and birthright blessings possessed by Israel, forfeited all of them through grievous sin shortly after Rachel's death.

Upon the death of Rachel, Israel chose to pitch his tent in the tent of Bilhah. She was given to him for a wife (concubine) by Rachel. Reuben was apparently angry and jealous that his mother Leah was not chosen, removed his fathers bed and lay with Bilhah. As a result of committing this sin the priestly, kingly and birthright blessings were removed from Reuben. The priestly office was given to Levi, the kingly office was given to Judah, and the birthright blessing was given to Joseph.

Deborah, (Rebecca's nurse on loan to Leah, Rachel, Bilhah and Zilpah) died and was buried beneath Bethel by Israel and company. Israel's mother Rebecca, wife of Isaac, apparently died in Hebron just prior to Israel's arrival. She was buried in the cave of Machpelah next to Abraham, and Sarah. Israel mourned much for these two great women in his life. Laban, his cousin and nemesis, also died. Esau and his family continued to live in Seir during this period.

Rebekah was remarkably faithful to the God of Abraham and Isaac. She had been raised in an idolatrous home, accustomed in her childhood to the incense burnt before idols. A beautiful young woman, she chose to accompany Eliezer from Haran to Canaan to marry Isaac, a man she had never before seen.

Living close to the spirit and possessing the gift of prophecy, Rebekah was able to guide the life of her righteous son Jacob, and at the same time, respect the priesthood of her nearly blind husband, Isaac. She had revealed to her at the birth of her twins that Jacob was the anointed one who would dedicate his life to the Lord. She departed neither to the right or to the left in pursuing that course, seeing to it he got the right blessings at the right time. There are eight references to Rebekah's gift of prophecy in the Legends. She was considered a woman of valor, devoted and true to Isaac.

In contrast to the pomp and ceremony accompaning the deaths of Sarah and Abraham, Rebekah's death and burial were quiet and without fan fare. About twenty five years Isaac's junior, Rebekah died at age 133 before Jacob and his family had yet arrived in Canaan. Isaac was nearly blind, Esau and his idolatrous wives did not believe in the resurrection of the dead. Consequently, Rebekah was buried at night in the Cave of Machpelah with little or no ceremony.[379]

---

379. Legends I:414, V:271

The Genesis account reports that Israel and his family came to see his father and limits any further reference to Isaac to mentioning his death at 180 years of age and that Esau and Jacob (Israel) buried him. Isaac nearly blind, still lived, however, during this 10 year period of Israel's life, and was 158 to 168 years of age at the time. Isaac blessed the sons of Israel and the sons of Esau before he (Isaac) died. Israel's family journeyed to Mamre which is Kireath -arba, in Hebron where Abraham and Isaac had sojourned. Israel and all belonging to him dwelt with his father for a time in Hebron during two different periods.

At approximately 105 years of age or about nine years dwelling in the land of Canaan again, and in Isaac's 165th year, Israel moved his family back to Shechem because of good pasture there. They dwelt in the part of the field purchased from Hamor, the father of Shechem, before his sons' had smitten the city.

The kings of the Canaanites were understandably nervous about Israel's return to Shechem. They prepared for war.

Israel prayed mightily that his small army and his sons might prevail. So powerful was his prayer and so great was God's response that the earth shook and the sun darkened and affrighted the Canaanites. Animated with the power of God, Judah and his brethren prevailed though badly out numbered. Further information about these experiences is contained in another work entitled THE TWELVE SONS OF ISRAEL.

Israel and his sons returned to Hebron the following year, to the dwelling of Isaac, his father, leaving behind their flocks and herds, which were fed daily in Shechem by Israel's servants. Israel's sons were sent to Shechem, from time to time, to check on the flocks and herds and to help feed them.

Leah, Israel's wife and mother of Reuben, Simeon, Levi, Judah, Issachar, Zebulum and Dinah, died in Hebron at age fifty one. The priesthood and kingly blessings which Reuben lost through sin were bestowed upon Levi and Judah. Like Sarah, Rebekah and Rachel, Leah possessed the gift of prophecy. Through her loins the power to act for God was continued through Levi. Among her posterity were to come kings of nations, the King of Kings and Lord of Lords, even Messiah who would save the world from the sins of its people. Israel buried her in the cave of the field of Machpelah. This burying place now contained Abraham, Sarah, Rebecca, and Leah. Rachel was also dead and buried in Ephrath or Bethlehem.

Genesis shifts its attention to the story of Joseph and Judah.

Exodus shifts to Levi, his priesthood and the leadership of his posterity Moses and Aaron. To reiterate; Joseph, Judah and Levi were heirs to the birthright, kingly and priesthood blessings respectively.

Joseph received the birthright blessing and therefore was the Lord's anointed servant through whom all Israel was to be blessed temporally and spiritually.

Israel's other sons had not caught the significance of Joseph's blessing of birthright which came to him as a result of Reuben's sin. Joseph's dream of sheaves of grain foretold his future role in saving all Israel from the famine of food. Joseph's dream of the eleven stars making obeisance to him also foretold his role and the role of his posterity in bringing salvation to all Israel, from the spiritual famine of the last days.

Jealousy and pride prevented his brothers from seeing and understanding his future role. They sold him instead. They deceived their father Israel. To Reuben's credit, Joseph's life was spared. Some of Joseph's brother's sought to kill him. Judah was the brother who proposed they sell Joseph to the Ishmael-ites. His brothers agreed. To Judah's credit, years later, he offered himself as surety for Benjamin and was willing to be a slave the rest of his life to permit Benjamin to be returned to Jacob (Israel). Joseph saved all Israel from famine years later. He also forgave his brothers. Joseph's life story is contained in the work previously mentioned entitled THE TWELVE SONS OF ISRAEL.

The life stories of the other sons of Israel, including Judah and Levi, are also contained in that work.

Little or no information exists on Jacob's life for the next twelve years age 108 to 120. The remaining Genesis account is devoted to Joseph and Judah.

Isaac's death approached in the 120th year of Israel's life and in the 29th year of the life of Joseph. Joseph was in prison in Egypt. Israel and his eleven sons and their families were with Isaac in Hebron. Esau and his sons, in Seir, received word that Isaac was about to die. They came to Canaan. Isaac requested Jacob (Israel) to come forward with his eleven sons. Isaac embraced, kissed them and invoked Abraham's blessing upon each one. The blessing included increase in their seed like the stars of heaven for number.

Isaac also blessed Esau's sons.

Isaac admonished Israel to:

"teach thy children and they children's children to fear the Lord, and to go in the good way which will please the Lord thy God, for if you keep the ways of the Lord and his statutes the Lord will also keep unto you his covenant with Abraham, and will do well with you and your seed all the days."[379]

Isaac then gave up the ghost and died. He was gathered unto his people and buried by his sons Esau and Jacob (Israel), in the cave of Machpelah along side Abraham, Sarah, Rebecca and Leah. Twenty seven years later Jacob (Israel) was also buried there.

Isaac was mourned as Abraham was, and the kings of Canaan showed him great honor at his death. Israel's and Esau's sons went barefooted round about, walking and lamenting on the way. They buried Isaac with very great honor as at the funeral of kings.

At the death of Isaac, he left his cattle and his possessions, land and all belonging to him to Esau and Israel. Isaac's estate was divided into two parts by Israel. Esau was invited to choose which part he was to take. One part was the land, the other part included riches, cattle and flocks. Esau was offered one or the other.

Esau counseled with Nebayoth, son of Ishmael. They reasoned that the land was really in control of the Canaanites, who dwelt securely there.

Better to take the riches, cattle and flocks and leave the land to Israel, they thought. Esau selected the riches, cattle and flocks and took them all back to Seir leaving the land to Israel as his inheritance.

Included in Israel's inheritance, then, was the cave of Machpelah the burial place of Abraham, Sarah, Isaac, Rebecca and Leah and where Israel later was buried. Also included in Israel's portion of the estate settlement was the land of Canaan and all the cities of the Hittites, the Hivites, the Jebusites, the Ammonites, the Perizzites and the Gergashites, all the seven nations from the river of Egypt unto the river Euphrates.

The city of Hebron, Kireatharba, and the cave which is in it did Jacob buy from Esau, according to the Legends.

All these things were written down in a book of purchase, signed

---

379. Legends I:414, V:271, Jasher XLVII:8

and testified to with four faithful witnesses. Jacob (Israel) took the book of purchase and the signatures, the commandment and the statutes and the revealed book, and he placed them in an earthen vessel in order that they remain a long time, and he delivered them into the hands of his children.[380]

While generally not recognized as being of the stature as Abraham, Isaac was certainly one of the great men of all the earth.

It has been written that Isaac:

- was born at a time set by the Lord God Jehovah Himself
- was also named by Him
- received revelation from God
- was a friend, servant and prophet of God
- received the priesthood or power to act for God and conferred it upon Jacob
- taught Levi in the law of the Priesthood
- bestowed his blessings upon Levi and Judah while Joseph was in Egypt
- was very much a proscelyte/missionary
- wore priestly garments
- loved the Lord God Jehovah with all his heart, offered sacrifices often and had no other gods before him
- loved his neighbor, gave to the poor of Gerar
- honored his father and mother
- did not kill, commit adultery, steal, covet, bear false witness or take the name of the Lord in vain
- was willing to give all he had, for and to the Lord including himself as a sacrifice

In summary, Isaac lived a righteous life, kept the covenants he had made with God, and passed all the tests put to him including the Akedah. For his efforts Isaac was granted his exaltation, and he Isaac, also sitteth upon his celestial throne. "Isaac did none other things than that which (he was) commanded, (he has) entered into his exaltation according to (God's) promises and sit/s upon thrones..."*

* Doctrine & Covenants 132:37

---

380. Jasher XLVII:15-29

AND GOD SENT ME BEFORE YOU TO PRESERVE YOU A POSTERITY IN THE EARTH, AND TO SAVE YOUR LIVES BY A GREAT DELIVERANCE

By way of review, Jacob was born in the 560th (550) year of the life of Shem, 450th year of Arphaxad, 415th year of Salah, 385th year of Eber, the 160th year of Abraham and 60th year of Isaac. Shem, Arphaxad, Salah, Eber, Abraham and Isaac all preceded Jacob in death.

The first fifteen years of Jacob's life along with Esau's is covered in Chapter 25:21-34 of Genesis. His birth was mentioned in verses 21-26. The purchase of the birthright in reviewed in verses 28-34. Genesis says nothing further about the twins until Esau is forty years of age. Genesis moves quickly to Isaac's blessing apparently when Jacob was about sixtythree, see Chapter 27:1-5. Chapter 28 describes events which take place some fourteen years later when Jacob is dispatched to Haran to obtain a wife from the house of Bethuel, his mother's father, and of Laban his mother's brother. The first seventy seven years of Jacob's life is covered in fifty eight verses.

Whatever else we know of Jacob's first seventyseven years is gleaned from other writings. Once again the Lord God Jehovah forecast the role one of His great spirits would play on earth, before he was born. The younger of the twins, which turned out to be Jacob, and his posterity were to be stronger than the other. The elder, Esau, and his posterity were to serve the younger, Jacob, and his posterity.

At 175 years of age just before his death, Abraham blessed his fifteen year old grandson Jacob. Jacob and Esau accompanied their parents Isaac and Rebekah to Gerar during a famine which lasted three years. Returning to Canaan, Jacob was sent on to the house of Shem and Eber where he stayed thirty two years from age eighteen to fifty.

Jacob resided near his father Isaac for thirteen more years after returning home to Hebron at the death of Shem. At age sixty three Jacob received Isaac's blessing. He returned again to Eber's house to escape Esau who wanted to kill him. He stayed another fourteen years with Eber. Jacob returned to Isaac and Rebekah where Esau again plotted to take his life. This time Jacob departed for Haran with instructions to obtain a wife. Twenty years later he returned with four wives, twelve children and many possessions. Jacob and his family settled in Canaan, had many trials including the deaths of his mother, Rebekah, his wives Rachel and Leah and his children's nurse Deborah during this ten year period from the age of 98 to 108.

During the 12 year period of Israel's life, age 108 to 120 (and Isaac's final twelve years) Joseph was sold into Egypt, served in Pharaoh's court, and subsequently was falsely imprisoned where he remained 10 years. Joseph's older brothers married and had families while he was imprisoned. Joseph, as the Lord's anointed, interpreted the dreams of the butler and the baker who had recently been imprisoned. Three days later the chief baker was killed. The chief butler was returned to the Pharaoh's service as prophesied by Joseph. Although Joseph asked to be remembered to the Pharaoh, the butler forgot to tell him. Another two years lapsed. During this period Isaac died and the Lord announced a forthcoming famine via the Pharaoh's dream and through his prophet Joseph's interpretation. A famine had also followed Abraham's death. To Pharaoh was revealed a dream, which no one could interpret to his satisfaction. The butler then remembered his dream that Joseph interpreted correctly. He told the Pharaoh about it. Joseph was summoned. He interpreted the Pharaoh's dream, with the help of the Lord, as prophets are sometimes called upon to do.

The Pharaoh was convinced. He put Joseph in charge of preparations during the seven years of plenty. The famine began. Two years into the famine Israel and his family felt the pinch. He sent his ten sons, (Benjamin stayed with Israel) to Egypt to buy corn.

Joseph was now the governor of the land of Egypt. He dressed in princely garments. His brothers were brought before him. Joseph accused them of being spies, and spoke roughly with them. The ten sons of Israel identify themselves. Joseph recognized them, but they did not recognize him.

Joseph sought to prove them by requesting they send one brother back to Jacob and bring Benjamin to Egypt as evidence they were telling the truth. Joseph confined his brothers three days, then brought them forth. He presented a different plan. The new plan called for all the brothers, save one, to take corn and provisions back to Jacob (Israel). One brother was to be left behind as a hostage, or surety. The nine brothers were to return to Canaan with instructions to bring Benjamin, Israel's youngest son, with them.

The brothers agreed, and Simeon was left behind. The sacks were filled with corn. Their money was secretly returned to them in the mouth of their sacks, by Joseph. The sons of Israel returned to Canaan to their father.

They related their experiences to Israel (Jacob) upon their return to Canaan. Israel wouldn't agree to send Benjamin back to Egypt. Time lapsed, perhaps more than a year, the corn and grains they had obtained from Egypt were consumed. Israel and his family again feel the pinch and were about to perish due to the famine.

An appeal was again made to allow Benjamin to go with Israel's other sons back to Egypt to buy more corn. Judah promised to be surety for Benjamin and to accept the blame, forever, if Benjamin were not safely returned to Israel.

Israel relented. He instructed them to take double money with them to repay that which was returned in the mouths of their sacks previously, and to take of honey, balms, spices, nuts and almonds (apparently some things did still grow in Canaan in spite of the famine) as a present for the governor of Egypt. Benjamin was taken along as required.

However, before his sons departure for Egypt, Jacob held family prayer. He spread forth his hands. He prayed unto the Lord on account of his sons saying:

"O Lord God of heaven and earth, remember thy covenant with our father Abraham, remember it with my father Isaac and deal kindly with my sons and deliver them not unto the hands of the king of Egypt; do it I pray thee O God for the sake of thy mercies and redeem all my children and rescue them from Egyptian power, and send them their two brothers. And all the wives of the sons of Jacob and their children lifted up their eyes to heaven, and they all wept before the Lord, and cried unto him to deliver their fathers from the hand of the king of Egypt".[382]

---

382. Jasher LII:26-27; Legends II:91-92

Israel (Jacob) sent a letter with them by way of Judah. He rehearsed his family history, from Abraham, and appealed for the safe return of all his sons.[383]

Upon reentry into Egypt Israel's sons were again brought before Joseph the governor. They still did not recognize their brother. Joseph's brethren made obesience to him. Joseph was delighted to see Benjamin. He inquired of the father Israel, and asked if he were still alive and well. Joseph was informed father Israel was yet alive and in good health.

A feast was prepared, the brothers were astonished as Joseph seated them in the order of their birth.

The sacks were again filled with corn. The silver cup was put in Benjamin's sack by Joseph's men. The journey back to Canaan was begun. The brothers were overtaken, the planted cup was found and the brothers were returned to Egypt to account for their alleged misdeeds.

Judah spoke in behalf of his brothers, and as surety for Benjamin promised to Israel. He offered to be a bondman for the governor of Egypt (Joseph) in order that Benjamin might be returned to father Israel.

Judah's willingness to serve as a bondman or slave in exchange for Benjamin'sfreedom and the happiness that would give Israel (Jacob), touched Joseph. He could not restrain himself any longer before them. He sent out the servants and while alone with the sons of Israel announced he was one of them, their brother, also son of Israel.

His brothers were afraid, but Joseph assured them all was forgiven, and announced that he believed it was in the Lord's plan that they sold him, "for God send (sent) me before you to preserve life".[384] In the words of Jasher:

"I am Joseph whom you sold into Egypt, now therefore let it not grieve you that you sold me, for as a support during the famine did God send me before you".[385]

---

383. Jasher LII:28-42; Legends II:91-93
384. Genesis 45:5 KJV, MT, JST
385. Jasher LIV:69; Legends II:112

Back to Genesis:

"And God sent me before you to preserve you a posterity in the earth, and to save your lives by a great deliverance. So now it was not you that sent me hither, but God: and he hath made me a father to Pharaoh, and lord of all his house, and a ruler throughout all the land of Egypt. Haste ye, and go up to my father and say unto him, Thus saith thy son Joseph, God hath made me lord of all Egypt: come down unto me, tarry not: And thou shalt dwell in the land of Goshen, and thou shalt be near unto me, thou and thy children, and thy children's children, and thy flocks, and thy herds, and all that thou hast:.... And ye shall tell my father of all my glory in Egypt, and of all that ye have seen: and ye shall haste and bring down my father hither."[386]

"And he fell upon his brother Benjamin's neck, and wept; and Benjamin wept upon his neck. Moreover, he kissed all his brethren, and wept upon them: and after that his brethren talked with him."[387]

The Pharaoh agreed to allow Israel and all his family to come to Egypt. Wagon loads of gifts were sent to Jacob (Israel) by Joseph who stayed in Egypt.

(From Genesis) "And the fame thereof was heard in Pharaoh's house, saying, Joseph's brethren are come: and it pleased Pharaoh well, and his servants. And Pharaoh said unto Joseph, Say unto thy brethren, This do ye; lade your beasts, and go, get you unto the land of Canaan; And take your father and your households, and come unto me: and I will give you the good of the land of Egypt, and ye shall eat the fat of the land. Now thou are commanded, this do ye; take you wagons out of the land of Egypt for your little ones, and for your wives, and bring your father, and come. Also regard not your stuff; for the good of all the land of Egypt is yours. And the children of Israel did so: and Joseph gave them wagons, according to the commandment of Pharaoh, and gave them provision for the way."

---

386. Genesis 45:7-13 KJV, MT, JST
387. Genesis 45:14-15 KJV, MT, JST

"To all of them he gave each man changes of raiment; but to Benjamin he gave three hundred pieces of silver, and five changes of raiment. And to his father he sent after this manner; ten asses laden with the good things of Egypt, and ten she asses laden with corn and bread and meat for his father by the way. So he sent his brethren away, and they departed: and he said unto them, See that ye fall not out by the way. And they went up out of Egypt, and came into the land of Canaan unto Jacob their father."[388]

The sons of Israel gently broke the news that Joseph was yet alive, with song and harp by way of Serach the daughter of Asher.

(From Jasher) "And Joseph ceased to command them, and he turned and went back to Egypt, and the sons of Jacob went to the land of Canaan with joy and cheerfulness to their father Jacob. And they came unto the borders of the land, and they said to each other, What shall we do in this matter before our father, for if we come suddenly to him and tell him the matter, he will be greatly alarmed at our words and will not believe us. And they went along until they came nigh unto their houses, and they found Serach, the daughter of Asher, going forth to meet them, and the damsel was very good and subtle, and knew how to play upon the harp. And they called unto her and she came before them, and she kissed them, and they took her and gave unto her a harp, saying, Go now before our father, and sit before him, and strike upon the harp, and speak these words. And they commanded her to go to their house, and she took the harp and hastened before them, and she came and sat near Jacob. And she played well and sang, and uttered in the sweetness of her words, Joseph my uncle is living, and he ruleth throughout the land of Egypt, and is not dead. And she continued to repeat and utter these words, and Jacob heard her words and they were agreeable to him. He listened whilst she repeated them twice and thrice, and joy entered the heart of Jacob at the sweetness of her words, and the spirit of God was upon him, and he knew all her words to be true. And Jacob blessed Serach when she spoke these words before him, and he said unto her, My daughter, may death never prevail over thee, for thou hast revived my spirit; only speak yet before me as thou hast spoken, for thou hast gladdened me with all thy words."

388. Ibid 45:16-25 KJV, MT, JST

200

"And she continued to sing these words, and Jacob listened and it pleased him, and he rejoiced, and the spirit of God was upon him. Whilst he was yet speaking with her, behold his sons came to him with horses and chariots and royal garments and servants running before them. And Jacob rose up to meet them, and saw his sons dressed in royal garmentsand he saw all the treasures that Joseph had sent to them. And they said unto him, Be informed that our brother Joseph is living, and it is he who ruleth throughout the land of Egypt, and it is he who spoke unto us as we told thee. And Jacob heard all the words of his sons, and his heart palpitated at their words, for he could not believe them until he saw all that Joseph had given them and what he had sent him, and all the signs which Joseph had spoken unto them. And they opened out before him, and showed him all that Joseph had sent, they gave unto each what Joseph had sent him, and he knew that they had spoken the truth, and he rejoiced exceedingly an account of his son. And Jacob said, It is enough for me that my son Joseph is still living, I will go and see him before I die."[389]

The Genesis account reads:

"And told him saying, Joseph is yet alive, and he is governor over all the land of Egypt, And Jacob's heart fainted, for he believed them not. And they told him all the words of Joseph, which he had said unto them: and when he saw the wagons which Joseph had sent to carry him, the spirit of Jacob their father revived: And Israel said, It is enough; Joseph my son is yet alive: I will go and see him before I die."[390]

The land of Canaan was promised to Abraham and to Isaac and to Israel and his posterity as an everlasting inheritance. Israel was understandably reluctant to leave it permanently. Instead he thought he would go to Egypt and visit Joseph, and then return to Canaan. The Lord had other plans for Israel and his family, however, as Israel found out when he came to Beersheba and offered sacrifices where Isaac and Abraham had previously offered them.

Before departing, however, Jacob (Israel) rose up and put on the

---

389. Jasher LIV:90-105, Legends II:115-116, V, Yashar Wa Yiggash 110a
390. Genesis 45:26-28 KJV, MT, JST

garments Joseph had sent him. He washed, shaved his hair and put on a turban Joseph had also sent him. His family donned the gifts they had received from Joseph and they rejoiced for three days in the news that Joseph was alive.[391]

The family of Israel departed Canaan for Egypt to visit Joseph. Enroute they stopped at Beersheba and offered sacrifices unto the God of his father Isaac.

> (From Genesis) "And God spake unto Israel in the visions of the night, and said, Jacob, Jacob, and he said, Here am I. And he said, I am God, the God of they father; fear not to go down into Egypt; for I will there make of thee a great nation: I will go down with thee into Egypt; and I will also surely bring thee up again; and Joseph shall put his hand upon thine eyes."[392]

Israel thusly received assurance that it was the Lord's will he move his entire family to Egypt and there become a great nation, and there would Israel die, and there would Joseph close Israel's eyes. The Lord God of Israel did indeed make a great nation of him during the next 215 years.* Israel came into Egypt with three score and six (66) souls, and departed with more than 600,000 men of Israel not counting children.[393]

---

391. Jasher LIV:107-110; Legends II:117, V, Yashar Wa-Yiggash, 110a
392. Genesis 46:2-4 KJV, MT, JST
393. Exodus 12:37 KJV, MT, JST

*Antiquities

202

AND ISRAEL SAID UNTO JOSEPH, NOW LET ME DIE, SINCE I HAVE SEEN THEY FACE, BECAUSE THOU ART YET ALIVE

Israel informed his family and their households that they should go to Egypt for the Lord had thus commanded them. ..."and Jacob rose up with his sons and all his household, and he went out from the land of Canaan from Beersheba with joy and gladness of heart, as they went to the land of Egypt."[394]

Genesis reads:

"And Jacob rose up from Beersheba: and the sons of Israel carried Jacob their father, and their little ones, and their wives, in the wagons which Pharaoh had sent to carry him. And they took their cattle, and their goods, which they had gotten in the land of Canaan, and came into Egypt, Jacob, and all his seed with him: His sons, and his sons' sons with him, his daughters, and his sons' daughters, and all his seed brought he with him into Egypt. And these are the names of the children of Israel, which came into Egypt, Jacob and his sons: Reuben, Jacob's firstborn. And the sons of Reuben; Hanoch, and Phallu, and Hezron, and Carmi. And the sons of Simeon; Jemuel, and Jamin, and Ohad, and Jachin, and Zohar, and Shaul the son of a Canaanitish woman. And the sons of Levi; Gershon, Kohath, and Merari. And the sons of Judah; Er, and Onan, and Shelah, and Pharez, and Zerah: but Er and Onan died in the land of Canaan. And the sons of Pharez were Hezron and Hamul. And the sons of Issachar; Tola,

---

394. Jasher LV:5; Legends II:118-119, V, Yashar Wa-Yiggash, 110a - 110b

and Phuvah, and Job and Shimron. And the sons of Zebulun; Sered, and Elon, and Jahleel. These be the sons of Leah, which she bare unto Jacob in Padanaram, with his daughter Dinah: all the souls of his sons and his daughters were thirty and three."

"And the sons of Gad; Ziphion, and Haggi, Shuni, and Ezbon, Eri, and Arodi, and Areli. And the sons of Asher; Jimnah, and Ishuah, and Isui, and Beriah, and Serah their sister; and the sons of Beriah; Heber, and Malchiel. These are the sons of Zilpah, whom Laban gave to Leah his daughter, and these she bare unto Jacob, even sixteen souls. The sons of Rachel Jacob's wife: Joseph, and Benjamin. And unto Joseph in the land of Egypt were born Manasseh and Ephraim, which Asenath the daughter of Poti-pherah priest of On bare unto him. And the sons of Benjamin were Belah, and Becher, and Ashbel, Gera, and Naaman, Ehi, and Rosh, Muppim, and Huppim, and Ard. These are the sons of Rachel, which were born to Jacob: all the souls were fourteen."

"And the sons of Dan;Hushim. And the sons of Naphtali; Jahzeel, and Guni, and Jezer, and Shillem. These are the sons of Bilhah, which Laban gave unto Rachel his daughter, and she bare these unto Jacob: all the souls were seven. All the souls that came with Jacob into Egypt, which came out of his loins, besides Jacob's sons' wives, all the souls were threescore and six.[395]

Israel sent Judah in advance of the family of sixty-six. Judah met Joseph and received instructions to settle in Goshen in the land of Egypt, where Joseph and the Pharaoh had assigned them. Judah returned to his father and family and led them to Goshen.

(From Genesis) "And he sent Judah before him unto Joseph,to direct his face unto Goshen; and they came into the land of Goshen. And Joseph made ready his chariot, and went up to meet Israel his father, to Goshen, and presented himself unto him, and he fell on his neck, and wept on his neck a good while."[396]

---

395. Genesis 46:5-27 KJV, MT, JST
396. Ibid. 46:28-29 KJV, MT, JST

Jasher amplifies the reunion:

"And Joseph harnessed the chariot and he assembled all his mighty men and his servants and all the officers of Egypt in order to go and meet his father Jacob, and Joseph's mandate was proclaimed in Egypt, saying, All that do not go to meet Jacob shall die. And on the next day Joseph went forth with all Egypt a great and mighty host, all dressed in garments of fine linen, and purple and with instruments of silver and gold and with instruments of war with them."

"And they all went to meet Jacob with all sorts of musical instruments, with drums and timbrels, strewing myrrh and aloes all along the road, and they all went after this fashion, and the earth shook at their shouting. And all the women of Egypt went upon the roofs of Egypt and upon the walls to meet Jacob, and upon the head of Joseph was Pharaoh's regal crown, for Pharaoh had sent it unto him to put on at the time of his going to meet his father."

"And when Joseph came within fifty cubits of his father, he alighted from the chariot and he walked toward his father and when all the officers of Egypt and her nobles saw that Joseph had gone on foot toward his father, they also alighted and walked on foot toward Jacob. And when Jacob approached the camp of Joseph, Jacob observed the camp that was coming toward him with Joseph, and it gratified him and Jacob was astonished at it."

"And Jacob said unto Judah, Who is that man whom I see in the camp of Egypt dressed in kingly robes with a very red garment upon him and a royal crown upon his head, who has alighted from his chariot and is coming toward us? and Judah answered his father saying, He is thy son Joseph the king; and Jacob rejoiced in seeing the glory of his son."

"And Joseph came nigh unto his father and bowed down to his father, and all the men of the camp bowed to the ground with him before Jacob. And behold Jacob ran and hastened to his son Joseph and fell upon his neck and kissed him, and they wept, and

Joseph also embraced his father and kissed him, and they wept and all the people of Egypt wept with him."[397]

Returning to Genesis:

"And Israel said unto Joseph, Now let me die, since I have seen thy face, because thou art yet alive."[398]

And Jasher's description:

"And Jacob said unto Joseph, Now I will die cheerfully after I have seen thy face, that thou art still living and with glory."[399]

The rest of Joseph's family also greet him:

"And the sons of Jacob and their wives and children and their servants, and all the household of Jacob wept exceedingly with Joseph, and they kissed him and wept greatly with him."[400]

Joseph took leave of Israel, returned and reported to the Pharaoh the arrival of Israel and his family in Goshen. Joseph arranged for some of his brethren to meet the Pharaoh in advance of Israel, including Reuben, Issachar, Zebublun, and Benjamin.

(From Genesis) "And Pharaoh said unto his brethren, What is your occu-pation? And they said unto Pharaoh, Thy servants are shepherds, both we, and also our fathers. They said moreover unto Pharaoh, For to sojourn in the land are we come; for thy servants have no pasture for their flocks; for the famine is sore in the land of Canaan; now therefore, we pray thee, let thy servants dwell in the land of Goshen. And Pharaoh spake unto Joseph, saying, Thy father and thy brethren are come unto thee: The land of Egypt is before thee; in the best of the land make thy father and brethren to dwell; in the land of Goshen let them dwell: and if

---

397. Jasher LV:7-15; Legends II:120-121, V, Yashar Wa-Yiggash 110b - 111a
398. Genesis 46:30 KJV, MT, JST
399. Jasher LV:16, Legends II:122, V, Yashar Wa-Yiggash 110b - 111a
400. Ibid LV:17

thou knowest any men of activity among them, then make them rulers over my cattle."[401]

Shepherds were an abomination to the Egyptians. By identifying themselves as such made it easier for Joseph to settle Israel in Goshen, apart from the Egyptians. The Pharaoh agreed, and the sons of Israel took leave.

Afterwards, Joseph brought Jacob to visit with the Pharaoh. The Pharaoh was blessed by Jacob (Israel). The Pharaoh enquired as to Jacob's age; and Jacob answered, one hundred thirty years, adding that he hasn't lived as long as his fathers (Isaac, Abraham, Eber, Shem) had lived.

Genesis states:

"And Joseph brought in Jacob his father, and set him before Pharaoh: and Jacob blessed Pharaoh. And Pharaoh said unto Jacob, How old art thou? And Jacob said unto Pharaoh, The days of the years of my pilgrimage are an hundred and thirty years: few and evil have the days of the years of my life been, and have not attained unto the days of the years of the life of my fathers in the days of their pilgrimage. And Jacob blessed Pharaoh, and went out from before Pharaoh."[402]

401. Genesis 47:3-6 KJV, MT, JST
402. Ibid. 47:7-10

CHAPTER XXVII

THOU SHALT CARRY ME OUT OF EGYPT

(From Genesis) "And Joseph placed his father and his brethren, and gave them a possession in the land of Egypt, in the best of the land, in the land of Rameses, as Pharaoh had commanded. And Joseph nourished his father, and his brethren, and all his father's household, with bread, according to their families."[403]

To which Jasher adds:

"And Joseph gave unto them the best part of the whole land; the best of Egypt had they all the days of Joseph; and Joseph also gave unto them and unto the whole of his father's household, clothes and garments year by year; and the sons of Jacob remained securely in Egypt all the days of their brother. And Jacob always ate at Joseph's table, Jacob and his sons did not leave Joseph's table day or night, besides what Jacob's children consumed in their houses...."

"And Jacob and his sons dwelt in the land of Egypt in the land of Goshen, and they took possession in it, and they were fruitful and multiplied in it."[404]

The famine worsened during the first five years of Israel's sojourn in Egypt. Joseph continued to parcel out the remaining food in the storehouses, selling it for whatever means of exchange was available, money until it ran out, silver and gold, horses and flocks and cattle, then the land he bought for Pharaoh.

---

403. Genesis 47:11-12 KJV, MT, JST
404. Jasher LV:27-28, 36

Jasher and the Legends indicate that Joseph collected the silver and gold and buried it. Some of it he buried near the Red Sea, some by the river Perath, some he gave to his brothers, and some he gave to the Pharaoh.

The seven years of famine came to an end. Seeds were given out and allowed to be planted. A fifth of the crop was to be given to the Pharaoh and four fifths retained unto themselves. Conditions returned to normal after the famine abated and there was sufficient food.

Except to report that "Israel dwelt in the land of Egypt, in the country of Goshen; and they had possessions therein, and grew, and multiplied exceedingly,"[405] nothing more is said of Israel's final seventeen years, until he approached death.

As the end of Israel's life nears much of significance transpires.

He obtained a promise from his sons that they would bury him in Machpelah in Hebron with his father Isaac and grandfather Abraham. He blessed all of his sons and some of his grandsons including Ephraim and Manasseh. Jasher and the Legends report that Israel prophesied the Lord would raise up a servant (Moses) among them that would deliver them from affliction and bring them back to the land of their fathers.

Jasher and the Legends also report that Israel identified those who were to carry his bier at his death. Joseph wasn't to help carry it, for he was a king. Levi was not to help carry Israel's bier either. Instead, he and his sons were to carry the Ark of the Covenant. Note that this is a reference to the Ark of the Covenant in Israel's day. It was Levi's posterity of the priesthood through Moses and Aaron who took care of the Ark of the Covenant and carried it, in their day and thereafter. Was this a prophesy of what was to come, or did the Ark of the Covenant exist in Israel's and Levi's day?

And now for the actual report.

(From Genesis) "And Jacob lived in the land of Egypt seventeen years: so the whole age of Jacob was an hundred forty and seven years. And the time drew nigh that Israel must die: and he called his son Joseph, and said unto him, If now I have found grace in thy sight, put, I pray thee, thy hand under my thigh, and deal kindly and truly with me; bury me not, I pray thee, in Egypt: But I

---

405. Genesis 47:27; Legends II:128-130

209

will lie with my fathers, and thou shalt carry me out of Egypt, and bury me in their buryingplace. And he said, I will do as thou hast said. And he said, Swear unto me, And he sware unto him. And Israel bowed himself upon the bed's head."[406]

From the Legends:

"Carry me out of the land of idolatry and bury me in the land where God hath caused His name to dwell..."[407]

And from Jasher:

"And Jacob lived in the land of Egypt seventeen years, and the days of Jacob, and the years of his life were a hundred and forty seven years. At that time Jacob was attacked with that illness of which he died and he sent and called for his son Joseph from Egypt, and Joseph his son came from Egypt and Joseph came unto his father. And Jacob said unto Joseph and unto his sons, Behold I die, and the God of your ancestors will visit you, and bring you back to the land, which the Lord sware to give unto you and unto your children after you, now therefore when I am dead, bury me in the cave which is in Machpelah in Hebron in the land of Canaan, near my ancestors. And Jacob made his sons swear to bury him in Machpelah, in Hebron, and his sons swore unto him concerning this thing."[408]

Knowing, therefore, his posterity would be brought back out of Egypt in the future, Israel sought to be buried in the land of his inheritance promised to Abraham, Isaac and himself and their posterity.

During this visit with Joseph, Israel bore testimony of the Lord God's appearance unto him in Luz (Bethel) and of the blessings God promised him there, before he was married and had children. God Almighty had promised Israel he would make of him a multitude of people and give his posterity an everlasting possession.

---

406. Genesis 47:28-31 KJV, MT, JST
407. Legends II:128
408. Jasher LVI:1-4

Genesis reads:

"And it came to pass after these things, that one told Joseph, Behold, thy father is sick: and he took with him his two sons, Manasseh and Ephraim. And one told Jacob, and said, Behold, thy son Joseph cometh unto thee: and Israel strengthened himself, and sat upon the bed. And Jacob said unto Joseph, God Almighty appeared unto me at Luz in the land of Canaan, and blessed me. And said unto me, Behold, I will make thee fruitful, and multiply thee, and I will make of thee a multitude of people; and will give this land to thy seed after thee for an everlasting possession."[409]

The Legends:

"The holy spirit made known to Jacob that Joseph was coming to him...He strengthened himself spiritually as well as physically, by prayer to God, in which he besought Him to let the holy spirit descend upon him at the time of his giving the blessings to the sons of Joseph."[410]

After testifying to Joseph of his experience and blessings in Luz (Bethel) years ago, Israel blessed his son Joseph and his grandsons Ephraim and Manasseh born through Rachel, whom he had buried near Ephrath (Bethlehem) years before. Israel prophesied concerning Joseph, blessed these two grandsons and made them equal by inheritance with his own sons. Israel also testified that God shall be with Joseph, and bring his posterity up to the land of his fathers, where Joseph's posterity would have one portion above his brethren.

Genesis reads:

"And now thy two sons, Ephraim and Manasseh, which were born unto thee in the land of Egypt, before I came unto thee into Egypt, are mine; as Reuben and Simeon, they shall be mine. And thy issue, which thou begettest after them, shall be thine, and

---

409. Genesis 48:1-4 KJV, MT, JST
410. Legends II:133

shall be called after the name of their brethren in their inheritance."[411]

To which JST Genesis adds:

"And now, of thy two sons, Ephraim and Manasseh, which were born unto thee in the land of Egypt, before I came unto thee into Egypt; behold they are mine, and the God of my fathers shall bless them; even as Reuben and Simeon they shall be blessed, for they are mine; wherefore they shall be called after my name. (Therefore they were called Israel)."

"And thy issue which thou begettest after them, shall be thine, and shall be called after the name of their brethren in their inheritance, in the tribes; therefore they were called the tribes of Manasseh and Ephraim. And Jacob said unto Joseph when the God of my fathers appeared unto me in Luz, in the land of Canaan; he sware unto me, that he would give unto me, and unto my seed, the land for an everlasting possession. Therefore, O my son, he hath blessed me in raising thee up to be a servant unto me, in saving my house from death; In delivering my people, thy brethren, from famine which was sore in the land; wherefore the God of thy fathers shall bless thee, and the fruit of thy loins, that they shall be blessed above thy brethren, and above thy father's house;

"For thou hast prevailed, and thy father's house hath bowed down unto thee, even as it was shown unto thee, before thou wast sold into Egypt by the hands of thy brethren; wherefore thy brethren shall bow down unto thee, from generation to generation, unto the fruit of thy loins forever; For thou shalt be a light unto my people to deliver them in the days of their captivity, from bondage; and to bring salvation unto them, when they are altogether bowed down under sin."[412]

The seed of Joseph then, was/is to bring salvation unto the house of Israel some time in the future when the house of Israel is bowed down under sin.

411. Genesis 48:5-6; Legends II:134
412. Genesis 48:5-11 JST

212

Returning to KJV Genesis:

"And as for me, when I came from Padan, Rachel died by me in the land of Canaan in the way, when yet there was but a little way to come unto Ephrath: and I buried her there in the way of Ephrath; the same is Bethlehem. And Israel beheld Joseph's sons, and said, Who are these? And Joseph said unto his father, They are my sons, whom God hath given me in this place. And he said, Bring them, I pray thee, unto me, and I will bless them. Now the eyes of Israel were dim for age, so that he could not see. And he brought them near unto him; and he kissed them, and embraced them. And Israel said unto Joseph, I had not thought to see thy face: and, lo, God hath shewed me also thy seed. And Joseph brought them out from between his knees, and he bowed himself with his face to the earth. And Joseph took them both, Ephraim in his right hand toward Israel's left hand, and Manasseh in his left hand toward Israel's right hand, and brought them near unto him. And Israel stretched out his right hand, and laid it upon Ephraim's head, who was the younger, and his left hand upon Manasseh's head, guiding his hands wittingly; for Manasseh was the firstborn. And he blessed Joseph, and said, God, before whom my fathers Abraham and Isaac did walk, the God which fed me all my life long unto this day. The Angel which redeemed me from all evil, bless the lads; and let my name be named on them, and the name of my fathers Abraham and Isaac; and let them grow into a multitude in the midst of the earth."

Continuing:

"And when Joseph saw that his father laid his right hand upon the head of Ephraim, it displeased him: and he held up his father's hand, to remove it from Ephraim's head unto Manasseh's head. And Joseph said unto his father, Not so, my father: for this is the firstborn; put thy right hand upon his head. And his father refused, and said, I know it, my son, I know it: he also shall become a people, and he also shall be great: but truly his younger brother shall be greater than he, and his seed shall become a multitude of nations. And he blessed them that day, saying, In thee shall Israel bless, saying, God make thee as Ephraim and as Manasseh: and he set Ephraim before Manasseh. And Israel said

213

unto Joseph, Behold, I die: but God shall be with you, and bring you again unto the land of your fathers. Moreover I have given to thee one portion above thy brethren, which I took out of the hand of the Amorite with my sword and with my bow."[413]

From these verses we learn that Ephraim received the greater blessing and responsibility, that his seed was to become a multitude of nations, and that Israel anticipated God would bring his posterity out of Egypt back to Canaan, the land of their inheritance, in the future.

The Legends add that Ephraim was receiving instruction from Jacob in the Torah (Law of the Gospel) and Ephraim was one of those who notified Joseph of Jacob's illness. They also report Ephraim's special blessing from his grandfather Jacob as follows:

"Ephraim, my son, thou art the head of the academy, and in the days to come my most excellent and celebrated descendants will be called Ephrati after thee."[414]

Israel brought his interview with Joseph, Ephraim, and Manasseh to a close and requested that all of his sons and their children be gathered together so that he could bless them also.

The first day with all his children and grandchildren in general assembly sitting before him, Israel blessed them and declared to them:

(From Jasher)..."Serve the Lord your God, for he who delivered your fathers will also deliver you from all trouble...The Lord God of your fathers shall grant you a thousand times as much and bless you, and may he give you the blessing of your father Abraham; and all the children of Jacob's sons went forth on that day after he had blessed them."

"And on the next day Jacob again called for his sons, and they all assembled and came to him and sat before him, and Jacob on that day blessed his sons before his death, each man did he bless according to his blessing; behold it is written in the book of the law of the Lord appertaining to Israel."[415]

---

413. Genesis 48:7-22 KJV, MT (48:12-28) JST
414. Legends II:132, 138
415. Jasher LVI:5-7

Genesis reads:

"And Jacob called unto his sons, and said, Gather yourselves together, that I may tell you that which shall befall you in the last days. Gather yourselves together and hear ye sons of Jacob; and hearken unto Israel your father."[416]

Back to Jasher:

"And Jacob again commanded his sons on that day, saying, Behold I shall be this day gathered unto my people; carry me up from Egypt, and bury me in the cave of Machpelah as I have commanded you. Howbeit take heed I pray you that none of your sons carry me, only yourselves, and this is the manner you shall do unto me, when you carry my body to go with it to the land of Canaan to bury me, Judah, Issachar and Zebulun shall carry my bier at the eastern side; Reuben, Simeon and Gad at the south, Ephraim, Manasseh and Benjamin at the west, Dan, Asher and Naphtali at the north. Let not Levi carry with you, for he and his sons will carry the ark of the covenant of the Lord with the Israelites in the camp, neither let Joseph my son carry, for as a king so let his glory be; howbeit, Ephraim and Manasseh shall be in their stead. Thus shall you do unto me when you carry me away; do not neglect anything of all that I command you; and it shall come to pass when you do this unto me, that the Lord will remember you favorably and your children after you forever."

Continuing:

"And you my sons, honor each his brother and his relative, and command your children and your children's children after you to serve the Lord God of your ancestors all the days. In order that you may prolong your days in the land, you and your children and your children's children for ever, when you do what is good and upright in the sight of the Lord your God, to go in all his ways. And thou, Joseph my son, forgive I pray thee the wrongs of thy brethren and all their misdeeds in the injury that they heaped upon thee, for God intended it for thine and they child-

---

416. Genesis 49:1-2 KJV, MT, JST

215

ren's benefit. And O my son leave not thy brethren to the inhabitants of Egypt, neither hurt their feelings, for behold I consign
them to the hand of God and in thy hand to guard them from the
Egyptians; and the sons of Jacob answered their father saying, O,
our father, all that thou hast commanded us, so will we do; may
God only be with us.

And Jacob said unto his sons, So may God be with you when
you keep all his ways; turn not from his ways either to the right or
the left in performing what is good and upright in his sight. For I
know that many and grievous troubles will befall you in the latter
days in the land, yea your children and children's children, only
serve the Lord and he will save you from all trouble. And it shall
come to pass when you shall go after God to serve him and will
teach your children after you, and your children's children, to
know the Lord, then will the Lord raise up unto you and your
children a servant from amongst your children, and the Lord will
deliver you through his hand from all affliction, and bring you out
of Egypt and bring you back to the land of your fathers to inherit
it securely."[417]

The Legends:

"According to my power did I bless you, but in future days a
prophet will arise, and this man Moses will bless you too, and he
will continue my blessings where I left off."[418]

Israel prophesied thus that his posterity would be afflicted and be
put in bondage and God would raise up a servant (Moses) who would
deliver them from that bondage.
Using allegories Israel gave each of is twelve sons a blessing and
prophesied what would befall them and their posterity in the last days.

To Judah, Israel declared:

..."Thou art he whom thy brethren shall praise: thy hand

---

417. Jasher LVI:10-21; Legends II:148, V, Yashar Wa Yehi 112a - 112b
418. Legends II:147

shall be in the neck of thine enemies; thy father's children shall bow down before thee. Judah is a lion's whelp; from the prey, my son thou art gone up; he stooped down, he couched as a lion, and as an old lion, who shall rouse him up? The sceptre shall not depart from Judah, nor a lawgiver from between his feet, until Shiloh come; and unto him shall the gathering of the people be."

"Binding his foal unto the vine, and his ass's colt unto the choice vine, he washed his garments in wine, and his clothes in the blood of grapes. His eyes shall be red with wine, and his teeth white with milk."[419]

To which Jasher adds:

"And Jacob said unto Judah, I know my son that thou art a mighty man for thy brethren, reign over them, and thy sons shall reign over their sons forever. Only teach thy sons the bow and all weapons of war, in order that they may fight the battles of their brother who will rule over his enemies."[420]

And the Legends:

"No people and no kingdom will be able to stand up against thee. Rulers shall not cease from the house of Judah, nor teachers of the law from his posterity, until his descendant Messiah come, and the obedience of all peoples be unto him, How glorious is Messiah of the house of Judah!"[421]

From Levi were to come the priesthood and the scholars that would expound the law of the Gospel (Torah) and render decisions according to its teachings. In other words, common judges in Israel were to be appointed among the peoples from the descendants of Levi, or who held the Levitical Priesthood.[422]

---

419. Genesis 49:8-12 KJV, MT, JST
420. Jasher LVI:8-9
421. Legends II:143
422. Ibid II:143

217

To Joseph, Israel declared:

"Joseph is a fruitful bough, even a fruitful bough by a well; whose branches run over the wall: The archers have sorely grieved him, and shot at him, and hated him: But his bow abode in strength, and the arms of his hands were made strong by the hands of the mighty God of Jacob; (from thence is the shepherd,* the stone of Israel:) Even by the God of thy father, who shall help thee; and by the Almighty, who shall bless thee with blessings of heaven above, blessings of the deep that lieth under, blessings of the breasts, and of the womb: The blessings of thy father have prevailed above the blessings of my progenitors unto the utmost bound of the everlasting hills: they shall be on the head of Joseph and on the crown of the head of him that was separate from his brethren."[423]

The Legends declare Joseph's blessing as having exceeded the blessing of all his brethren. Jacob spoke:

"O son whom I bred up, Joseph, whom I raised, and who wast strong to resist the enticements of sin, thou didst conquer all the magicians and the wise men of Egypt by thy wisdom...May the blessing of thy father giveth thee now, and the blessing that his father's Abraham and Isaac gave him - may all these blessings be a crown upon the head of Joseph, and...yet diminish(ed) not the honor due his brethren."[424]

The blessings Israel gave to his other sons along with the story of their lives and the lives of Judah and Joseph are contained in another work, previously mentioned, entitled THE TWELVE SONS OF ISRAEL.

Israel closed his blessings on his twelve sons and charged them again to bury him in the cave of Machpelah in Hebron in the land of Canaan with his parents Isaac and Rebekah and grandparents Abraham and Sarah; and with his wife Leah.

423.Genesis 49:22-26 KJV, MT, JST *It is from the lineage of Jacob that the
   Messiah comes.
424. Legends II:146

Genesis reads:

"All these are the twelve tribes of Israel: and this is it that their father spake unto them, and blessed them; every one according to his blessing he blessed them. And he charged them, and said unto them, I am to be gathered unto my people: bury me with my fathers in the cave that is in the field of Ephron the Hittite, In the cave that is in the field of Machpelah, which is before Mamre, in the land of Canaan, which Abraham bought with the field of Ephron the Hittite for a possession of a buringplace. There they buried Abraham and Sarah his wife; there they buried Isaac and Rebekah his wife; and there I buried Leah. The purchase of the field and of the cave that is therein was from the children of Heth. And when Jacob had made an end of commanding his sons, he gathered up his feet into the bed, and yielded up the ghost (expired), and was gathered unto his people."[425]

---

425. Genesis 49:28-33 KJV, MT, JST

CHAPTER XXVIII

AND JOSEPH WENT UP TO BURY HIS FATHER

The twelve sons of Israel led by Joseph carried out the wishes of their father. After he was embalmed, a great mourning, a seventy day mourning, was held for Israel in Egypt. Following the days of mourning in Egypt, Israel's sons and all their families traveled to Canaan and buried him there in the cave of Machpelah.

Genesis reads:

"And when Jacob had made an end of commanding his sons, he gathered up his feet into the bed, and yielded up the ghost, and was gathered unto his people."[426]

"And Joseph fell upon his father's face, and wept upon him, and kissed him. And Joseph commanded his servants the physicians to embalm his father: and the physicians embalmed Israel. And forty days were fulfilled for him; for so are fulfilled the days of those which are embalmed: and the Egyptians mourned for him threescore and ten days. And when the days of his mourning (weeping) were past. Joseph spake unto the house of Pharaoh, saying, If now I have found grace in your eyes, speak, I pray you, in the ears of Pharaoh, saying, My father made me swear, saying, Lo, I die: in my grave which I have digged for me in the land of Canaan, there shalt thou bury me. Now therefore let me go up, I pray thee, and bury my father, and I will come again. And Pharaoh said, Go up, and bury thy father, according as he made thee swear."[427]

---

426. Genesis 49:33 KJV, MT, JST
427. Ibid 50:1-6 KJV, MT, JST

Jasher adds:

"And his sons' wives and all his household came and fell upon Jacob, and they wept over him, and cried in a very loud voice concerning Jacob. And all the sons of Jacob rose up together, and they tore their garments, and they all put sackcloth upon their loins, and they fell upon their faces, and they cast dust upon their heads toward the heavens. And the thing was told unto Osnath Joseph's wife, and she rose up and put on a sack and she with all the Egyptian women with her came and mourned and wept for Jacob. And also all the people of Egypt who knew Jacob came all on that day when they heard this thing, and all Egypt wept for many days. And also from the land of Canaan did the women come unto Egypt when they heard that Jacob was dead, and they wept for him in Egypt for seventy days. And it came to pass after this that Joseph commanded his servants the doctors to embalm his father with myrrh and frankincense and all manner of incense and perfume, and the doctors embalmed Jacob as Joseph had commanded them. And all the people of Egypt and the elders and all the inhabitants of the land of Goshen wept and mourned over Jacob, and all his sons and the children of his household lamented and mourned over their father Jacob many days.

And after the days of his weeping had passed away, at the end of seventy days, Joseph said unto Pharaoh, I will go up and bury my father in the land of Canaan as he made me swear, and then I will return. And Pharaoh sent Joseph, saying, Go up and bury thy father as he said, and as he made thee swear; and Joseph rose up with all his brethren to go to the land of Canaan to bury their father Jacob as he had commanded them. And Pharaoh commanded that it should be proclaimed throughout Egypt, saying, Whoever goeth not up with Joseph and his brethren to the land of Canaan to bury Jacob, shall die. And all Egypt heard of Pharaoh's proclamation, and they all rose up together, and all the servants of Pharaoh, and the elders of his house, and all the elders of the land of Egypt went up with Joseph, and all the officers and nobles of Pharaoh went up as the servants of Joseph, and they went to bury Jacob in the land of Canaan."[428]

---

428. Jasher LVI:24-34; Legends II:149-151

The funeral procession must have stretched for miles for not only did it include the house of Israel but the servants of Pharaoh and all the elders of the land of Egypt.

Genesis reads:

"And Joseph went up to bury his father: and with him went up all the servants of Pharaoh, the elders of his house, and all the elders of the land of Egypt, And all the house of Joseph, and his brethren, and his father's house: only their little ones, and their flocks, and their herds, they left in the land of Goshen. And there went up with him both chariots and horsemen: and it was a very great company."[429]

To which Jasher adds:

"And the sons of Jacob carried the bier upon which he lay; according to all that their father commanded them, so did his sons unto him. And the bier was of pure gold, and it was inlaid round about with onyx stones and bdellium; and the cover of the bier was gold woven work, joined with threads, and over them were hooks of onyx stones and bdellium. And Joseph place upon the head of his father Jacob a large golden crown, and he put a golden sceptre in his hand, and they surrounded the bier as was the custom of kings during their lives. And all the troops of Egypt went before him in this array, at first all the mighty men of Pharaoh, and the mighty men of Joseph, and after them the rest of the inhabitants of Egypt, and they were all girded with swords and equipped with coats of mail, and the trappings of war were upon them. And all the weepers and mourners went at a distance opposite to the bier, going and weeping and lamenting, and the rest of the people went after the bier. And Joseph and his household went together near the bier barefooted and weeping, and the rest of Joseph's servants went around him; each man had his ornaments upon him, and they were all armed with their weapons of war. And fifty of Jacob's servants went in front of the bier, and they strewed along the road myrrh and aloes, and all manner of perfume, and all the sons of Jacob that carried the bier walked

429. Genesis 50:7-9 KJV, MT, JST

upon the perfumery, and the servants of Jacob went before them strewing the perfume along the road. And Joseph went up with a heavy camp, and they did after this manner every day until they reached the land of Canaan...."[430]

The procession stopped at the threshing floor of Atad in the land of Canaan where they were joined by the Canaanites and together the house of Israel, the Egyptians and the Canaanites mourned for Jacob (Israel) and lamented another seven days.

From Genesis:

"And they came to the threshing floor of Atad, which is beyond Jordan, and there they mourned with a great and very sore lamentation: and he made a mourning for his father seven days. And when the inhabitants of the land, the Canaanites, saw the mourning in the floor of Atad, they said, This is a grievous mourning to the Egyptians: wherefore the name of it was called Abel-mizraim, which is beyond Jordan."[431]

To which Jasher adds:

"....and they came to the threshing floor of Atad, which was on the other side of Jordan, and they mourned an exceeding great and heavy mourning in that place. And all the kings of Canaan heard of this thing and they all went forth, each man from his house, thirty-one kings of Canaan, and they all came with their men to mourn and weep over Jacob. and All these kings beheld Jacob's bier, and behold Joseph's crown was upon it, and they also put their crowns upon the bier, and encircled it with crowns. And all these kings made in that place a great and heavy mourning with the sons of Jacob and Egypt over Jacob, for all the kings of Canaan knew the valor of Jacob and his sons."[432]

Genesis reports that Israel's sons buried him in the cave of Machpelah as he requested and returned to Egypt. The remaining eleven

---

430. Jasher LVI:35-42; Legends II:152-3
431. Genesis 50:10-11 KJV, MT, JST
432. Jasher LVI:42-45; Legends II:153-4

verses of Genesis are devoted to Joseph and his brethren. The Genesis account of Jacob's (Israel's) life ends as follows:

> "And his sons did unto him according as he commanded them: For his sons carried him into the land of Canaan, and buried him in the cave of the field of Machpelah, which Abraham bought with the field for a possession of a burying place of Ephron the Hittite, before Mamre."[433]

Jasher and the Legends, on the other hand, report that as the huge funeral procession neared its destination, Esau received a report saying Jacob, his brother, had died in Egypt, and that his sons and all Egypt were conveying him to the land of Canaan for burial. Esau's wrath was rekindled, he assembled his substantial followers including the sons of Ishmael and Keturah under the pretense they too would mourn for Jacob (Israel). After feign mourning with all those assembled, Esau and his followers blocked the entrance of the cave of Machpelah as he stood before Joseph, his brethren and all that came with him from Egypt.

Joseph and his brethren inquired of Esau as to why they were blocking the cave. Esau claimed that the cave belonged to him and his fathers (Isaac and Abraham). Joseph responded by saying his father Israel had title to the cave and that the transaction of purchase was back in Egypt. Esau advised that the records be brought to Canaan, and that he Esau would abide by them. Naphtali, Joseph's brother, was swift of foot and he it was that was sent back to Egypt to get the records including those which contained "all the transactions of the birthright which are written, fetch thou."

Naphtali departed for Egypt, and Esau increased his resistance. He began a battle with Joseph and his brethren. Forty of Esau's men were slain.

Chushim, son of Dan, son of Jacob, watched the battle from a hundred cubits distant. Chushim was deaf, understanding only the voice of consternation among them. He inquired "Why do you not bury the dead and what is this consternation?" Chushim then quickly

---

433. Genesis 50:12-13 KJV, MT, JST

224

ran into the battle and slew Esau and cut off his head. The loss of Esau disoriented his followers and the sons of Jacob prevailed.[434]

(From Jasher) "And Jacob was buried in Hebron, in the cave of Machpelah which Abraham had bought from the sons of Heth for the possession of a burial place, and he was buried in very costly garments. And no king had such honor paid him as Joseph paid unto his father at his death, for he buried him with great honor like unto the burial of kings."[435]

So Israel's life came to a close, the mantle of leadership fell upon Joseph whom Israel had anointed and blessed as the leader of the Lord's covenant people. They continued to reside in Egypt at the discretion of the Pharaoh.

It has been written that Israel

- was chosen for his role on earth before he was born in the flesh
- was accorded the privilege of asking God what he would
- was a priest before God, having the power to act for Him
- wore priestly garments
- was named by the Lord Himself
- gave tithes of his possessions
- received revelations from the Holy Spirit/God
- was a friend, servant and prophet of God
- foretold the future of Israel through his sons
- was a proscelyte/missionary
- loved the Lord God Jehovah with all his heart, offered sacrifices often and had no other Gods before Him
- honored his father and mother

For his efforts Israel was granted his exaltation, and he Israel also sitteth upon his celestial throne. "And Jacob did none other things than that which (he was) commanded, (he has) entered into his exaltation, according to (God's) promises and sit/s upon thrones..."*

*Doctrine & Covenants 132:37

---

434. Jasher LVI:46-65; Legends II:153-54
435. Ibid LVI:66-67

EPILOGUE

Reviewing the lives of Abraham, Isaac and Israel and their relationship to the Mighty God Jehovah (Yahweh), we have learned that:

(1) Jehovah is the living God of planet earth, which He created under the direction of His Father.

(2) There was a spiritual creation which preceded the physical creation of life on this earth.

(3) Life on earth represents a second stage of existence for human beings.

(4) Men and women existed as spirits in the presence of God in the first stage, before receiving physical bodies.

(5) Those who come to earth and take physical bodies qualified to do so by the choices they made and the lives they lived while they were spirits.

(6) Some spirits were/are greater than others, and Jehovah was/is the greatest of them all.

(7) Freedom of choice is part of the Lord's plan. He will not pre-empt mankinds agency to choose.

(8) The purposes of God are to bring to pass the immortality and eternal life of men and women.

(9) The purpose of earth life is to prove each soul to see if s/he will do all that has been commanded of her/him, thereby qualifying for an eternal life.

(10) God has chosen to work through covenant peoples to achieve His purposes.

(11) The covenant people through whom the Lord God Jehovah works had their origins in Noah, Shem and Eber, but came into fruition through Abraham, Isaac, Jacob, Levi, Judah and Joseph, and their posterity.

(12) Abraham, Isaac and Jacob (Israel) were among the great spirits who were chosen for the roles they were to play in the earth, before they were born in the flesh. Each was named by Him.

(13) The Lord's commands to walk uprightly before Him and be perfect, given Abraham, Isaac and Jacob and their posterity are part of a test to qualify each soul for eternal life.

226

(14) The covenants God made with Abraham, Isaac, and Jacob and their posterity are consonant with His purposes.

(15) The Lord God will intervene in the lives of men and women as required to achieve His purposes, but He will not pre-empt any man or woman's agency to choose. Men and women are free to obey God's commandments and reap the consequences in benefits and blessings. Men and women are also free to sin against God's commandments and reap the consequences in anguish, guilt, sorrow, pain, and denial of God's blessings. Sin is overcome only through complete repentance and God's forgiveness.

(16) God answers the prayers of those who truly seek Him and have faith in Him.

(17) When offended, men and women should be easily appeased, slow to anger, and as soon as those who have sinned asks for pardon, the offended party should forgive the sinner with all his/her heart. Even if deep and serious injury has been done to him/her, s/he should not be vengeful, nor bear his/her brother or sister a grudge in his/her heart.

(18) Priesthood blessings were to be continued by the Lord from Abraham, Isaac and Jacob through Levi and later through Aaron, Moses, and others, whereby men may act for God. Men are permitted to act for God, not to achieve their vain ambitions, or to gratify their personal pride, or to control or compel the souls of the children of men in any degree of unrighteousness. Rather, those who hold this priesthood were/are to let personal righteousness be the guiding principle for handling and controlling its power. Priesthood power given to man is for the purpose of assisting God in achieving His purposes, and for blessing the lives of others.

(19) Where ever he lived, Abraham, using priesthood power won souls for the living God Jehovah, starting each on the road to immortality and eternal life. He exercised his priesthood not by compulsion, but by persuasion, long suffering, by gentleness, meekness, by love unfeigned, by kindness and with pure knowledge, as revealed from heaven.

(20) The kingly blessings were continued through Judah, whose physical posterity was/is to include the King of Kings, and the Lord of Lords whose spirit was/is to be enveloped with flesh. He would/did come to save the world from the sins of its people, to break the bonds of death and redeem all mankind from the fall of Adam.

(21) The Lord God Jehovah's purposes, i.e. to bring to pass the immortality of mankind. All mankind would be redeemed from the fall of Adam, by the King of Kings and Lord of Lords. He would also be known as the Son of Man and the Son of God when He came/comes in the flesh.

(22) The birthright blessings were continued through Joseph and his posterity, who were also given the priesthood through whom spiritual salvation would be made possible to the house of Israel and to all the world in the latter days.

(23) Spiritual salvation or eternal life of souls would be determined by the quality of life each soul lived while on earth, the standard being perfection, as defined by the Lord, undergirded by personal righteousness, and by keeping the covenants each has made with the Lord. Obedience is the first law of Heaven.

Shall we not go therefore, and do the works of Abraham, Isaac and Jacob and worship Him whose name Isaiah declared shall be called Wonderful, Counselor, The Mighty God, the Everlasting Father and the Prince of Peace?*

(NOTE) These themes are continued in subsequent works tracing Abraham's, Isaac's and Jacob's posterity through the twelve sons of Israel, especially through Levi, Judah and Joseph, and in later generations through Moses, Aaron, Ephraim, Manasseh, and Joshua; David, Solomon, Daniel, Isaiah, Ezekial, Elijah Malachi, Lehi, Nephi, Mosiah, Alma, Helaman, Mormon, Moroni and others.

Sources for such volumes are those books God has caused to be written for He said, "For I command all men, both in the east and in the west, and in the north and in the south, and in the islands of the sea, that they shall write the words which I speak unto them; for out of the books which shall be written I will judge the world, every man according to their works, according to that which is written." For an elaboration see Appendix A.

*Isaiah 9:6, (Pele-joez-el-gibbor-Abi-ad-sar-shalom, That is Wonderful in Counsel is God the mighty, the everlasting Father, the Ruler of peace).

Appendix A

Selected Book of Mormon and Doctrine & Covenants references to Abraham, Isaac and Jacob (Book of Mormon peoples in America were descendants of Abraham, Isaac, Jacob and Joseph).

"But behold, there shall be many-at that day when I shall proceed to do a marvelous work among them, that I may remember my covenants which I have made unto the children of men, that I may set my hand again the second time to recover my people, which are of the house of Israel; And also, that I may remember the promises which I have made unto thee, Nephi, and also unto thy father, that I would remember your seed; and that the words of your seed should proceed forth out of my mouth unto your seed; and my words shall hiss forth unto the ends of the earth, for a standard unto my people, which are of the house of Israel."

"And because my words shall hiss forth-many of the Gentiles shall say: A Bible! A Bible! We have got a Bible, and there cannot be any more Bible. But thus saith the Lord God: O fools, they shall have a Bible; and it shall proceed forth from the Jews, mine ancient covenant people. And what thank they the Jews for the Bible which they receive from them? Yea, what do the Gentiles mean? Do they remember the travels, and the labors, and the pains of the Jews, and their diligence unto me, in bringing forth salvation unto the Gentiles?"

"O ye Gentiles, have ye remembered the Jews, mine ancient covenant people? Nay; but ye have cursed them, and have hated them, and have not sought to recover them. But behold, I will return all these things upon your own heads; for I the Lord have not forgotten my people."

"Thou fool, that shall say: A Bible, we have got a Bible, and we

229

need no more Bible. Have ye obtained a Bible save it were by the Jews? Know ye not that there are more nations than one? Know ye not that I, the Lord your God, have created all men, and that I remember those who are upon the isles of the sea; and that I rule in the heavens above and in the earth beneath; and I bring forth my word unto the children of men, yea, even upon all the nations of the earth?"

"Wherefore murmur ye, because that ye shall receive more of my word? Know ye not that the testimony of two nations is a witness unto you that I am God, that I remember one nation like unto another? Wherefore, I speak the same words unto one nation like unto another. And when the two nations shall run together the testimony of the two nations shall run together also."

"And I do this that I may prove unto many that I am the same yesterday, today, and forever; and that I speak forth my words according to mine own pleasure. And because that I have spoken one word ye need not suppose that I cannot speak another; for my work is not yet finished; neither shall it be until the end of man, neither from that time henceforth and forever."

"Wherefore, because that ye have a Bible ye need not suppose that it contains all my words; neither need ye suppose that I have not caused more to be written. For I command all men, both in the east and in the west, and in the north, and in the south, and in the islands of the sea, that they shall write the words which I speak unto them; for out of the books which shall be written I will judge the world, every man according to their works, according to that which is written."

"For behold, I shall speak unto the Jews and they shall write it; and I shall also speak unto the Nephites and they shall write it; and I shall also speak unto the other tribes of the house of Israel, which I have led away, and they shall write it; and I shall also speak unto all nations of the earth and they shall write it."

"And it shall come to pass that the Jews shall have the words of the Nephites, and the Nephites shall have the words of the Jews; and the Nephites and the Jews shall have the words of the lost tribes of Israel; and the lost tribes of Israel shall have the words of the Nephites and the Jews."

"And it shall come to pass that my people, which are of the house of Israel, shall be gathered home unto the lands of their possessions; and my word also shall be gathered in one. And I will show unto them that fight against my word and against my people, who are of the house of Israel, that I am God, and that I covenanted with Abraham that I would remember his seed forever." 2 Nephi 29:1-14 Book of Mormon.

"Wherefore, our father hath not spoken of our seed alone, but also of all the house of Israel, pointing to the covenant which should be fulfilled in the latter days; which covenant the Lord made to our father Abraham, saying: In thy seed shall all the kindreds of the earth be blessed." 1 Nephi 15:18 (600 to 592 BC) Book of Mormon.

"Behold, the Lord esteemeth all flesh in one; he that is righteous is favored of God. But behold, this people had rejected every word of God, and they were ripe in iniquity; and the fulness of the wrath of God was upon them; and the Lord did curse the land against them, and bless it unto our fathers; yea, he did curse it against them unto their destruction, and he did bless it unto our fathers unto their obtaining power over it. Behold, the Lord hath created the earth that it should be inhabited; and he hath created his children that they should possess it...He ruleth high in the heavens, for it is his throne, and this earth is his footstool. And he loveth those who will have him to be their God. Behold, he loved our fathers, and he covenanted with them, yea, even Abraham, Isaac, and Jacob; and he remembered the covenants which he had made; wherefore, he did bring them out of the land of Egypt." 1 Nephi 17:35-40 (about 591 BC) Book of Mormon.

"...for it appears that the house of Israel, sooner or later, will be scattered upon all the face of the earth, and also among all nations. ...And after our seed is scattered the Lord God will proceed to do a marvelous work among the Gentiles, which shall be of great worth unto our seed; wherefore, it is likened unto their being nourished by the Gentiles and being carried in their arms and upon their shoulders. And it shall also be of worth unto the Gentiles; and not only unto the Gentiles but unto all the house of Israel, unto the making known of the covenants of the Father of heaven unto Abraham, saying: In thy seed shall all the kindreds of the earth be blessed." 1 Nephi 22:3-9 (588 to 570 BC) Book of Mormon.

"And it shall come to pass that my people, which are of the house of Israel, shall be gathered home unto the lands of their possessions; and my word also shall be gathered in one. And I will show unto them that fight against my word and against my people, who are of the house of Israel, that I am God, and that I covenanted with Abraham that I would remember his seed forever." 2 Nephi 29:14 (559 to 545 BC) Book of Mormon.

"...but we can write a few words upon plates, which will give our children, and also our beloved brethren, a small degree of knowledge concerning us, or concerning their fathers—Now in this thing we do rejoice; and we labor diligently to engraven these words upon plates, hoping that our beloved brethren and our children will receive them will thankful hearts, and look upon them that they may learn with joy and not with sorrow, neither with contempt, concerning their first parents. For, for this intent have we written these things, that they may know that we knew of Christ, and we had a hope of his glory many hundred years before his coming; and not only we ourselves had a hope of his glory, but also all the holy prophets which were before us. Behold, they believed in Christ and worshiped the Father in his name, and also we worship the Father in his name. And for this intent we keep the law of Moses, it pointing our souls to him; and for this cause it is sanctified unto us for righteousness, even as it was accounted unto Abraham in the wilderness to be obedient unto the commands of God in offering up his son Isaac, which is a similitude of God and his Only Begotten Son." Jacob 4:2-5 (544 to 421 BC) Book of Mormon.

"Yea, humble yourselves even as the people in the days of Melchizedek, who was also a high priest after this same order which I have spoken, who also took upon him the high priesthood forever. And it was this same Melchizedek to whom Abraham paid tithes; yea, even our father Abraham paid tithes of one-tenth part of all he possessed." Alma 13:14-15 Book of Mormon.

"And now behold, Moses did not only testify of these things, but also all the holy prophets, from his days even to the days of Abraham. Yea, and behold, Abraham saw of his coming, and was filled with gladness and did rejoice. Yea, and behold I say unto you, that Abraham not only knew of these things, but there were many before the days of Abraham who were called by the order of God; yea, even after the order of his Son;...And now I would that ye should know, that even since the days of Abraham there have been many prophets that have testified these things; yea, behold, the prophet Zenos...also Zenock, and also Ezias, and also Isaiah, and Jeremiah." Helaman 8:16-20 Book of Mormon.

The Savior proclaimed himself to be the prophet spoken of as like unto Moses and refers to his covenant with Abraham.

"Behold, I am he of whom Moses spake, saying: A prophet shall the Lord your God raise up unto you of your brethren, like unto me; him shall ye hear in all things...Verily I say unto you, yea, and all the prophets from Samuel and those that follow after, as many as have spoken, have testified of me. And behold, ye are the children of the prophets; and ye are the house of Israel; and ye are of the covenant which the Father made with your fathers, saying unto Abraham: And in thy seed shall all the kindreds of the earth be blessed...And I will remember the covenant which I have made with my people; and I have covenanted with them that I would gather them together in mine own due time, that I would give unto them again the land of their fathers for their inheritance, which is the land of Jerusalem, which is the promised land unto them forever, saith the Father. And it shall come to pass that the time cometh, when the fulness of my gospel shall be preached unto them; And they shall believe in me, that I am Jesus Christ, the Son of God, and shall pray unto the Father in my name. Then shall their watchmen lift up their voice, and with the voice together shall they sing; for they shall see eye to eye.Then will the Father gather them together again, and give unto them Jerusalem for the land of their inheritance. Then shall they break forth into joy-Sing together, ye waste places of Jerusalem;for the Father hath comforted his people, he hath redeemed Jerusalem." 3 Nephi 20:23-33 Book of Mormon.

..."marvel not, for the hour cometh that I will drink of the fruit of the vine with you (Joseph Smith) on the earth, and with Moroni, whom I have sent unto you to reveal the Book of Mormon, containing the fulness of my everlasting gospel, to whom I have committed the keys of the record of the sick of Ephraim; And also with Elias, to whom I have committed the keys of bringing to pass the restoration of all things spoken by the mouth of all the holy prophets since the world began, concerning the last days;"

"And also John the Son of Zacharias, which Zacharias he (Elias) visited and gave promise that he should have a son, and his name should be John, and he should be filled with the spirit of Elias; Which John I have sent unto you, my servants, Joseph Smith, Jun., and Oliver Cowdery, to ordain you unto the first priesthood which you have received, that you might be called and ordained even as Aaron;"

"And also Elijah,unto whom I have committed the keys of the power of turning the hearts of the fathers to the children, and the hearts of the children to the fathers, that the whole earth may not be smitten with a curse;"

"And also with Joseph and Jacob, and Isaac, and Abraham, your fathers, by whom the promises remain; And also with Michael, or Adam, the father of all, the prince of all, the ancient of days; And also with Peter,and James, and John, whom I have sent unto you, by whom I have ordained you and confirmed you to be apostles, and especial witnesses of my name, and bear the keys of your ministry and of the same things which I revealed unto them; Unto whom I have committed the keys of my kindgom and a dispensation of the gospel for the last times; and for the fulness of times, in the which I will gather together in one all things,both which are in heaven, and which are on earth; And also with all those whom my Father hath given me out of the world." Doctrine and Covenants 27:5-14

"Which Abraham received the priesthood from Melchizedek, who received it through the lineage of his fathers, even till Noah; And from Noah till Enoch, through the lineage of their fathers; and from Enoch to Abel, who was slain by the conspiracy of his brother, who received the priesthood by the commandments of God, by the hand of his father Adam, who was the first man-Which priesthood continueth in the church of God in all generations, and is without beginning of days or ends of years." Doctrine & Covenants 84:14-17

"For whoso is faithful unto the obtaining these two priesthoods of which I have spoken, and the magnifying their calling, are sanctified by the Spirit unto the renewing of their bodies. They become the sons of Moses and of Aaron and the seed of Abraham, and the church and kingdom, and the elect of God." Doctrine & Covenants 84:33-34

"Behold, this is the law I gave unto my servant Nephi, and thy fathers, Joseph, and Jacob, and Isaac, and Abraham, and all mine ancient prophets and apostles. And again, this is the law that I gave unto mine ancients, that they should not go out unto battle against any nation, kindred, tongue, or people, save I, the Lord, commanded them. And if any nation, tongue, or people should proclaim war against them, they should first lift a standard of peace unto that people, nation, or tongue; And if that people did not accept the offering of peace, neither the second nor the third time, they should bring these testimonies before the Lord; Then I, the Lord, would give unto them a commandment, and justify them in going out to battle against that nation, tongue or people." Doctrine & Covenants 98:32-36

"I, the Lord, have suffered the affliction to come upon them wherewith they have been afflicted, in consequence of their transgressions; Yet I will own them, and they shall be mine in that day when I will come to make up my jewels. Therefore, they must needs be chastened and tried, even as Abraham, who was commanded to offer up his only Son. For all those who will not endure chastening, but deny me, cannot be sanctified." Doctrine & Covenants 101:2-5

"For ye are the children of Israel, and of the seed of Abraham, and ye must needs be led out of bondage by power, and with a stretched-out arm. And as your fathers were led at the first, even so shall the redemption of Zion be." Doctrine and Covenants 103:17-18

In prayer of dedication offered by Joseph Smith Jr. for Kirtland Temple March 27, 1836:

"But thou knowest that thou hast a great love for the children of Jacob, who have been scattered upon the mountains for a long time, in a cloudy and dark day. We therefore ask thee to have mercy upon the children of Jacob, that Jerusalem, from this hour, may begin to be redeemed; And the yoke of bondage may begin to be broken off from the house of David; And the children of Judah may begin to return to the lands which thou didst give to Abraham, their father." Doctrine & Covenants 109:61-64

(Vision of Joseph Smith Jr., the Prophet and Oliver Cowdery):

235

"After this vision closed,the heavens were again opened unto us; And Moses appeared before us, and committed unto us the keys of the gathering of Israel from the four parts of the earth, and the leading of the ten tribes from the land of the north. After this, Elias appeared, and committed the dispensation of the gospel of Abraham, saying that in us and our seed all generations after us should be blessed. After this vision closed, another great and glorious vision burst upon us; for Elijah the prophet, who was taken to heaven without tasting death, stood before us, and said: Behold, the time has fully come, which was spoken of by the mouth of Malachi-testifying that he [Elijah] should be sent, before the great and dreadful day of the Lord come-To turn the hearts of the fathers to the children, and the children to the fathers, lest the whole earth be smitten with a curse-Therefore, the keys of this dispensation are committed into your hands; and by this ye may know that the great and dreadful day of the Lord is near, even at the doors." Doctrine & Covenants 110:11-16

"And as I said unto Abraham concerning the kindreds of the earth, even so I say unto my servant Joseph: In thee and in thy seed shall the kindred of the earth be blessed." Doctrine & Covenants 124:58

"Abraham received all things, whatsoever he received, by revelation and commandment, by my word, saith the Lord, and hath entered into his exaltation and sitteth upon his throne. Abraham received promises concerning his seed, and of the fruit of his loins-from whose loins ye are, namely, my servant Joseph-which were to continue so long as they were in the world; and as touching Abraham and his seed, out of the world they should continue...This promise is yours also, because ye are of Abraham...Go ye, therefore, and do the works of Abraham; enter ye into my law and ye shall be saved. But if ye enter not unto my law ye cannot receive the promises of my Father, which he made unto Abraham." Doctrine & Covenants 132:29-33

"Abraham was commanded to offer his son Isaac; nevertheless, it was written: Thou shalt not kill. Abraham, however, did not refuse, and it was accounted unto him for righteousness." Doctrine & Covenants 132:36

"For I am the Lord thy God, and will be with thee even unto the end of the world, and through all eternity; for verily I seal upon you your exaltation, and prepare a throne for you in the kingdom of my Father, with Abraham your father." Doctrine & Covenants 132:49

"Therefore, marvel not at these things, for ye are not yet pure; ye can not yet bear my glory; but ye shall behold it if ye are faithful in keeping all my words that I have given you, from the days of Adam to Abraham, from Abraham to Moses, from Moses to Jesus and his apostles, and from Jesus and his apostles to Joseph Smith, whom I did call upon by mine angels, my ministering servants, and by mine own voice out of the heavens, to bring forth my work; Which foundation he did lay, and was faithful; and I took him to myself." Doctrine & Covenants 136:37

(Vision of the Redemption of the Dead)

"Among the great and mighty ones who were assembled in this vast congregation of the righteous were Father Adam, the Ancient of Days and father of all, And our glorious Mother Eve, with many of her faithful daughters who had lived through the ages and worshipped the true and living God. Abel, the first martyr, was there, and his brother Seth, one of the mighty ones, who was in the express image of his father, Adam. Noah, who gave warning of the flood; Shem, the great high priest; Abraham, the father of the faithful; Isaac, Jacob, and Moses, the great law-giver of Israel; And Isaiah, who declared by prophecy that the Redeemer was anointed to bind up the broken-hearted, to proclaim liberty to the captives, and the opening of the prison to them that were bound were also there."

"Moreover, Ezekial, who was shown in vision the great valley of dry bones, which were to be clothed upon with flesh, to come forth again in the resurrection of the dead, living souls; Daniel, who foresaw the establishment of the kindgom of God in the latter days...Elias who was with Moses on the Mount of Transfiguration; And Malachi; the prophet who testified of the coming of Elijah-of whom also Moroni spoke to the Prophet Joseph Smith, declaring that he should come before the ushering in of the great and dreadful day of the Lord-were also there."

"The Prophet Elijah was to plant in the hearts of the children the promises made to their fathers, Foreshadowing the great work to be done in the temples of the Lord in the dispensation of the fulness of times, for the redemption of the dead, and sealing of the children to their parents, lest the whole earth be smitten with a curse and utterly wasted at his coming."

"All these and many more...waited for their deliverance, For the dead looked upon the long absence of their spirits from their bodies as a bondage. These the Lord taught, and gave them power to come forth, after his resurrection from the dead, to enter into his Father's kingdom, there to be crowned with immortality and eternal life, And continue thenceforth their labor as had been promised by the Lord, and be partakers of all blessings which were held in reserve for them that love him...The dead who repent will be redeemed, through obedience to the ordinances of the house of God. And after they have paid the penalty of their transgressions, and are washed clean, shall receive a reward according to their works, for they are heirs of salvation. Thus was the vision of the redemption of the dead revealed to me, and I bear record, and I know that this record is true, through the blessing of our Lord and Savior, Jesus Christ, even so. Amen" (Joseph F. Smith) Doctrine & Covenants 138:38-60

Appendix B

Extrapolations of dates from the fall of Adam to Jacob (Israel's) death.

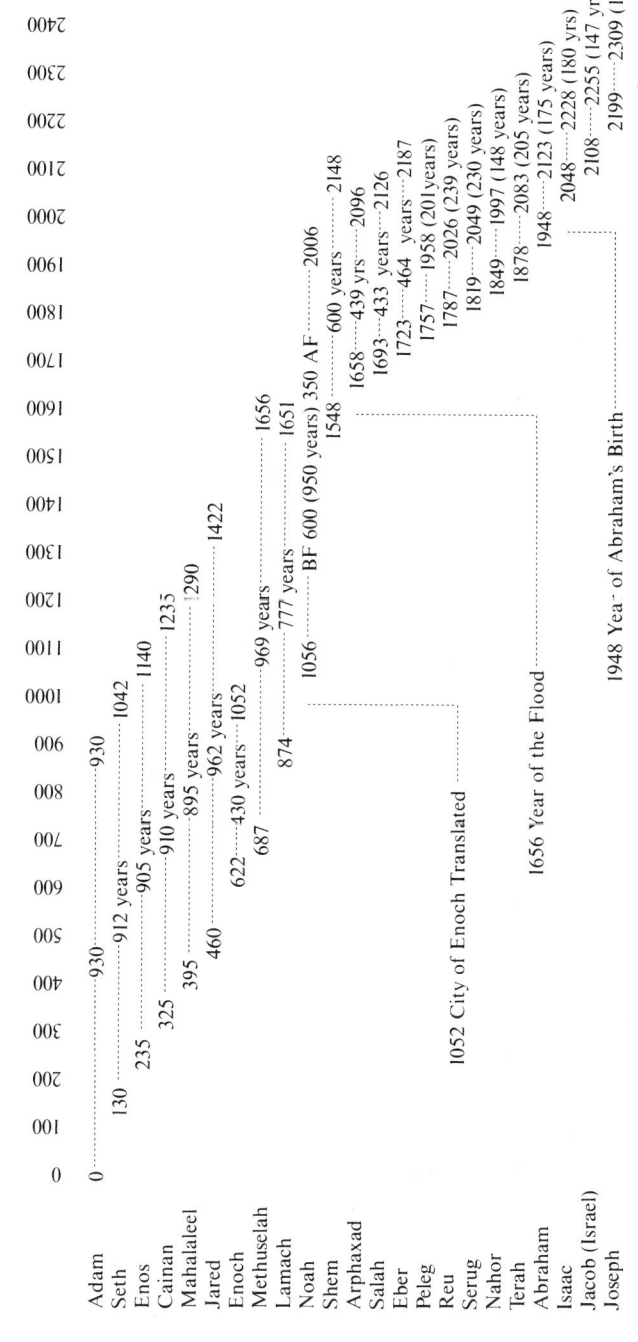

Bibliography

1. The Holy Bible, Authorized King James Version, Old & New Testaments, The Church of Jesus Christ of Latter Day Saints, Salt Lake City, 1979.

2. *The Holy Scriptures, According To The Masoretic Text,* The Jewish Publication Society of America, Philadelphia, 1955.

3. *The Holy Scriptures Containing The Old & New Testaments,* Board of Publication of The Reorganized Church of Jesus Christ of Latter Day Saints, Independence, Tenth Printing, 1964.

4. Charlesworth, James H., *The Old Testament Pseudepigrapha Volume,* 1, Doubleday & Company, Inc., Garden City, 1983.

5. Ginzberg, Louis, *The Legends of the Jews,* Philadelphia, The Jewish Publication Society of America (7 volumes), 1910.

6. Glueck, Nelson, *Rivers in the Desert,* The Jewish Publication Society of America, New York 1959.

7. Nibley, Hugh, *Abraham in Egypt,* Deseret Book Company, Salt Lake City, 1981.

8. Smith, Joseph, Jr. Translator, *The Book of Mormon,* The Church of Jesus Christ of Latter Day Saints, Salt Lake City, 1977

9. Smith, Joseph Jr., The Pearl of Great Price, A Selection from the Revelations, Translations, and Narrations of Joseph Smith - Book of Abraham, The Church of Jesus Christ of Latter Day Saints, Salt Lake City, 1974.

10. Smith, Joseph Jr., Prophet, Seer & Revelator, *The Doctrine and Covenants,* The Church of Jesus Christ of Latter Day Saints, Salt Lake City, 1979.

11. *The Book of Jasher,* J.H Parry Company, Salt Lake City, 1887, 1973.

12. *The Antiquities of the Jews,* Complete Works of Flavius Josepheus, Whiston, William Translator, Kregel Publications, Grand Rapids 1978.